Business for Beginners

From research and business plans to money, marketing and the law

Frances McGuckin

SOURCEBOOKS, INC.®
NAPERVILLE, ILLINOIS

Published by Sourcebooks, Inc.
P.O. Box 4410, Naperville, Illinois 60567-4410
(630) 961-3900
Fax: (630) 961-2168
www.sourcebooks.com

Library of Congress Cataloging-in-Publication Data

McGuckin, Frances.
Business for beginners : from research and business plans to money, marketing and the law / Frances McGuckin.
p. cm.
Originally published: Toronto: Productive Publications, c1997.
Includes index.
1. New business enterprises. 2. Small business--Management. I. Title.

HD62.5.M387 2005
658.1'1--dc22

2005003351

Printed and bound in the United States of America
VP 10 9 8 7 6

More Praise for *Business for Beginners*

"McGuckin has crafted a wise and thorough introduction to an exciting but challenging human endeavor. Some would go as far as to call her book indispensable."

PAUL LUKE, SUCCESS MONEY, *THE PROVINCE*

"The most popular book in our resource library is Frances McGuckin's *Business for Beginners*. When our clients are accepted into our entrepreneurship program, they automatically receive this book as part of their start-up supports."

SELF-EMPLOYMENT CONNECTOR

"When searching for a well-written financial manual to include with our business plan software, the obvious choice was *Business for Beginners*. Frances McGuckin has produced a thorough, easy-to-read guide to personal finances that even beginners, with the most basic understanding of business needs, can use effectively."

DAMIAN CRISTIANI, PRESIDENT, *GLOBAL STAR SOFTWARE*

"Hallelujah! At last, someone has offered a thorough course in business start-up that's understandable by the neophyte. I congratulate Fran, because *Business for Beginners* fills the niche that no one seemed to want to fill."

TONY WANLESS, MONEY AND SMALL BUSINESS WRITER, *THE PROVINCE*

Praise from college and entrepreneurship programs

"The book is exactly as promised—a simple step-by-step guide for starting your own business! The easy-to-read style makes it seem like anyone is able to start a business. Congratulations on a job well done! We feel privileged and proud we are able to feature such a wealth of information in our Career Center."

MARY ELLEN-KUEHL, TRINITY WESTERN UNIVERSITY

"The easy-to-read formula and back-to-basics approach is just what we have been looking for in training material. I commend Frances on her excellent book."

SUSANNA LACHANCE-WATSON, PROGRAM COORDINATOR

"We have found this book to be a valuable resource in business start-up...very informative and easy to understand. Starting a business has never been the easiest task to accomplish. *Business for Beginners* makes the task achievable."

CAL PURCELL, VP GOVERNMENT RELATIONS, SPROTT-SHAW COMMUNITY COLLEGE

"The book has an excellent format....It's very easy to read and be understood by the various ethnic groups whose first language is not English.... Please accept my congratulations on your efforts to contribute to the development of entrepreneurship."

KOFI OHENE-ASANTE, EASE PROGRAM MANAGER

"*Business for Beginners* is an excellent resource guide for new entrepreneurs.... It is clearly written, concise, and filled with valuable information that both my students and I have greatly benefited from. I recommend this book to anyone wanting to achieve success in their entrepreneurial endeavors."

CRYSTAL FLAMAN, ENTREPRENEUR & PROGRAM FACILITATOR

"*Business for Beginners* is in the right place at the right time, providing practical, easy-to-read advice and guidance for start-up companies. Well done, Frances!"

PETER THOMSON, DIRECTOR, BCIT VENTURE DEVELOPMENT CENTER

"It is one of the best, if not *the* best, books on small business that I have read—and I've read a lot. Most small biz books are too institutional, which creates confusion, not clarity. I think it would be safe for me to say that there is genius in your simplicity."

MIKE PHIPPS, MARKETING MANAGER, DELTA CHAMBER OF COMMERCE

Praise from satisfied readers

"I would like to thank you for *Business for Beginners*.... I have used it extensively and it's a great reference."

"I would like to compliment you on this excellent book. I teach entrepreneurship at U.S. public schools and at a university. I would like permission to use part of this text in my classes."

"I just purchased *Business for Beginners*. It is terrific! Now my future business partner is reading it, taking note of everything I underlined."

This book is dedicated to all new entrepreneurs.
The road to success is paved with speed bumps and potholes.
Some prefer a smooth ride and turn around to find an easier route,
but those people never experience the satisfaction
of realizing their dream.

There is no easy route when you are self-employed,
but the rewards of hard work, perseverance, focused goals,
and dreams will be yours if you travel this road
equipped with knowledge, drive, a true
entrepreneurial spirit—and a plan.

Follow your dreams.

Contents

Acknowledgments

Since 1997, the continued success and popularity of *Business for Beginners* has taken it into six countries and multiple editions. I extend my deepest thanks to the many colleges, institutions, entrepreneurship programs, and entrepreneurs across North America who use the book and who have been generous in their support, feedback, and testimonials.

Knowing you have written a book that helps people is the ultimate inner reward. It's like giving birth—a painful and tedious process that in this case involves months of research, writing, editing, proofing, and suffering sore eyes. But when you give birth, you quickly forget the pain.

Because change is a constant factor and teachers must reflect these changes in their materials, this edition has expanded to cover areas that came to light during keynotes, consultations, and workshops. I thank all the wonderful people I spoke to for your questions, enthusiasm, and positive responses.

I have to give special recognition to my dynamic literary agent, Catherine Fowler of Redwood Agency in California, who jumped right in and was committed to seeing both my books published in the United States. Her industry knowledge, professionalism, and expertise in matching me with the right publisher are a credit to her and greatly appreciated.

I must also thank Peter Lynch, editor at Sourcebooks Inc., and the editorial staff for welcoming me aboard as one of their business authors. It is a privilege to work with such a reputable company; they really care about their authors and are committed to seeing their works succeed. Peter, I'll do everything in my power to make this a successful and profitable partnership.

All major projects involve a dedicated team working together, and this book would not have become the success it is today without the help of my production team, Heidi LeRossignol, Tita Zierer, Shirley Olson, Naomi Pauls, and Lee Fodi, who have stuck by me through many editions, numerous reprints, and sales of over 130,000 books.

An author does not usually complete a work without help from outside resources and experts. A very special thanks to two professionals who live and work in Blaine, Washington: Donald Starr, certified public accountant, and Christopher Fletcher, attorney at law. Don's twenty years of experience allowed him to patiently answer dozens of my accounting and tax questions in great detail, plus review and give great input into Chapters 3, 8, and 9. Christopher has twenty-eight years of experience in business law, and kindly reviewed and gave invaluable input into Chapter 5, "Why Do You Need a Lawyer?"

The wonderful support from the Nevada, Kentucky, and New Jersey Small Business Development Centers and the Seattle U.S. Small Business Administration offices gave birth to the success stories in Chapter 13. Thank you to directors and managers Becky Naugle, Michael Graham, Sharon Fusco, Dennis Rasugu, and Roger Hopkins for putting me in touch with some of their special clients who are now an important part of this book. Thank you to each person who shared their story with me; it was a great pleasure getting to know you all. I have affectionately dubbed you "the SmallBiz Success Team" and know that your experiences will inspire others to reach for their dreams.

Thank you to Russell Smart of IDC Insurance Group (www.lifeinsurancequote.com), who contributed invaluable insurance information to Chapter 6. A special thanks is extended to his associate, John Frazier, vice president of estate and business planning in the Bellevue office of Parker, Smith & Feek, Inc., for reviewing and checking the information. To my many friends, clients, and associates who I may have forgotten to thank—thank you for your input and support.

To my wonderful mother, beautiful teenage daughter, Katrina, and awesome son, Richard—what can I say? They are used to Mom being buried in the office burning the midnight oil writing. Without their understanding, it would be a difficult road to travel. Thank you for being the special family that you are. I am blessed.

Preface

Follow Your Entrepreneurial Dream

As we hurtle into the new millennium, the number of people who want to start their own business continues to grow. With technology leaping ahead at a dizzy pace, more people have the option of starting a small or home-based business, with wonderful tools at their fingertips.

There is nothing like being your own boss. It gives one a feeling of supreme power and confidence—or does it? For some, the experience is lonely and isolating. Being self-employed requires a myriad of skills, so the more skills you develop, the more successful you will be. It takes courage, determination, expertise, long hours, and commitment, but the rewards of owning a business are well worth the effort. You gain knowledge, build confidence and expertise, and—let's hope—grow your bank balance. Ah, but there is so much to learn, so much to do, so little money to do it with—and an abundance of unanswered questions.

What is the first step? Which business is right for you? What will it cost? Where will you get the money? Is your idea viable? How should you market? How much competition is out there? The questions continually spin in your mind. You are probably eating and sleeping the thought of owning your own business—but where to start?

Love What You Do

Not everyone is born an entrepreneur, but you *can learn* to be a truly great one. But whereas most skills can be learned, one "skill" can't—passion. So start by choosing a business that you love, because without passion, the novelty soon wears off. Clients sense a passionate entrepreneur, and it's contagious. You must work hard to develop good organizational, financial, administration, sales, and marketing skills, plus be positive and practical. A good sense of humor will often be your lifesaver.

When I was writing the sequel to this book, *Taking Your Business to the Next Level,* I developed a list of sixty jobs that an entrepreneur is responsible for. As a business owner, you need to have your finger on the pulse of them all. To achieve this, formulate a practical business plan, acknowledge your areas of weakness, work to improve on these areas, and don't procrastinate. Many new (and not so new) entrepreneurs make the mistake of becoming "too busy" to network and learn how to grow their businesses. Wrong! As you formulate this exciting new idea, plan time for these important tasks.

Find a Mentor

To achieve great heights and turbocharge your business, find a mentor within your community who is willing to help you. There are many people who will share their knowledge and experiences with you—sometimes all you have to do is ask. If you are not sure where to look, contact your local Chamber of Commerce, U.S. Small Business Administration (SBA) or Small Business Development Center (SBDC). If you can't find a mentor, read this book carefully and refer to it often. I'd be pleased to be your silent mentor.

Reap the Rewards of Success

The businesses that succeed today focus on keeping up with technology and industry knowledge and offer superior service coupled with sound management planning and drive. Flying by the seat of your pants is no longer an option.

Take the right steps—baby steps—one at a time, and you will succeed. This book helps you take these right steps and understand that the decision you have made is one of the biggest of your life. It takes time for the road to become smooth, but each wise step taken is a step in the right direction. Once you have successfully run your own business, you will never want to be an employee again.

I sincerely wish you an exciting trip down the road to success. I hope that this book maps out a safe route for you or enables you to avoid a few potholes. Often the journey is more exciting than the final destination. Enjoy your entrepreneurial trip and never let go of your dreams.

Chapter 1

Where Do You Start?

There are those who dream—and then there are those who make their dream happen.

- **Are you ready to be an entreprenuer?**
- **Why are you starting your own business?**
- **The downside of self-employment**
- **Seven skills for success**
- **Do you have management skills?**
- **Why do businesses fail?**

Are You Ready to Be an Entrepreneur?

Welcome to the wonderful world of entrepreneurship, one of the leading global trends. What an exciting opportunity to explore your creativity, be your own boss, and build a little gold mine—you hope. It is an exciting challenge, a whole new world of doors and knowledge opening for you. If you do it right, being self-employed can be the most rewarding experience of your life.

It's hard work though, taking commitment, dedication, constant learning, and persistence to succeed. With the proliferation of home-based businesses over the last few years, some believe that you can sit in your pajamas and make a bundle. That idea is a fallacy. Whether you are home-based or operate out of a storefront, being your own boss requires you to take your business seriously and work to maintain disciplined routines and deadlines.

The failure rate for small businesses is high—in the first few years, it is as much as 80 to 90 percent. The first two years are traditionally the most difficult. You have to establish a client base, an effective marketing plan, viable products or services, and a reputation within your community. This all takes time and patience.

So where do you start? Take a look at what is involved in being an entrepreneur so you can better assess whether or not you are ready. When you read about entrepreneurs who are considered successful, they don't talk about money as the focus of their success. Instead, they talk about achieving a balance in their lives, freedom, passion, happiness, excitement, achieving goals, helping others, hard work, and focus.

What is an entrepreneur?

Dictionaries describe an entrepreneur as "a person who starts or organizes a business company, especially one involving risk." These days, we tend to associate entrepreneur more with a person striking out on his or her own, usually equating the word with a successful venture. A successful entrepreneur is not a particular type of person, but someone with a well-rounded combination of talents that enables the business to progress.

Some people thrive on the challenge, and some have a natural aptitude for business. Others study hard, take courses, and read extensively. A true entrepreneur will have a passion for business and an unquenchable desire to learn, absorb, explore, and grow. Anyone can be self-employed, but it takes a certain type to fulfill the true entrepreneurial requirements. An entrepreneur will have, or will develop, some or all of these qualities. Figure 1.1 allows you to determine which entrepreneurial traits already apply to you. If you can already check off more than four, you have a great head start.

Figure 1.1: **EIGHT ESSENTIAL ENTREPRENEURIAL TRAITS**

Do you have a real entrepreneurial spirit? Are you:

	Yes	No
1. **A risk-taker:** Usually taking calculated risks, entrepreneurs will not hesitate to seize the moment and run with their intuition.	☐	☐
2. **A decision-maker:** The word "procrastination" does not exist in an entrepreneurial vocabulary. They are comfortable with their decisions and know where they are going.	☐	☐
3. **A dream-maker:** Entrepreneurs have their dreams and are aggressive at making those dreams become reality. They don't say "I wish," but instead "I will."	☐	☐
4. **A visionary:** Instead of looking just one step ahead, entrepreneurs can visualize the whole big picture, both now and in the future.	☐	☐
5. **Driven:** Because they have a vision and a dream, entrepreneurs are usually driven and motivated people who let nothing stand in the way of their goals.	☐	☐
6. **Passionate:** Consumed as entrepreneurs are by their dreams, passion plays a large part in making their dreams become reality. You can feel the passion radiate from a true entrepreneur.	☐	☐
7. **Confident:** Entrepreneurs know where they are going and why, and are confident that they will succeed.	☐	☐
8. **Energized:** Full of drive and motivated by their dreams, entrepreneurs usually have an abundance of energy and thrive on seeing each step of their dream take them closer to a reality.	☐	☐

Do you have what it takes?

As you research your business, review these traits and assess whether your business idea generates these feelings in you. If you choose the right business, you should feel passionate and driven to succeed. Having the dream is key, but if you are a procrastinator or not comfortable in making decisions or in taking calculated risks, perhaps you are not cut out to be an entrepreneur. Now is the time to admit to your challenges and decide how you can overcome them. A true entrepreneur loves to continually learn and grow.

It takes a dedicated person to handle the successful start-up and running of a business, but it's well worth the effort. The rewards of doing it yourself are bountiful. You will gain self-confidence, knowledge, and emotional satisfaction. If you love what you are doing and do it well, you will be motivated to persist toward your future goals.

Figure 1.2 lists thirty questions designed to give you insight into the qualities an entrepreneur needs or should develop. Answer them honestly now, before reading on.

QUICK Tip

Learn How to Think on Your Feet: If you lack confidence and communication skills, take a course through Toastmasters. It will teach you necessary verbal and time management skills, how to think on your feet, and how to carry on a winning conversation—all in a supportive and positive environment. To find out more about Toastmasters, visit www.toastmasters.org.

Why Are You Starting Your Own Business?

Self-employment did not evolve in the last century; it is the way people have survived and made money almost since the beginning of time. Small and microbusinesses constitute a huge percentage of American—and global—businesses. When times get tough and the word "recession" emerges—in other words, they are forced to make their own. There is usually an increase in self-employment as people can't find a job.

Figure 1.2: **YOUR ENTREPRENEURIAL CHECKLIST**

Answer the following questions to determine what business qualities you already have and which ones you need to develop.

	Yes	No
1. Are you a timely decision-maker?	☐	☐
2. Do you trust your intuition?	☐	☐
3. Do you relate well to people on all levels?	☐	☐
4. Can you join in a conversation in a room full of strangers and feel at ease?	☐	☐
5. Can you pick up the phone and ask a direct question in an uncomfortable situation?	☐	☐
6. Could you call a client and ask for a late payment?	☐	☐
7. Can you direct others to carry out your orders without being too aggressive or overbearing?	☐	☐
8. Can you start a project and follow it through?	☐	☐
9. Are you a good verbal communicator?	☐	☐
10. Do you like yourself and who you are?	☐	☐
11. Do you start each day in a positive manner?	☐	☐
12. Can you maintain a positive attitude in adverse situations?	☐	☐
13. Do you have the appropriate technical expertise for the business you are considering?	☐	☐
14. Are you willing to expand on these skills?	☐	☐
15. Do you keep up with global and financial current affairs?	☐	☐
16. Can you cold-call or sell yourself over the phone?	☐	☐
17. Do you have a sound financial knowledge of how a business operates?	☐	☐
18. Can you express yourself well in writing?	☐	☐
19. Can you work without direction?	☐	☐

continued

	Yes	No
20. Are you willing to work long, hard hours?	☐	☐
21. Can you work without getting easily distracted?	☐	☐
22. Do you understand terms such as cash flow, assets, liabilities, equity, depreciation, and working capital?	☐	☐
23. Do you keep legible notes and pay attention to details?	☐	☐
24. Do you keep appointments and arrive on time?	☐	☐
25. Are you usually well-organized?	☐	☐
26. Do you enjoy people?	☐	☐
27. Do you have patience with people?	☐	☐
28. Do you enjoy meeting new people and networking?	☐	☐
29. Could you keep the pressures of business away from your family life?	☐	☐
30. Will you continue to pursue your hobbies and interests?	☐	☐

Ideally you have been able to answer yes to at least twenty of these questions. You need a variety of skills so you can control a multifaceted operation by yourself. If you answered no to any questions, ask yourself how you could improve in these areas, and make a note of them below.

____

____

____

____

As words such as "layoff," "downsize," "capsize," "pint-size," and "reorganize" resound around corporate walls, they all mean the same thing in plain English: "You're fired!" "You're redundant," or "We aren't hiring." People tend to take the skills they have developed over the years to start a business, but sometimes, they are starting in a far from ideal climate.

As the world constantly changes, so do the reasons for business start-ups. The increase in technology and Internet-based businesses means that now millions of workers are telecommuting, working at home, moonlighting in a second part-time business, or struggling in their first endeavor.

If you start your business for the right reasons, you are on your way to success. But some start for the wrong reasons, making it a difficult road. People starting up out of desperation risk making hasty decisions. Some are just not suited to self-employment. Some have spent many years working for one employer, feeling stressed, unmotivated, and depressed, and view self-employment as a solution to all their problems. Some find themselves needing an immediate income replacement when they are often tired and burnt-out. What they really need is a good long rest with time to research their new venture thoroughly. If you are in a similar situation, please proceed with caution.

Others may not be used to decision-making after decades of working for an employer who did it all for them. Some have no time to take the necessary courses needed to expand their knowledge. The two most important steps—preparing a proper business plan and thoroughly researching the market—are often not taken, and they jump in with both feet without first checking the depth of the water.

Let's face it, there's no easy way to make money. Business means hard work, diligence, patience, and careful planning. That doesn't mean you shouldn't start your own business, but it does mean you must think about what lies ahead. Most important of all, consult professionals for advice.

The short questionnaire in Figure 1.3 on the next page helps you determine why you are starting your business. Complete it and carefully analyze why you are exploring self-employment. The first eight reasons on this list can create difficulty for you if you are thinking of starting your business to solve these problems. Be sure your reasons are the right ones and that you have the emotional stamina, sufficient financial resources, knowledge, and time that this venture requires.

The Downside of Self-Employment

People who make time to take an in-depth course on self-employment and business management significantly increase their chances of success. The new business that is thrown together on a hope and a dream without being thoroughly researched, or that started without enough working capital, could sadly become a failure statistic.

Figure 1.3: WHY I AM STARTING MY BUSINESS?

Answer the following questions honestly to determine why you are starting your own business.

	Yes	No
1. I need more money; my wages don't stretch far enough.	☐	☐
2. I am depressed because I cannot find a job.	☐	☐
3. My work situation is unbearable—my boss doesn't appreciate me.	☐	☐
4. I was laid off and feel that I am ready to be my own boss.	☐	☐
5. I am tired of working for an incompetent boss.	☐	☐
6. I can better organize my family life by working at home.	☐	☐
7. I have to care for my aging parents at home.	☐	☐
8. I want to be my own boss. I'm tired of working for one.	☐	☐
9. I can start a technology-based business at home.	☐	☐
10. I retired early and have the funds and time to explore this option.	☐	☐
11. I have the experience and time to research this thoroughly.	☐	☐
12. I have the skills, time, passion and money to start a business.	☐	☐

When economies experience a downturn, self-employment usually increases as people look to making their own job to survive when they can't find a traditional one. As economies stabilize, self-employment often decreases. In good economic times, those finding the entrepreneurial road a bumpy one return to the workforce and a regular paycheck.

Learn and Earn: Those people who don't do their homework or learn the appropriate skills too often face business failure, with devastating results. Often, former owners are left with huge, high-interest consumer debts to pay off.

Who do you think suffers from a failed business? Not just the family, but the whole economy. A failed business means fewer dollars circulating in the local, state, and national economy, with suppliers left with bad debts that they can ill afford. Business failure is often the cause of divorce, so the more you are aware of what you are up against, the better armed you will be.

Leaving the traditional workplace

With all these challenges facing aspiring entrepreneurs, why do so many people want to leave their traditional jobs? Here are the most common reasons—and the reality behind them.

More work, less pay Wages have not kept pace with inflation in the last few years, and in some cases, workplace conditions have become unbearably stressful for many employees. Forced to take on increased workloads through layoffs, they have worked under these stressful conditions for long periods. The pressure to have material "stuff" and to keep up with the Joneses is media-driven and relentless. Just visit any shopping mall in the evenings and over the weekend and observe North American shopaholics in action.

There comes a point for many when the measly paycheck is not worth the job-related stress. People opt for self-employment with the vision of controlling their destiny and experiencing profitable returns. If your new business is well planned, you'll profit only after a couple of years of hard work. If you don't plan properly, you work harder than in a salaried position and make less money.

Stress-related illness and depression More employees are now taking stress leave, which has been recognized by doctors and employers as a serious by-product of this new millennium. Heart attacks at an earlier age are often linked to work pressures. Marriage failures are on the increase, one factor being financial problems caused by cutbacks and layoffs.

Unemployment can lead to depression. I can relate, first-hand, to the feelings of worthlessness, futility, and good old self-pity. Many people hope that owning their own business will solve their stress problem. However, being your own boss involves a high level of stress, too. You have no corporate pensions and benefits, and in most cases, no future retirement plans—

all good reasons for you to set practical goals for your business and plan it out in detail. Planning will help to reduce negative stress by taking the guesswork out of your new venture.

Unappreciative employers These days, people with secure positions are considered the lucky few. Some employees are treated abominably. Verbal abuse, sexual harassment and low wages are common complaints in today's workforce. Financial pressures of struggling businesses are passed on to employees who are not getting the rewards and positive strokes necessary for sustained job motivation. Some corporations are now aware of these effects on employees and are taking steps to increase employee motivation, but many are not. The time eventually comes when one says, "Enough! I'm quitting! I'll start my own business! I don't deserve to be treated like this."

Layoffs, downsizing, or no work The slowdown in the U.S. economy after 9/11 was felt for quite a few years. Many businesses did not survive, as is evident in the statistics on business start-ups and closures. In 2001 and 2002, business closures far exceeded business startups for the first time in many years, forcing many into self-employment. Government restructuring and changing technology both contribute to corporate downsizing. In these situations, many people turn to self-employment as an opportunity to generate income.

Fewer opportunities for youth For educated young people, entrepreneurship is an exciting alternative to working for an employer for minimum wage when they have maximum qualifications. Young people have much to offer our economy with their new and innovative ideas, energy, and technological knowledge. There are many subsidized programs that encourage our youth to seek self-employment as a job alternative. However enthusiastic they may be, it is crucial for young people to be business-savvy before they make this important decision, because although they have great enthusiasm, they may lack the necessary experience. Young people often face the added frustrating challenge of not being taken seriously by adults and other businesspeople.

Incompetent employers Experienced employees often feel that their employers are not particularly competent. Some get tired of working under these conditions, feeling that they have the experience and ability to strike out on their own. However, being an expert in one area does not constitute expertise as a businessperson. When you switch from a job with one area of responsibility—such as head of human resources—to managing all aspects of your own business, it is quite a change of wardrobes.

Family juggling and home-based businesses Operating a home-based business has become a popular way for people juggling family responsibilities to earn an income and attend to family needs. More women are operating from home and trying to achieve a balancing act. Many find themselves caught up in a constant struggle for time, are usually stressed, and are always "too busy." It works for some, but it takes discipline and commitment to strive for that perfect balance. I haven't quite found it yet.

Many baby boomers are also facing the responsibility of looking after aging parents in their home and choose self-employment as a way to juggle yet another family ball. Coping with my ninety-five-year-old mother, I can honestly say that it is quite a time-consuming responsibility.

Home-based businesses are also promoted as great tax write-offs, but they do have their disadvantages. See Chapter 12 for an in-depth discussion on this subject.

Get Help: If you are starting a business to accommodate juggling family jobs, explore services available in your community to help you. You may need a babysitting exchange, a home-care nurse, or even a gofer to do some running around. You cannot do it all, and your business—and you—will suffer if you try.

Leaving the boss behind No one enjoys being told what to do. When you are your own boss, you, and you alone, are responsible for all decisions. There is a certain pride in the words, "I have my own business," or "I am going into business for myself." As much as you may not enjoy being told what to do, at least you had direction in your old job. As an entrepreneur, you are the one who makes all the decisions. What a responsibility! Who shoulders the blame when things go wrong? You, of course.

That's a heavy load to place upon yourself, so let's hope you are not a procrastinator, and that you have confidence in your business acumen. It can be lonely at the top.

Fingertip technology With the advent of the home computer and continual new advances in technology, many new and exciting businesses can be operated from home or with a small capital outlay. With the Internet comes easier accessibility to information, clients, and, for many, a career. Webpage design and online business-to-business ventures didn't really exist ten years ago. The world is at your fingertips. Using technology to operate your business is essential these days, but if you are looking to start a Web-based business, tread carefully. Remember that many dot-coms are now not-dot-coms.

The baby boomer upsurge North America is quickly becoming populated by geriatrics. Many corporations who downsize offer early severance packages to long-term employees, who at fifty-something don't feel ready to put up their feet and plant petunias. To many, self-employment is an attractive option, particularly as they have the time and usually the buyout financial resources to explore this option. The downside is that many have been employees with attractive benefit packages for dozens of years, and the transition to becoming an entrepreneur is a difficult one.

Seven Skills for Success

By completing the exercises in this chapter, you should now have a better indication of some of the skills necessary for entrepreneurial success. You should also have some idea of your strengths and weaknesses and know where you need to focus your efforts to improve. The key skills you need can be broken down into seven areas, as explained in the following list. Read this section carefully, then complete all the checklists in this chapter to identify your strengths and weaknesses.

1. Interpersonal skills

Owning a business is all about dealing with people, so your number one priority is to determine whether you like people or not. There are many people operating businesses who make it painfully obvious that they are not people persons. Everyone has a story to tell of being treated rudely at a business they are patronizing. Remember four important words: YOU are your business. The way you deal with people will determine much of your success. How many times have you decided not to return to a store because the cashier, clerk, or manager was rude to you? How many times have you been impressed by a businessperson going out of his or her way to help you?

Politeness Pays Off: Good manners, politeness, and attentiveness to your customers' needs ensure repeat business. Customers need to feel that they are important to you. The same principles apply to dealing with your trade suppliers, employees, business contacts, and even the competition. Never burn your bridges by treating people badly, and respect those with whom you deal.

With the competitiveness of the big-box stores—who don't always have a reputation for good service—your ace in the hole will be wonderful customer service. You will need to develop patience, as some people are more difficult to please, or even understand, than others. You may be dealing with senior citizens, new immigrants to the country, disgruntled consumers, tradespeople, or the mayor of your community. Part of developing your customer service skills is learning to listen to—and not just hear—your customers' needs. Listening is an art, and coupled with great service, is a winning combination.

A good sense of humor is also an important survival tool, as is a smile. A smile or a little joke in a tense situation can do wonders in turning a problem around. Maintaining a positive outlook will keep you motivated and your customers coming back. No one wants to talk to a negative person. If you maintain a positive outlook, you will transmit this to your customers. They will want to be associated with and do business with you.

2. Self-confidence

If you suffer from a lack of confidence or self-esteem, entrepreneurship can become a difficult challenge. You are the only person who can blow your own horn. Confidence does grow as you establish yourself as an expert and build on the other vital skills. Yet there are many who never make it past first base because they don't have that all-important confidence and self-esteem.

You will spend a great deal of time working alone and do not need negative thoughts to distract you. Sometimes it is difficult to stay motivated. There are many tools, counselors, and courses to help you overcome these stumbling blocks. Hypnotherapy can help remove negative thoughts and allow you to

CASE STUDY: Going That Extra Mile

My pride and joy Jeep was involved in an accident in the snow (no, my husband was driving, not me), and the rear panel with a special Grizzly edition sticker had to be replaced.

"Unfortunately, you will lose the sticker," said Lawrence, the owner of Bodycraft Collision. "They aren't available now."

I liked the sticker and repeatedly grumbled about losing it, muttering something about male drivers. When I picked up the Jeep ten days later, beautifully de-dented and shiny, there was a new Grizzly sticker on the back. I was ecstatic! Lawrence tracked down the manufacturer of the stickers and had one especially made. I was so impressed with his service that I tell everyone about his special caring and attention to detail. Now that is wonderful customer service and great listening.

stay on track and keep positive. Remember, you are selling yourself first to your clients—your business follows.

3. Financial skills

Business is all about dollars and cents. Although you are doing something that you love, the underlying reason is to generate an income. You have to understand financial figures and the business end of business. Most people hate this area and mistakenly avoid it. You don't want to learn the hard way by making serious mistakes. Your knowledge should include basic accounting, organizational, and administrative skills, an understanding of all tax laws, federal and state requirements, and an in-depth knowledge of the business that you are about to undertake. (See Chapter 3 for more on financial statements.)

Sounds like a lot to learn, and it is. But take heart—you can learn everything you need to know. No one was born a business hotshot, and there are many courses available offering business management training, most of which can be tailored to fit your schedule.

4. Technical skills

Anyone can hang out their business shingle, but without sound technical knowledge of your trade or profession, it isn't fair to you or your customers. As a businessperson, you have a responsibility to perform the best service in an expert manner, so please don't start or purchase a business until you have the necessary skills.

Start in an area where you can best utilize your talents. Your skills may need to be expanded through evening courses or additional reading. Never cease to keep up with the changing technology within your chosen field.

Attend seminars, workshops, trade shows, and conferences to add to your knowledge and keep an edge on your competitors. Don't become so engrossed in working at your business that you forget to work on your business.

Avoid the "Technician Trap": Michael Gerber wrote in his bestselling book, *The E-Myth Revisited,* that "the typical small business owner is only 10 percent Entrepreneur, 20 percent Manager, and 70 percent Technician." He states that an ideal entrepreneur is an equal mix of all three. Read his book as you plan your business. It will help you become more aware of avoiding the "technician trap."

Your customers will look to you as the expert, and that is what you have to be. For example, when you look in the Yellow Pages for a plumber or an electrician, you assume the companies advertised there are run by professional and skilled people. As a consumer, you put your trust in them. Your customers put the same trust in your skills, and you should never let them down. Be the expert, or don't be in business. With the stiff competition out there, your expertise is one of the few advantages that allows you to compete with similar businesses, and consumers are becoming picky about where they spend their money.

5. Communication skills

The secret to both a successful business and an enriching life is learning to effectively communicate. Everything you do is about communicating something to someone in some manner. How you communicate verbally to potential clients will make the difference in whether they choose to do business with you, both now and in the future.

QUICK Tip

Improve Your Writing Skills: People are quickly judged by their written skills, or the lack of them. When letters or flyers are received with obvious grammatical errors, 99 percent immediately judge that company as unprofessional and recycle the literature. This is your first—and often last—foot in the door. If you need to tune up your written skills, take a course or read books on writing business letters. A course on creative writing can be a tremendous benefit for marketing your business.

In this electronic era, we communicate using voice mail, faxes, answering machines and email. Therefore, every form of communication that transpires through your office should be polite, professional, and positive. Your telephone should always be answered quickly and pleasantly, and all correspondence written without grammatical errors. "Leave a message after the beep" doesn't cut it in business. Voice mail and answering machine greetings should convey a feeling of "we care" and should imply that messages will be promptly returned, not within a few hours. These days, people are stressed and impatient. They want to talk to you now, so always be available either by pager or cell phone.

You may need to communicate with lawyers, accountants, bank managers, loan companies, or venture capitalists. You may have to negotiate leases or contracts and work with building inspectors, county officers, government and various tax officials, suppliers, advertising agencies, and employees. Some may be difficult to deal with, so good verbal and written communication skills will reduce the chances of being misunderstood.

Speak with Power: If you lack confidence, it often shows in your conversations by the overuse of "ers" and "ums." The listener's immediate perception of you is that you lack knowledge. Your messages should be clear, concise, confident, and competent.

The ability to communicate effectively at a variety of levels in a variety of ways to a variety of people is a skill few people naturally possess, and this is where Toastmasters International can help. Many prominent business people owe a good part of their success to this highly effective organization.

6. Marketing skills

You may have the best business in town, but how are you going to get your message across to potential customers? Marketing is not just putting an advertisement in the local paper or flyers in the mail. In a nutshell, marketing refers to the various strategies you use to reach potential customers, informing them of your products or services. Effective marketing encompasses using communication skills, knowing how to define and target your market, and then utilizing the right marketing mix to reach potential customers.

It's easy to spend valuable dollars on ineffectual methods. Study your competitors and decide if their marketing techniques will work for you. You will have to read books, talk to others in a similar field, and observe how other businesses successfully market. No one has the magical marketing answer—usually, effective marketing is a combination of many techniques that can change from time to time. Your job will be to define which works best for you. Marketing is explained in more detail in Chapter 10. For in-depth marketing information, including how to use written and verbal skills for long-term effectiveness and to enhance your reputation as "the expert," read my book *Taking Your Business to the Next Level.*

7. Technological skills

Today's businesses must be online and technologically terrific. Because time is today's most valuable commodity, most businesses need to use email. Many people now prefer to communicate using email rather than the telephone. I was surprised recently when I used the services of a small business that relies heavily on computers for production purposes, yet which did not use email. Having to save a graphic file on a disk and deliver it is not an acceptable option for today's busy clients.

Consumers like to surf 'n' shop in the evenings on their home computers, so a well-designed website can be an important marketing tool. You don't have to sell over the Internet, but your site can describe your service or products and give the consumers what they want—information.

Stay in Touch: There is nothing more frustrating to a customer than not having telephone calls or emails promptly returned. Make it a practice to check messages and emails regularly and return calls. This is an important part of customer service and your customers will appreciate you going that extra mile.

Word processing and publishing programs allow you to prepare professional letters and marketing information. Accounting and spreadsheet programs allow you to keep your costing, forecasting, and bookkeeping up-to-date at the click of a mouse. A database or contact management system streamlines administrative functions and is a wonderful marketing tool. Research which technology will help your business save time and keep current with the business world.

Do You Have Management Skills?

To help you identify where you may need to develop your managerial skills, complete Figure 1.4 and see how you score. Do you have what it takes? You need to answer yes to these twelve important questions.

If you didn't answer yes to all the questions in Figure 1.4, you now have a guide as to where to focus your management training efforts. Some of these skills will take time to learn while others increase with experience.

Figure 1.4: **MANAGEMENT SKILLS CHECKLIST**

Using the following questions, determine whether you have the management skills necessary to run your own business.

	Yes	No
1. Could I cope with constant pressures and deadlines?	☐	☐
2. Could I handle stressful situations without "losing my cool"?	☐	☐
3. Could I fire an incompetent employee?	☐	☐
4. Could I maintain strict credit control?	☐	☐
5. Could I refuse credit to a good but slow-paying client?	☐	☐
6. Could I adapt to constant change?	☐	☐
7. Could I maintain control of my daily, weekly, and monthly finances?	☐	☐
8. Do I understand how my business is taxed?	☐	☐
9. Do I know what a break-even point is?	☐	☐
10. Could I delegate responsibilities to others?	☐	☐
11. Am I willing to increase my skills in the areas that are lacking?	☐	☐
12. Will I use a business plan and regularly revisit it?	☐	☐

The important question to ask yourself is: Am I willing to learn? It's important to be the very best manager you can be to ensure that your first business will be an exciting and successful venture.

Why Do Businesses Fail?

No one likes to think of failure, yet business failure statistics are high. If you know why businesses fail, you can avoid making these mistakes. There are seven main reasons why the majority of businesses fail:

1. No planning and poor management
2. Lack of cash flow and capital
3. Wrong location
4. Inadequate marketing plan
5. Competition not researched
6. Wrong choice of business
7. Business grows too quickly

Any one of these reasons can cause your business to fail, but combine two or more and your business will be in hot water. Let's look at each in turn.

No planning and poor management

The previous exercises have shown that you need to be multifaceted in your entrepreneurial abilities. Just as an architect must work to blueprints, so your business must work to a plan. The key to business success is in the development of a sound and well-researched business plan, discussed in Chapter 7.

You only have to drive around your own community to see "the revolving door syndrome" of retail outlets closing down after a few months and a new venture starting. Service industries suffer the same fate. The usual reason for these failures is lack of planning. No matter which business you pursue, it needs a great manager at the helm. Good management encompasses everything from customer service to running an efficient office. Review the strategies on page 21 and see if you are ready for this challenge.

Lack of cash flow and capital

"Cash flow" describes the flow of money within a business. Businesses are often started by people with very little money to invest in the start-up and not enough to see the business through the first two fragile years. Without enough capital investment, important corners are cut. Shoestring budgets make survival and growth difficult. Without money to purchase the necessary equipment, support monthly overhead, or spend on marketing to launch the business, the enterprise cannot get off to a positive start.

WHAT IS GOOD BUSINESS MANAGEMENT?

- ☐ Providing the right service or product at the right time, in the right location, at the right price
- ☐ Knowing that profit margins can support overhead, pay salaries, and meet personal commitments
- ☐ Ensuring that the business provides a steady year-round income and that you have a plan B for quieter months
- ☐ Astute inventory management to ensure a regular turnaround
- ☐ Keeping accounting records up-to-date and closely monitoring financial figures
- ☐ Regularly reviewing marketing strategies for their effectiveness
- ☐ Changing with consumer trends, technology, and the changing economy
- ☐ Making time daily for follow-up, marketing, and paperwork
- ☐ Monitoring accounts receivable and keeping in touch with slow-paying clients
- ☐ Understanding all aspects of your business and the industry
- ☐ Providing a better service than your competitors
- ☐ Becoming known as the expert in your field
- ☐ Being an active member in your community
- ☐ Diversifying—not putting all your eggs in one basket
- ☐ Continual networking and follow-up
- ☐ Planning for growth and having an exit strategy

The average business is started with minimum capital, often borrowed from family, banks, credit cards, or high-interest loans. Some people increase home mortgages, an inadvisable step, because if the business fails, the home could be lost and the marriage or other personal relationships would be put to the test. Know where your financing will come from, what the terms of repayment will be, and whether the business can afford the repayments. If you can't afford to borrow—then don't. Rethink your business plan.

Start with a Capital Cushion: The very minimum capital you will need is enough to support the business and personal commitments for the first three months—or longer. This is the barest necessity, based on a business that has a guaranteed and immediate cash flow. The ideal would be a financial reserve that covers all expenses for the first nine months.

Wrong location

With the competition from big-box stores and large malls, location is key for retail businesses to succeed. Is it practical to have a hairdressing salon in an industrial area? Or a restaurant tucked into a small strip mall frequented mainly by seniors? Despite this self-evident logic, people often locate their businesses in the wrong areas. "But the rent is so cheap!" they cry in delight.

Studies show that the average consumer will travel no more than three blocks out of their way, particularly if the same product can be purchased closer. No amount of advertising will entice customers to an out-of-the-way location if they can buy the product more conveniently elsewhere. Walk-by traffic, visibility, and parking are all vital to a retail location. There is no such animal as "cheap rent."

Inadequate marketing plan

A marketing plan is an integral part of a business plan, yet many people don't plan how they will market their new business. "Oh, I'll put some flyers out, put an advertisement in the local paper, and wait for the phone to ring" is not a marketing plan. You need a structured marketing plan—one where you research which marketing techniques best suit your business. With small and home-based businesses, marketing is usually cited as one of the largest hurdles faced by the owners.

Competition not researched

Many budding entrepreneurs take their specific talent and dive into starting a business without first assessing their competition. Take the time to thoroughly research this aspect of your business. With the proliferation of home-based

QUICK Tip

Find Your Niche: Identify whether your business is filling both a *need* and a *niche* in the marketplace, which you will only discover after thorough market research. Then move on to how you can best fill that niche and attract customers to your business.

service businesses, knowing who and where your competition is can be time-consuming. Your hidden competitors will be the unlicensed ones. Most county offices and your chamber of commerce can give you a list of licensed businesses in your field.

Only so much business can be generated in one geographic area. Too many stores offering the same service means that all will struggle to make a living, offering profit-draining specials to entice consumers. Study your town or marketing area intimately *before* starting your business to access how successful your competitors are. Ask yourself:

- Why are they successful? What are they *not* doing?

Also consider the future. What would happen to your business if a large store selling your product or service for less money opened up a few blocks away? There are no regulations prohibiting businesses offering similar services from opening up near each other. Just take a look at your own hometown.

QUICK Tip

Fill the Industry Gaps: Ask yourself two questions: What can I offer that the competition can't? What can they offer that I can't? This will help you to focus on the niche that your business should be filling. Can you compete with large chain stores or well-established smaller businesses? Chapter 4 discusses researching your business in depth.

Wrong choice of business

Be an expert in your field and love what you do (you will hear this message many times; it's important). Choosing a business because it seems like an easy way to make money is foolhardy. Review consumer, economic, and long-term trends and assess your business community. If you are buying into a "business investment opportunity" or purchasing an existing business, you need an accountant to review the proposal.

Many unprofitable businesses have been positively presented through professional presentation, skilled wording, and a good sales pitch. A professional portfolio often glosses over the real reasons for the business sale—lack of profits. Some people think they can take a business and do better than the last person. If it's your first business purchase, don't be so sure that you can create miracles. Advertised promises of a quick return for little outlay and minimal work belong in the fiction section.

Business grows too quickly

Business growth doesn't sound like a reason for business failure, but it is often the case. If a business is started with minimum cash flow, particularly one involving a large inventory, rapid growth can create all kinds of problems. Sudden growth may mean that your location is no longer suitable, and moving a business is costly. Additional inventory requirements, staffing, machinery, or equipment upgrading must be paid for with profits. There is always a delay between needing extra cash and the eventual cash flow back into the business from sales. Sudden growth puts extra demands on your management abilities as you adjust to the changes.

What Is the Next Step?

In this chapter, you learned about being an entrepreneur and some of the desirable traits, skills, and qualities you should apply to your business. Have you identified some areas where you need to round out your skills? Knowing why businesses fail will help you avoid pitfalls as you start planning. The next step is to look at the different types of businesses available to you and the steps involved in buying a business.

Chapter 2

How Do You Find the Right Business?

If it's as easy to make money as the advertisements say, why aren't we all rich in a year and a day?

- **What types of businesses are available?**
- **Which business is right for you?**
- **Why are businesses sold?**
- **What is a business opportunity?**
- **How do you assess a potential business?**
- **Seven rules for a successful purchase**

What Types of Businesses Are Available?

The business that best suits your needs and experience will take time to research. The more time you spend, the wiser choice you will make, as you will discover that very few will fit your personal criteria.

At first, the idea of buying your first business is exciting, although the choices can be overwhelming. There are few gems in a mountain of silt, so to make your mining for gold easier, start sifting through your personal criteria. For example, if you don't like cold-calling, opt for an established business with an established clientele. If you are uncomfortable selling to friends and family, don't enter into a multilevel situation. If working seven days a week is not for you, avoid retail.

Businesses come in all shapes and sizes, with close to 70 percent being in the service sector. Following is an outline of the six main types of businesses that you may be researching:

1. Service
2. Retail
3. Franchising
4. Manufacturing
5. Distribution
6. Multilevel and network marketing

1. Service businesses

The majority of new entrepreneurs start a service business because it is the easiest way to generate income utilizing their many years of expertise. What is a service business? Quite simply, one that performs a service in return for a fee, which is usually calculated on an hourly or contract fee basis. Service businesses include consulting, accounting, bookkeeping, Web design, all the trades, teaching, and tourism, to name just a few. Clients pay for your expertise and knowledge.

Being that expert is a key component to a successful service business. Once you advertise and open the doors, you are representing yourself as a professional in your field. Unless you belong to an accredited association—mandatory for doctors, lawyers, and accountants—the consumer has little recourse except to sue if you offer wrong advice or perform inadequately.

A service business should offer just that. Service. Clients expect it, so you'd better be prepared to offer excellent service plus a little bit more at a reasonable price. Guarantee your work, as this gives the message that you stand by and take pride in what you do. Consumers, now more than ever, expect quality service at the best price. Don't hang out your shingle until you are sure you can offer a professional product—you. Ask yourself:

- Do I feel comfortable calling myself an expert?
- Will others perceive of me as "an expert"?

QUICK Tip

Ensure Customer Satisfaction: Punctuality, reliability, and follow-up are three major components of a service business. Be on time for appointments. Call if you are unavoidably detained, then always follow up afterward, asking if everything is to the client's satisfaction. This one call will earn you credit and gives you the opportunity to address any problems before an unsatisfied client starts complaining to others. Bad word-of-mouth referrals travel much faster than good referrals.

Isn't it amazing how one hears the negative service business stories more than the positive ones? We read about home renovators performing substandard work, mechanics who don't adequately fix a vehicle's problem, or bookkeepers who operate without proper accounting knowledge. Imagine what could happen if a gas appliance was not properly installed. An improperly wired house could cause a devastating house fire, and a brake failure could cause someone's death.

Your clients should receive the same professional expertise and service that you would expect to receive. You are taking the lives, property, and welfare of your clients into your hands. Before you open your doors, consider taking out liability insurance for protection from unforeseen disasters (see Chapter 6). Serious errors can lead to lengthy and costly legal battles, causing irreparable damage to the business.

UPS AND DOWNS OF SERVICE BUSINESSES

Service businesses often appear glamorous, but they do have their downside. Review this list of advantages and disadvantages and see which ones may apply to you.

The advantages

- They usually require less start-up capital.
- You can apply your skills to generate income.
- Many can be operated from a home-based office.
- Overhead costs are considerably lower.
- You have some flexibility in setting appointments.
- You usually don't have to carry a large inventory, if any.
- There's less paperwork and accounting.

The disadvantages

- If you are ill or injured, the job doesn't get done.
- You work longer hours catching up on administrative functions.
- It is easy to become isolated from the business world.
- There is a high liability factor involved.
- If you make a mistake, your reputation is threatened.
- Some businesses experience drastic seasonal peaks and ebbs.
- Competitors often price-cut to stimulate business.

2. Retail

Welcome to the mega-millennium, the world of big-box, humungous, cold, poorly serviced but cheap discount stores. What a difficult climate for small retail stores. All the more reason to do thorough homework before embarking on a retail venture. The competition is fierce, with many small retail businesses hardly making an acceptable living. Retail outlets not only compete with each other, they also compete with large chain stores, manufacturers' outlets, and multilevel, Internet, and mail-order sales.

However, if you carefully target your market, your chances of success will increase. Future trends indicate that baby boomers are opting for service and stress-free shopping, tired of the mega-monsters. Barbara Caplan, a New York–based consumer trends expert, states that "people want to hit the bull's eye every time they do something or buy something. They want pleasure, enjoyment, connection with people, an experience—and they want to be taken seriously." Caplan calls it the "affluent attitude," and baby boomers, along with teenagers, will drive the future consumer economy. Baby boomers have higher disposable incomes and teenagers demand a lot of that income from their baby-boomer parents.

Although Internet sales are making small inroads into retail shopping, recent consumer research indicates that more than 60 percent of potential on-line shoppers abandon a site before buying. Websites must be easy to use and "surfer-friendly," which many are not. So although retail competition has increased from these two sectors—big-box and the Internet—service is still the winning factor that will entice consumers into your store, because in most cases, you can't compete with pricing.

Here are some factors to consider that are unique to retail stores:

a) Location Prime retail locations are expensive for a good reason. If a store is located in a large shopping mall, rents can be disproportionately high, with advertising dollars paid to the mall property managers each month. You have to sell a lot of doughnuts to pay $2,000 or $3,000 a month for rent. If your store is located in an out-of-the-way location, you will not experience the volume of walk- and drive-by traffic necessary to generate enough sales. Before deciding on a location, find out how many other stores in that location moved on or closed up shop.

b) Employees Both you and your employees should have thorough product knowledge. Remember—be the expert. Your employees should also have excellent customer service skills. Consumers expect and demand both. Many customers have been lost to the competition because of incompetent sales staff. That being said, finding good employees is the biggest problem experienced by both small and large businesses.

The retail trade requires excellent people skills. You need patience to deal with a variety of temperaments. You will have to serve teenagers, seniors, immigrants, tourists with language difficulties, parents with screaming children and some rather disagreeable customers who seem to enjoy giving sales staff a difficult time.

c) Inventory control Well-stocked shelves and attractive displays entice customers to browse. A small retail store can easily carry a minimum of $60,000 in inventory, equating to large amounts of cash sitting on the shelves. Poor inventory purchasing means that slow-moving products will eventually have to be discounted. Select your lines carefully to facilitate a quick turnaround. Find out how many times a year your inventory should "turn" or sell by your industry's standards. Monitor your inventory turnover and watch for the slow-moving products.

d) Hours Retail stores are often open seven days a week, with extended trading hours. You can't work seven days and order supplies, restock shelves, and manage all the accounting and administrative work. You need help. First, determine the hours you can manage to work regularly without overextending yourself, decide for which work you are best suited, and then fill the gaps with additional staff. Be prepared for long days.

e) Marketing Many retail stores waste money on ineffective marketing methods. Study how similar stores advertise in your area. Note how their advertising appeals to you as a consumer. Visit the stores both before and during an advertised sale, noting whether traffic has increased or not.

Know Your Profit Margins: You need to use a mix of marketing techniques, including specials, clearance sales, and special events to keep your business in the consumers' eyes. Sales may increase on clearance and sale items, but profit margins will decrease. Calculate how much you can reduce the cost of an item before losing money.

f) Consumer spending cycles Keep up-to-date with consumer trends as they vary with the economic climate. As the nation seems to be working harder and getting poorer, tailor inventory to your target market. Unless you specialize in strictly high-end products, maintain an inventory that appeals to the pockets of lower- and middle-income brackets. Retail outlets are totally vulnerable to consumer spending cycles. Your sales can be affected by weather, post-Christmas financial woes, summer vacations, the back-to-school rush, the economic climate, and political changes. Learn the cycles that will both increase and decrease sales so you can better plan your cash flow and marketing strategies.

g) Overhead and profit margins A good portion of your profit will be going into other people's pockets, particularly to your staff and landlord. If you employ family members, at least the money stays in the family. Standing overhead costs—that is, overhead costs that do not decrease whether or not you make a sale—must still be met. Advertising, rent, telephones, power, and wages eat up a good percentage of profits. If you are starting a new store, know the break-even point (the amount of sales you must make each month to cover the bills), calculate how much you must sell, and determine how you are going to achieve this figure. (See Chapter 11 for information on calculating your break-even point.)

More Is Better: If you are purchasing an existing store, use an accountant to thoroughly review two-years' financial statements, which must be up-to-date and professionally prepared. For example, a store with six-month-old statements could be trying to cover up a recent decrease in sales and profits. Your accountant can compare sales fluctuations and cost variances to reveal the true picture.

h) Pricing Tough competition in the retail sector means that you must know your prices and regularly review them. Not many businesses can boast total product exclusivity—even specialty stores have competition. A smaller store's buying power is weaker than the larger ones, and you can only corner a certain percentage of the market, unless you sell a unique product line. Few businesses enjoy this luxury.

Keep normal retail prices in line with the competition. At the same time, they must be high enough to support your overhead. It is easy to fall into the trap of offering continuous sales that realize very little profits. Profit pays for the overhead.

3. Franchising

It seems that everyone is franchising everything these days, from coffee shops to tanning salons. Those with a solid reputation who have perfected their business strategies over the years will be asking a fair price for a franchise. Traditionally, established franchise business failures are significantly rarer than independent business failures because they have designed effective sales, marketing, and administration systems. This is what you pay for, along with the company's good name.

Investing in a relatively new franchise company is as risky as starting your own business, as is buying one that is riding a current popular trend. Your market research will indicate whether the trend is predicted to be short-lived or long-term. Definitely consult your accountant before making a decision.

Well-established and profitable franchises are expensive, and there are many reasons for this:

- They have spent the time and money on in-depth marketing research and their products and services are usually proven.
- They have perfected their marketing and advertising methods.
- Locations are researched for viability.
- They have built their reputation and are trusted by consumers.
- Profit margins, products, and operating expenses have been established and refined.

If you have a strong and creative entrepreneurial spirit, you may find a franchise too restrictive and regulated, as you must abide by their rules. Uniformity is the secret to their success. A McDonald's hamburger in Mexico tastes exactly like one in North America. They have designed an operational plan and a formula that work. Although you are an independent, you are controlled by the head office. You pay for goodwill on purchase, and a percentage of profits or sales volume each year. You must purchase their own brand of supplies and raw materials, paying more than if you shopped around. A good franchise is an expensive proposition, but in most cases, a profitable business is the end result.

CASE STUDY: Licked by Ice Cream

Norma and Joseph, an early-retired couple, pursued their dream of owning a family business. They purchased an ice cream franchise, thinking it would be a good investment and also create jobs for their teenage children. It was located in a large shopping mall, so they had to be open long hours, pay high rent, advertising, and royalty percentages to both the mall and the franchise, and of course, pay top dollars for the business.

After two years of operation, Norma and Joseph were tired—and not any richer. Because of the high overhead costs, after all expenses, the business was making substantially less than $20,000 a year, not an acceptable income for two hard-working people. Disillusioned, they sold the franchise for a loss. It takes a lot of licking ice creams to get rich.

4. Manufacturing

Manufacturing is defined as anything produced from raw materials, from candles to cameras. As a manufacturer, you are responsible for the end product and its safety in the marketplace, therefore you should be an expert in the industry. During you market research, check local, North American, and overseas markets producing similar products. Often, locally manufactured goods cannot match the prices of internationally produced goods because of our higher salaries and living standards.

Starting a manufacturing business It takes years to establish a new name in an industry, so you will need enough working capital to maintain the new business for up to two years or until regular profits roll in. If you need a loan for manufacturing purposes, contact your nearest Small Business Administration office (www.sba.gov). They will walk you through the various lending options and criteria and help you ascertain the viability of your business idea and plan, saving you both valuable time and money.

Allow adequate time and money to talk to the various government agencies and to confer with your accountant or a business consultant. You need a sound business plan that you have prepared—with professional advice—so that you are fully conversant with its contents. Manufacturing can require a lot of money, as you may need to purchase tools, packaging supplies, and equipment or incur legal costs for patents and trademarks. You will need an experienced team working together to cover production, sales, shipping, marketing, and administration.

Buying a manufacturing business Most vendors will provide a training period after purchase, but their expertise usually comes from many years in the industry. Are they going to take the time and teach you all the tricks of the trade? You may purchase a business with dependable, well-trained employees already in place, but you cannot rely solely on your employees—they are transient. You have to rely on your own experience and good judgment.

Get the Scoop from Staff: Before purchasing a business, if possible, talk to the key employees. Ascertain their long-term goals with the company and listen to any complaints or suggestions about the current operation. Employees are the backbone of every business and usually know the inside scoop that you may not hear from the vendor. Observe their enthusiasm for the business; it can be an important indicator.

If you plan to export a product or import raw materials, you must learn about the various methods and costs of shipping, customs documentation, and letters of credit. Products have to be costed to allow for fluctuations in currencies, particularly as some countries' economies can be unstable, with their currency values changing almost overnight. No matter how small or large your manufacturing business will be, don't do it alone. There is a lot of help available to you through various government agencies (see www.business.gov). A well-run manufacturing concern can make healthy profits as well as increase the goodwill value over time.

5. Distribution

Distribution (or wholesaling) usually operates on small profit margins, relying on volume to support a profitable business. A distributor acts as a link between the manufacturer and retail outlets. Be knowledgeable about the products you are distributing; most manufacturers offer support or training to their distributors.

The size and variety of lines you distribute will dictate the type and size of the premises you will need. Larger items may require a warehouse, dock-loading facilities, shelving, forklifts, special equipment for moving materials, and an efficient shipping and receiving system with dependable, honest employees.

During the research process, find answers to the questions in Figure 2.1.

Figure 2.1: **PRODUCT EVALUATION**

A thorough product evaluation requires you to carefully think about each of the following considerations.

	Yes	No
1. Have the products been available for a few years?	☐	☐
2. Could they become obsolete?	☐	☐
3. Does the manufacturer have a good reputation?	☐	☐
4. Do you know how large the market is?	☐	☐
5. Do you know all your major competitors?	☐	☐
6. Are prices competitive?	☐	☐
7. Does the manufacturer honor warranties?	☐	☐
8. Are the products easily serviceable or repairable?	☐	☐
9. Do you know the products' seasonal sales cycles?	☐	☐
10. Are there any reoccurring problems with the products?	☐	☐

If you are purchasing an existing business, the retail client base should be established. You will need to review the financial information to see whether the client base needs expanding, what the current terms of payment are, how slowly clients pay, and whether there are any bad credit risks. If you are starting a distribution business, you must find potential clients and evaluate their interest in your products. It's no use distributing products that move slowly, as they take up valuable warehouse space and restrict your cash flow.

Profits and overhead costs Your business plan will help determine if there is enough profit margin in your products to cover overhead. Average gross profit margins (i.e., profit after the sale less the cost of the product) can range from 10 to 30 percent of selling price. A profit margin of less than 20 percent doesn't leave much room to cover overhead costs. Calculate how much you must sell monthly to cover your break-even costs before making a final decision.

6. Multilevel and network marketing

Starting a multilevel or network marketing business—perhaps part-time at first—is one way to get your feet wet. The start-up costs can be low and the business operated from home. It is a transient type of business. Approximately 0.6 percent of beginners make it to the top level and earn an excellent income. One well-known, reputable direct sales company estimates that they have 30 percent of their people starting the business, 40 percent operating it on a part-time, "dabbling" basis, and 30 percent "on their way out."

It is certainly one way of discovering what type of sales and business person you are. You need the type of personality that can sell and total confidence in the products. Be prepared to market those products at every opportunity. You will need to find people to join your down-line or team, as you earn commission off their sales. This is where the real money kicks in.

It takes commitment Your social life can be affected. Instead of enjoying a social event, you may instead see a room full of potential clients. You may even find friends avoid you if you constantly grind away at them. If you are outgoing, an extrovert and a person with a lot of business, social, and networking contacts, multilevel could be for you. Those who succeed are usually passionate and driven entrepreneurs, committed to their products and their company.

Most multilevel companies require that you attend training sessions, motivational seminars, and weekly "bring a friend" sales sessions. Their products are often distributed through in-home parties, so be prepared to work nights and weekends. These companies tend to come and go, so find one with a solid history. There are many disreputable companies distributing through this system—and there are some quite reputable, popular ones that have been around a long time. Talk to others who have been in the same company for a while and listen carefully to their feedback.

Answer the questions in Figure 2.2 before you make a commitment.

Figure 2.2: **IS DIRECT SELLING FOR ME?**

Consider the following questions before deciding whether direct selling and the company in question are a good match for you.

	Yes	No
1. Is the company secure?	☐	☐
2. Does it have a good reputation?	☐	☐
3. Do the company principals have sound credentials?	☐	☐
4. Are their track records credible?	☐	☐
5. Does the corporate management regularly change? (If yes, why?)	☐	☐
6. Can I feel comfortable approaching friends and family for sales?	☐	☐
7. Has the company been in business a few years?	☐	☐
8. Are the products of good quality and reasonably priced?	☐	☐
9. Am I confident enough to involve friends and family?	☐	☐
10. Will family life suffer because of evening/weekend commitments?	☐	☐
11. Am I able to attend out-of-town and out-of-country conferences?	☐	☐
12. Can I quickly close a deal?	☐	☐
13. Do I have enough money to purchase the start-up inventory?	☐	☐

Each company has its own set of rules, but usually you will need to buy sample kits or inventory, brochures, videos, magazines, and promotional items. You will need credit card facilities and will be charged shipping and handling costs, approximately 4 percent of the dollar value of the order. Some companies restrict how and where you can sell their products. Some want you to market only through home parties or prohibit displaying at trade shows. Be aware of these restrictions before making a final decision.

Multilevel marketing is like any other self-employed business, with the normal start-up costs and monthly overhead. Talk to a few people who have succeeded in the business and review start-up costs with them, including the continuing costs of remaining successful.

Which Business Is Right for You?

Ultimately, only you can decide which business will work best for you, so the next step is to further narrow down the possibilities by doing more research and evaluating. Figure 2.3 outlines some important considerations to think about as you toss and turn at night, dreaming about owning your first business. Think carefully about each one and write down your answers and concerns.

Figure 2.3: TEN FACTORS TO CONSIDER BEFORE DECIDING ON A BUSINESS

1. **Why I want to start a business:** Are you starting for the right reasons? Figure 1.3 in Chapter 1 will help you to better define this.
2. **My health and mental attitude:** Entrepreneurship takes long hours and can be stressful. If you are a Type A personality or easily depressed, self-employment can be a challenge.
3. **My future goals:** Be clear about your short-, mid-, and long-term goals for yourself, your family, and the business. Do you foresee a comfortable work-at-home situation, or do you want to grow? You need these goals to sustain your motivation.
4. **Family and quality of life:** These are the two most important facets of our lives. How will your business detract from or add to both?
5. **Suitability of your skills:** Are you experienced and knowledgeable enough for this business? Are you willing to continually upgrade your expertise and knowledge? Of course, you love people—right?

6. **Time:** You need extensive time to research and get this venture going. Then you'll be married to it, particularly for the first year or two. How much time are you prepared to devote to this business?
7. **Industry track record:** It may sound like a wonderful opportunity, but you need to research the past performance of this type of business. Trends come and go.
8. **Current and future trends:** Chapter 4 is devoted to market research and researching trends. You need to know where this business is going in the next decade.
9. **Financial considerations:** How much will you need, when will you need it, and where is it coming from? Chapter 7 addresses these questions.
10. **Personal cash needs:** You will need the business to provide you with an income. Have you reviewed your family and personal budget? Some businesses don't generate a profit for a year or two. How will you manage?

Work with professionals

When a business piques your interest, use professionals to help you make informed decisions. If you feel that you can't afford their fees, then you are not quite ready to start a business. Economizing in the wrong places will cost you later on. You will need the help of an accountant or business consultant, and should use a lawyer for all legal work and to review contracts and leases.

Ask friends in business if they are happy with their accountant, lawyer, or consultant. Be careful with referrals though—what works for one person may not be the best for another. Work within your budget, as many professionals charge an expensive hourly rate. If you have access to a U.S. Small Business Administration office, community business, or economic development office, call them for advice and referrals, or visit www.sba.gov.

You must feel comfortable with the professional you work with, so don't be scared to ask questions. Remember the old saying, "A question is only a dumb question until you find out the answer." Prepare a list of questions before you meet each time, and write down or record the answers. A good professional will fill in all the other gaps and tell you what you need to know. Listen carefully to their words of wisdom as they usually come from years of experience of counseling countless business owners.

Why Are Businesses Sold?

You can purchase two types of businesses, either an existing one or a "business opportunity," which will be discussed next in this chapter. Finding the perfect business is an exercise in patience, time, and frustration. Having traveled this road and worked with other entrepreneurs on the same path, I have seen the process take months. It requires professional advice and a practical approach because the wrong choice may cost you thousands of dollars.

Established businesses sell for a variety of reasons, the most common of which follow.

1. The business runs out of money

Poor planning, administrative difficulties, or new competitors are the usual reasons why businesses run out of money. Most small businesses struggle when they first open, and if costs exceed expectations or sales do not meet them, bank accounts quickly deplete. Owners become desperate to sell and will appear eager to persuade you that their business is the best thing since the invention of the microchip.

QUICK Tip

Know the Difference: Some businesses are excellent opportunities to acquire a business at a fair price. Perhaps all that is needed is a competent manager to turn it around. But first do your homework. It's no use buying someone else's troubles if they can't be remedied.

2. Illness, death, or family problems

Illness is a common reason for selling a business, particularly if there are no staff or family members to continue the operation. Seventy-five percent of small businesses close after the principal owner dies or becomes seriously ill. Some businesses cause too much stress on the family relationship, and the decision has to be made between keeping the business or maintaining the family's health. If it is being sold because of family pressures, find out why the work created these pressures in the first place. If the business is so stressful, do you really want to inherit someone else's problems?

3. Business burnout

It happens to many business owners—they just get really tired after many years of doing the same thing. It's like any other job. When the challenge has gone or the daily stresses are too great, the passion is lost. I personally know of many people who have closed up shop for these reasons. Baby boomers are frequently ready for a change of lifestyle. If the business has adequately supported the owner for many years, it may be a worthwhile proposition. It should have a well-established clientele and reputation, along with a solid financial history.

4. Increased competition

It's difficult to keep one step ahead of the competition, particularly for many smaller retail businesses. The arrival of a new supermarket, big-box store, or shopping mall is often their ultimate demise. Even if the vendor doesn't admit to this reason, it should be obvious if you thoroughly research the competition. If this appears to be the main reason for selling, pass this one by, because you will only inherit someone else's failing business.

What Is a Business Opportunity?

A business opportunity is just that—an opportunity to make money using a concept or idea that someone has developed. Businesses such as multilevel, network marketing, distributorships, vending routes, janitorial contracts, franchises, mail order, and Internet or computer-related businesses are considered business opportunities. Many can be operated from home. You purchase a concept that may or may not already be proven. Its success depends entirely on your business acumen and your ability to establish clients. The purchase price usually includes the necessary tools, such as vending machines, inventory, or samples.

Many of these businesses will present you with an idea that is made to sound so exciting and profitable, you just can't wait to sink your teeth into it. *Be cautious.* Seek professional advice, as these businesses are advertised in a manner that readily attracts people wanting a quick return and who have little cash. Those promises of big money usually don't pan out.

Beware of scams

Advertisements are designed to focus on five key attractions to potential buyers. They will tout:

- Low start-up costs
- Quick returns with high profits
- Part-time work
- No experience necessary
- The ability to work from home

Take a look in your newspaper under the business opportunities section on a Saturday, and read the tempting offers of quick, easy money. Here are just some advertisements, taken from a daily newspaper in one weekend edition:

- **LOOK! A minimum $10K investment can earn $65K** a year immediately. Guaranteed.

- **EMAIL PROCESSORS required immediately.** Use your own computer to earn income from home. No experience necessary.

- **AMAZING OPPORTUNITY.** Open the hottest franchise in North America. Low investment, high returns.

- Earn up to **2.5 million annually.** Investment required.

- Earn **$900 a month**, work only **10 hours a week**. Up to $2,500 a month for 25 hours' work.

- **Awesome** Internet Business. Home-based, no computer or exp. necessary. Huge profit potential.

- **Retire in three years!** Incredible income, low start-up costs, huge market!

- **$100,000 year** potential, computer earns you money 24 hours a day!

- **$20K investment, six-figure return**, huge market, no selling.

Advertisers reel in unsuspecting victims, preying on their desire for quick, easy cash with minimum investment. People who want to operate a home-based business are often their target. It's hard for the eager not to get excited with these wonderful promises. But if all these businesses were as simple as they sound, then why aren't more people rich? There are some not-so-honest people who are ready to take your money and run, or sell you an unprofitable business that makes money for no one except the vendors.

If you are not sure about with whom you are dealing, spend some time researching. Follow these five simple rules to put your mind at ease. Even if you are purchasing what appears to be a viable and reputable business, a thorough background check is time well invested. A resourceful site for conducting background checks is www.backgroundcheckgateway.com.

Rule #1: Perform a company name search

A legitimate business should be registered in your state with the Secretary of State. Are the owners really who they say they are? What is the corporate structure? In most states, you can perform a cost-free, online company search by business name to find out the corporate structure and ownership, and in some cases, even view and print out their corporate documents. As an example, visit www.sos.state.ia.us/dbsearch/index.html.

Rule #2: If in doubt, check them out

If you are not sure about the vendor's honesty, play super sleuth. Note the license plate and personal telephone numbers. See which name the phone line is registered under. If the person claims to own property, do a title search. Ensure you have both their home and business addresses.

Rule #3: Check references

Ask the vendor for both business and personal references, but be wary of personal references unless they come from a reputable source. Friends can provide glowing references for often shady characters. Ask for three recent trade references and ensure that the vendor is paying bills on time. Their bank may provide a credit reference with the vendor's permission. Ask for the vendor's bank manager's name.

Rule #4: Check the vendor's credentials

Checking a vendor's credentials is important, particularly if you are considering investing money into a new venture or a partnership. People seeking venture capital will often tell you anything to get their hands on your money. Some become quite desperate. Ask for a résumé and a list of previous employers, and check all references or contacts.

Rule #5: Check with other agencies

It is a simple procedure to check with the Better Business Bureau, where you can complete an online application (www.bbb.org), for previous complaints about a business. If you are a member of a credit bureau, have a credit check performed on the company. If the vendor is a member of any associations, call them and ask for a reference. If the vendor is trustworthy, they won't mind you asking these questions. If there is any hesitation, take it as a warning.

How Do You Assess a Potential Business?

A motivated vendor should have prepared information on the business for sale, called a business proposal. They come in many shapes and sizes, and you may have to wade through a lot of information to find out whether this business is right for you. You will undoubtedly look at many proposals before getting excited about a particular one. As most people can't afford to consult their accountant about each one, learn to first analyze them yourself. Then you can weed out those that do not meet your criteria and give the ones of interest to your accountant.

A well-presented business proposal should contain all or most of the following information:

1. History and detailed operation of the business
2. Profiles and résumés of the company owner(s)
3. Profiles and résumés of key employees, if any
4. Summary of current and future markets
5. Details of relevant competitors
6. Details of property leases, description of location and its benefits
7. Full description of the assets for sale, including any training period and other services or guarantees offered with the business
8. Asking price and terms of payment
9. Financial statements (prepared by a reputable accountant) for the previous two years
10. Projected income and expenses for one to two years
11. Letters of reference from clients and suppliers
12. Any pending contracts or letters of intent from clients

Many proposals don't contain all this information, so it's up to you to ask the vendor the right questions to fill in the gaps. Bear in mind that the vendor will present the business in its most positive light and probably play down any negative aspects. You need the information above for your accountant to make a fair assessment of the business. By analyzing all aspects of the business, including past history and current performance, you can both work together to make an informed decision about the business.

Twelve important questions to ask

As you review the proposal, there are twelve significant areas that you need to analyze. Once you feel satisfied that you have answered all the following questions and still feel positive about the proposal, make an appointment with your accountant or business consultant and review the proposal together. If you do not understand some of the terminology, turn to the glossary of terms in Chapter 3.

1. Is this business profitable? A business' profitability can be greatly determined by interpreting the financial statements. Therefore, ensure that they are prepared by a reputable accounting company. If possible, obtain two years' statements. They will show the assets, liabilities, equity and growth of the business, sales, cost of sales, operating expenses, the wages paid to staff and owners, and subsequent profits or losses. Your accountant can help you analyze them.

Pay for the Profits: Be prepared to pay for a well-established, profitable business. It's worth it, because you will have an immediate guaranteed income. Take into account the hard work that someone else has put into the business. They have experienced the mistakes and the learning curves—that alone has to be worth something.

2. Can the business support your wage requirements? If a business is not incorporated, the financial statements will not show the wages paid to the owners. Instead, the business should reflect a bottom line net profit high enough to satisfy the wage that you would like to take from the business. If it is incorporated, owners' wages will show as management fees. Wages will also be broken down into the various employee categories, such as manufacturing, sales, and office.

First decide which role you and your family or partner will play in the business. Then look at the wages paid out each year on the financial statements. This gives you an idea of how much wage overhead the business can support. Take into account the profits (if any) after all expenses and your wage. They can be used as additional wages, as long as your wage requirement does not negatively affect the business' cash flow. To ensure the business can support your wage requirements, draw up an annual household budget to determine the amount that the business must provide you with. Examine your personal expenses and include expenses that will occur in the near future.

3. Are sales seasonal, increasing, or decreasing? When you look at the annual sales on a financial statement, they don't reflect seasonal or month-by-month fluctuations. Ask the vendor to supply a two-year monthly sales breakdown so that you can assess seasonal fluctuations and decreases or increases in sales. The case study about Mel's Bookkeeping and Tax Services on the next page gives an example of a business that when closely examined, experiences definite sales fluctuations.

CASE STUDY: Mel's Bookkeeping and Tax Services

Mel was selling a small bookkeeping and tax business showing annual sales of $68,5000. The business incurred monthly costs of $2,000, and Mel drew $2,500 a month. The sales looked good, but when analyzing them month-by-month, this was the picture.

Monthly Sales for Mel's Bookkeeping and Tax Services

January	*$ 6,000*	*July*	*$3,500*
February	*$ 7,000*	*August*	*$2,500*
March	*$ 9,000*	*September*	*$4,000*
April	*$12,000*	*October*	*$5,000*
May	*$ 9,000*	*November*	*$3,000*
June	*$ 6,000*	*December*	*$1,500*

Analysis

Because the bulk of the bookkeeping income was from small businesses having their annual books and income taxes prepared, the first few months of the year were busy. But for five months, the business did not make enough to cover overhead and wages. Not only would the first six months be stressful with a heavy workload, it would also be difficult to plan cash flow to keep the business going for the rest of the year and plan to pay personal tax installments. One solution would be to train clients to bring in their books quarterly to even out the workload. Many businesses experience these seasonal fluctuations.

4. Are you paying too much for this business? The sale price of a business is based on the value of the assets—equipment, buildings, furniture, and inventory—plus goodwill. The business should reflect the ability to generate a steady wage. There is usually room to negotiate on the pricing, particularly if you and your accountant have performed a thorough analysis of the proposal.

5. Are the assets worth what is being asked? If you purchased the shares of an incorporated company, the assets are usually sold at book value as listed on the financial statements. "Book value" is the cost of the assets less accumulated depreciation over the years. With a proprietorship, the vendor may put an unrealistically high value on the assets or show you misleading appraisals for the value of larger equipment. Never pay more than fair market value.

No matter what an appraisal says, equipment is really worth no more than its book value at the time of sale. This is how banks evaluate assets on loan applications. Some vendors and purchasers arrive at an agreed purchase price somewhere between book and market values. Evaluating the inventory will require astute knowledge of what you are buying. People inevitably end up with worthless inventory or overpriced equipment. See Rule #2 under "Seven rules for a successful purchase" later in this chapter for more information.

6. Is the goodwill realistically priced? "Goodwill" is the term used to place a value on the intangible worth of the business. The figure is based on the business' reputation, its stability, and its ability to generate both profits and a reasonable wage for the owners. Your accountant can help you decide whether the goodwill price is reasonable. If you are purchasing a franchise, the goodwill is usually a set amount and there is little room for negotiation.

One common calculation bases goodwill on the money the business generated as an owner's wage within a one-year period (although some vendors use a two-year calculation), plus any net profits. If the vendor is drawing an annual wage of $40,000, or $65,000 with a spouse, then the goodwill could be as high as $65,000. If the business is still making a profit after these wages are drawn, then the goodwill may be worth even more. If it is losing money after these wages are drawn, then the goodwill amount should be reduced.

7. Do you have the experience to keep the business profitable? A new business is a challenge, and as the owner, you are responsible for its success. Ask the vendor about the role he or she plays in the business. Can you adequately fill these shoes or afford to pay someone else to? Remember to address those four main roles in business—operations, administration, sales, and marketing.

CASE STUDY: Missing the Mechanics of Business

Tony and Pradeep purchased a mechanical repair business. Pradeep had some mechanical experience, gained mainly from tinkering and a short night school course, while Tony was meticulous at paperwork. He had operated his own microbusiness for many years.

When they took over the store, things didn't go quite as planned. The operation required a vast knowledge of different components, and the paperwork, accounting, inventory management, sales, and marketing were more than a full-time job. Extra staff was hired to keep the business operational. The first two years produced a dramatic loss due to mismanagement at all levels. The stress caused Tony and Pradeep to argue and led to the eventual downfall of the business.

8. Could this business be expanded? Diversification is the key to growth, and planned growth is the key to success. How else could this business expand or diversify into other areas? If it is a retail store, what other lines or services could be introduced? For a service business, how could you expand, increase, or improve this service? For a seasonal business, how could you diversify during the quieter periods? If you cannot expand or diversify, what else can you do to increase sales?

9. What mistakes did the owners make that you should avoid? Your accountant will highlight any areas of concern in the financial statements. The balance sheet may show too much inventory, a growing bank overdraft, or perhaps too many outstanding accounts receivables. Government taxes may be overdue. The statement of income and expenses will highlight areas of overspending, such as wages or advertising. The profit margins after cost of sales may not be as high as you have been told. Ask the vendor these questions. From there, you have to decide whether you could run the business more efficiently. What would you change? What can be changed? What will take time to change? What would such changes cost?

10. What is the life expectancy of this business? Your business needs a built-in longevity to survive. Research the history of the industry, study consumer trends, and be reasonably certain that your business will still be performing profitably in the next five to ten years. For example, one long-term business trend is computer servicing, repair, and customer education. Few businesses can survive without technology these days, and many owners do not fully understand how to use the various software programs.

Consumers are fickle. They drive the world trends and trends change quickly. Some businesses do not continue to grow because they refuse to keep up with both trends and technology. Is the business you are purchasing keeping up with these changes? How will future trends affect its growth?

11. Who makes the most profit—the franchiser or you? With a franchise, you need to know exactly what percentage of profits is going into the franchiser's pocket. You will probably pay a percentage of gross sales as a royalty or toward advertising costs. Some franchises require an annual fee for overhead costs. With an existing franchise chain, those numbers will already be available to study.

You will pay a franchise fee, or goodwill on purchase, and depending on the franchise's reputation, this can be tens of thousands of dollars. In some cases, franchises make more money than their operators. Think about how much ice cream or how many cups of coffee you have to sell to cover these costs and the time and labor involved.

12. Are projections realistic? Projections of future income, expenses, and profits should be based on past performance, factoring in the present and future economy and trends. Few projections live up to their claims because too many factors can change at any moment. So don't take them at face value. It makes more sense to study past financial statements. If they reflect a loss, yet the projections reflect healthy profits in the coming year or two, ask what magic formula the business will be using to achieve these figures and market that formula yourself—you'll get rich a lot quicker!

Seven rules for a successful purchase

If after answering all these questions you still have a burning desire to buy this business, the next step is to delve even further.

Question a Projection: Projections are just one person's idea of how the business may perform in the next one or two years. It's amazing what one can do with numbers and a spreadsheet. They are only as good as the substantiated reasoning behind them, so ensure that they are based on past history, current performance, and relevant current and future market trends, expansion potential, and sales and marketing strategies.

Here are seven rules to help you to further evaluate the business' viability.

Rule #1: Take a thorough inventory of the premises

The reputation of the business in the marketplace is important to your success. A good reputation is based on management and technical expertise, quality products, and customer service. If you would be taking over an existing location, it's time for a field trip. Take note of the overall appearance of the premises. They should be a clean, cheery, well-decorated, and comfortable. Ask yourself: Is this a business that I would like to do business with? Answer the questions in Figure 2.4 on your field trip.

Talk to the employees and ask lots of questions. Take someone experienced with you for a second opinion. It's too easy to view a business through rose-colored glasses when you are excited about buying your first business; you need an outside, practical, experienced person to help you. You need to be sure that equipment is in good working order and that the internal operation is efficient. Ask to see the lease and talk to the landlord.

Rule #2: Perform a physical inventory of the assets

The proposal should contain a list of assets and inventory for sale with the business. Take it with you and physically check each asset, ensuring that you see everything on the list. Note model and serial numbers of larger pieces of equipment. You can phone around later to verify that you are paying a fair price. Ask what type of regular repairs and maintenance the equipment requires and when it last broke down or was serviced.

Figure 2.4: **HOW TO EVALUATE THE PREMISES**

Take an inventory of the premises and ensure all these questions are answered.

	Yes	No
1. Is the staff friendly?	☐	☐
2. Are the products attractively displayed?	☐	☐
3. Do prices seem competitive?	☐	☐
4. Is there sufficient, up-to-date inventory?	☐	☐
5. Are the employees happy in their work?	☐	☐
6. Will they stay on after a change of ownership?	☐	☐
7. Do you know their areas of expertise?	☐	☐
8. Is the location suitable for this type of business?	☐	☐
9. Do you know what improvements are needed?	☐	☐
10. Are these improvements costly?	☐	☐
11. If leased, do you know when the rent will increase?	☐	☐
12. Do you know how long the lease is for?	☐	☐
13. Will you have the first option to renew the lease?	☐	☐
14. Have you checked with the city or county's zoning department?	☐	☐
15. Is there adequate parking?	☐	☐
16. Is there adequate heat and ventilation?	☐	☐

As a new purchaser, you may not be aware of what sells and what does not. You don't want to purchase inventory that will not turn quickly, as this depletes your operating capital and cash flow. If in doubt, contract a company to evaluate the inventory (see "Inventory Services" in the Yellow Pages). They may also be able to suggest an appraiser for your equipment.

Don't Buy Junk: Ensure that the inventory is all marketable and that no obsolete or unsaleable items are included. If there are useless products, make a deal to either purchase them at a low cost or have the book value deleted from the final inventory purchase price. Then it is the vendor's responsibility to dispose of these items.

For example, one client of mine was buying a business, including a piece of equipment valued at $6,500. When I requested the financial figures, the equipment turned out to be quite old, having a book value of only $2,300. My client then offered the book value price for the equipment, saving $4,200.

CASE STUDY: Outdated and Obsolete

Sid and Ray were interested in buying a store that carried a large inventory worth nearly $100,000. It was a well-established business, with much of the inventory consisting of rebuilt stock and used spare parts. Their knowledge of this equipment was basic, so under their accountant's advice, they spent three weeks thoroughly physically checking the inventory, finally arriving at a price reduction. What they didn't do was take along someone who had expertise with that type of equipment. After the first year of operation, they realized that much of it was useless. Of the remaining inventory, large, expensive pieces sat on the floor without moving all year. These pieces had to be reduced to cost to regain some cash flow. Sid and Ray finally dumped the old stock at a loss of $30,000. The business bankrupted the following year.

Rule #3: Discuss all information with your accountant

Professionally prepared proposals can boggle your mind with hype, exciting words, facts, and figures. Don't buy a business without some pertinent written information and financial figures. Be wary of financial figures prepared by the business, as people can be extremely creative with their accounting. They must use a professional accountant to validate the financial statement's authenticity.

You *have* to use an accountant to review a proposal. He or she will prepare a list of questions to be asked or will ask those questions for you. Accountants can read the whole history of a business in financial statements. Your accountant will contact the accountant who prepared the statements and will know the right questions to ask. As an example, if just one outstanding supplier account for $3,000 is not entered into the books, the profits will be overstated by $3,000.

Rule #4: Have a proper agreement for sale prepared

Don't purchase any business without having a legal agreement for sale prepared. It will protect both you and the vendor. Without this document, you have no recourse when trouble arises—and it can. Your agreement becomes a valuable document in court. (This subject is covered in more depth in Chapter 5.)

Two women went into partnership and opened a high-end shoe store. The store flourished, but after four years, one partner wanted to sell her share of the store. There was a legal agreement in place, and after the issue was resolved, the other partner ended up leaving. She commented that she was so glad there was a solid agreement in place to protect her interests.

Rule #5: Visit your local city or county office

A visit to local city or county offices enables you to check that the company has not infringed on or broken any local regulation or environmental laws. Check pending or possible future regulations that could be detrimental to the business. Planning and engineering departments can tell you whether there are pending changes to zoning regulations or traffic route changes. New road construction may involve cutting off store access, sending customers to competitors. There may be new malls being built near you. You don't need a new competitor opening a sparkling new store next door a few months down the road.

QUICK Tip

First Know the Home-Based Regulations: If the business you are considering will be home-based, become familiar with the home-based regulations. Most have restrictions on retail sales, manufacturing, the type of business, traffic generation, office size, and building usage, and regulations differ in each city and county. Many home-based businesses have been closed down due to regulation infractions, and it's usually your friendly neighbor who will report you.

Rule #6: Research your competition and the market

No matter how well the business appears to be doing physically and on paper, presume that the competition is still fierce. Find out who your competitors are, what type of products they sell, and what their pricing structures are. What does this business offer that is better than the competition?

The business may be seriously affected by consumer spending trends, continued downturns in the economy, environmental issues, or advancing technology. It may have performed adequately to date or may show a slight drop in sales over the previous year or two. No matter what the vendor tells you, thorough market research will indicate current and future trends. (Chapter 4 deals with market research and strategies in depth.)

Rule #7: Don't start a business on a shoestring

Purchasing or starting a business on a shoestring budget or with big loans is usually a formula for disaster. Prepare a business plan that includes projections and cash flow forecasts. See Chapter 7 for more information on business plans. Your business has to meet loan payments one month after you open your doors. Allow time for take-over or start-up, a period when revenues may drop or expenses may be higher than normal. If you ruin your credit rating by defaulting on loan payments, it will take years to repair. You are also threatening the growth and success of your business if you can't spend the necessary dollars to keep it fully operational.

As you research this business, consider the questions in Figure 2.5 on the following page.

Figure 2.5: BUSINESS PURCHASE CHECKLIST

Use this checklist to guide you through the purchase so that you don't miss any important steps.

	Yes	No
1. I've searched the company name and had it validated.	☐	☐
2. I've validated the vendor's personal credentials.	☐	☐
3. I've validated business and trade references.	☐	☐
4. I've researched the business location, the lease, and employees	☐	☐
5. I've evaluated the assets and inventory and they are satisfactory.	☐	☐
6. I've discussed the business proposal with my accountant.	☐	☐
7. My lawyer has prepared the agreement for sale.	☐	☐
8. The city/county approval and research are completed.	☐	☐
9. I've researched the competition and market.	☐	☐
10. I have sufficient funds available to start and operate this business.	☐	☐
11. This business is definitely a profitable concern.	☐	☐
12. This business can pay me a satisfactory wage.	☐	☐
13. The sales figures are steady and not declining.	☐	☐
14. I can operate the business competently.	☐	☐
15. My accountant agrees that the price is satisfactory.	☐	☐
16. The assets are fairly evaluated.	☐	☐
17. The goodwill is fairly priced.	☐	☐
18. This business could be diversified or expanded.	☐	☐
19. I am aware of mistakes made by the previous owner.	☐	☐
20. This business has a definite long-term life.	☐	☐
21. This franchise makes acceptable profits.	☐	☐
22. The projected returns are realistic and attainable.	☐	☐

What Is the Next Step?

Before you progress any further, you now need to understand the ins and outs of financial figures, because that's what being in business is all about—making sales and making profits. It is difficult to make informed decisions or prepare a business plan if you don't understand accounting terminology and financial statements. The next chapter gives you a crash course in both these areas. As most people hate accounting, you had better make a fresh cup of coffee and grit your teeth—the more you know, the better prepared you will be for success.

Chapter 3

What Is a Financial Statement?

A balanced life is one where the assets far outweigh the liabilities.

- **Why do we need accounting?**
- **How do the figures get there?**
- **What information is in a financial statement?**
- **Accounting terms and definitions**
- **How to analyze a financial statement**
- **The five-minute financial test**

Why Do We Need Accounting?

Accounting is one of the few languages that is universally understood. Businesses throughout the world record their transactions using what is called the double-entry bookkeeping method. I believe this system was invented by an ancient Greek. No wonder people look at their financial statements and mutter, "It all looks like Greek to me." Yet to survive and succeed in business, you should learn this foreign language, its terminology, and its unique bookkeeping methods. Once you get the hang of it, it makes a lot of sense. Bottom line, you *are* in business to make money.

The majority of business owners glance at their financial statements when their accountant prepares them annually, and then throw them into the filing cabinet, usually after complaining about both their tax and accounting bills. Yet these documents are the lifeline of a business and the only true tool that monitors the performance of a business to the cent—if the bookkeeping is accurate.

Learn to love financial statements

Running a business is no different from running your household. Your home and contents are your assets and the mortgage and unpaid bills are liabilities. The difference between the value of your assets less the debts is called "equity." We all know what equity in our home means. Your paycheck is the income that should accommodate the home expenses such as food, mortgage or rent, clothing, and utilities. The money you have left over (if any) is your profit.

QUICK Tip

Definition of a Financial Statement: A financial statement is a snapshot taken of your business at a given time. Usually this picture is taken at a month-end. It will tell you what the business owns (its assets), what it owes (its liabilities), your capital and equity in the business, what the sales were, what it cost to make those sales, what the business overhead was, and how much profit (or loss) the business made.

Financial statements are essential business management tools because you will be making many decisions based on this information, including whether to buy an existing business or not. Just as you would not buy a used vehicle without having a mechanic do a thorough check or purchase an expensive jewel without an appraisal, you wouldn't buy a business without first establishing the accuracy of the financial figures. Financial statements paint a vivid picture of your business' progress and will guide you toward making sound decisions. So learn to treat them as your friend, not a necessary evil.

Think Ahead: The smart operator will review financial statements at least quarterly. You can catch mistakes and review problem areas before they worsen and use the statements to plan ahead. You can review the results of certain strategies, marketing campaigns, or changes in consumer and electronic trends.

As a consultant, clients don't leave my office until they have received a thorough lesson in interpreting their statements. It may take a few cups of coffee, but you cannot operate a business without understanding what is happening to it. Those few clients who refused to take financial responsibility are no longer in business.

Financial statements can be prepared monthly, quarterly, half-yearly, or annually. Most small businesses only have an annual statement prepared for tax purposes. This is seat-of-the-pants management, which leads to large holes and is one main reason why so many businesses fail. Problem areas develop, but no one takes the time to notice or analyze why.

To make this fun subject a little easier, each term found on a financial statement is defined in this chapter. Understanding financial statements is probably the most difficult subject to digest, so hang in there—the reading gets easier once you have grasped the basic concepts.

Don't Ignore the Numbers: Financial statements show you sales fluctuations, profit margin changes, cost increases, overhead fluctuations, and changes in net profit. They will tell you whether you are further in debt or have too much cash tied up in inventory or receivables. You can plan your personal tax position and strategies for growing your business.

How do the figures get there?

Financial statements don't just magically appear at the press of a button. A full accounting cycle must first be completed. To better understand how financial statements are produced and the importance of accurate paperwork and bookkeeping, let's examine the accounting cycle.

1. Source documents

The first rule of accounting is to keep a receipt for everything, from the research stage through to start-up and onward. (See Chapter 11 for your record-keeping and accounting lesson.) These papers are called "source documents," and include invoices, checks, credit card accounts, bank deposits, bills, and receipts. Each month, these source documents are recorded into various books, or "ledgers," using the double-entry bookkeeping system.

2. Double-entry bookkeeping system

When source documents are recorded into the various ledgers, either manually or using an accounting software program, one entry is always a debit and one a credit. As Figure 3.1 shows, one entry describes the transaction and the other acts as a control, for example, when your checks are reconciled to the bank statement. At the end of each month, all transactions are totaled, with debit columns equalling credit columns. The balances are then transferred to a general ledger, which is set up in order of the financial statement's accounts. The general ledger is used to prepare financial statements. Figure 3.1 gives an example of paying an account and entering it to the check disbursements journal.

Figure 3.1: PHONE PAYMENT USING DOUBLE-ENTRY BOOKKEEPING

Date	Paid to	Check #	Bank out	Telephone
			(Credit)	(Debit)
06/26/xx	AT&T Telephone Co.	7824	165.00	165.00
			(Control)	**(Expense description)**

3. The six-step accounting cycle

Without giving you a complete bookkeeping lesson, Figure 3.2 shows how those source documents are turned into a financial statement in six steps. An error recording a source document carries through all of the six steps.

Figure 3.2: THE SIX-STEP ACCOUNTING CYCLE

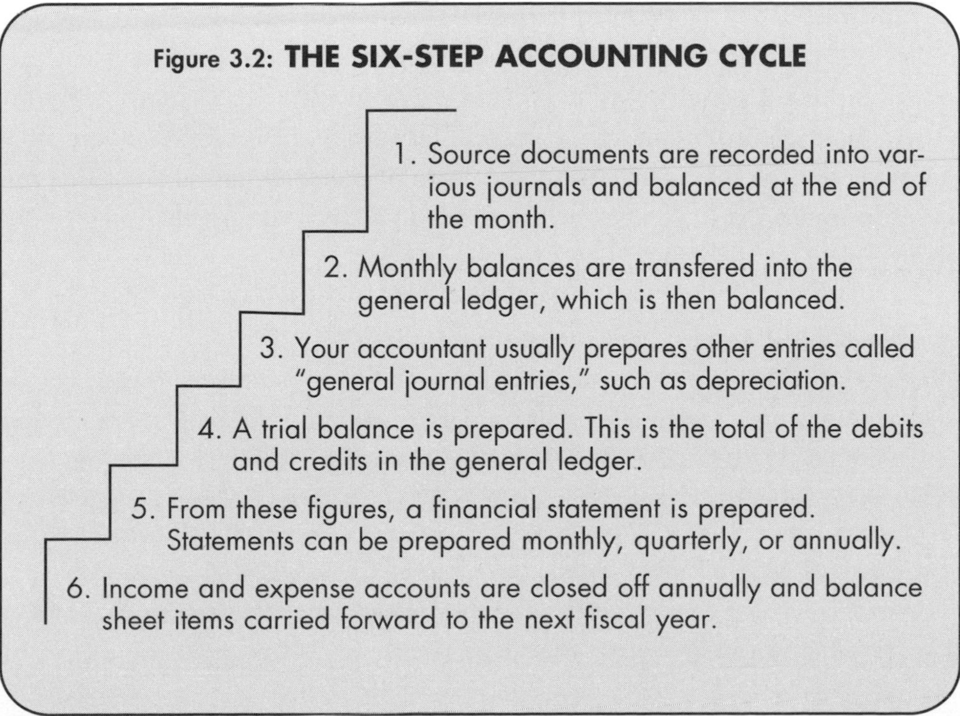

What Information Is in a Financial Statement?

A financial statement follows a set format, consisting of the following sections:

1. Compilation or review engagement report
2. Balance sheet
3. Statement of retained earnings (if incorporated)
4. Statement of income and expenses
5. Notes to financial statements
6. Statement of changes in financial position

1. Compilation or review engagement report

A financial statement opens with either a compilation or a review engagement report disclaimer, which must be prepared by a CPA for that title to be legally valid. This is a statement from the accountant to the business owner telling you which method was used to prepare the statements.

A compilation report disclaimer states that the accountant has prepared the information provided from the records of the business, but has not reviewed, audited, or otherwise attempted to verify the accuracy or completeness of such information or determined whether the statements contain departures from generally accepted accounting principles. Some may say that the statements are for internal use of management and for income tax purposes only, so readers are cautioned that the statements may not be appropriate for their purposes.

QUICK Tip

Choose Carefully: Most small businesses have a compilation report prepared, as a review engagement report is a more expensive and time-consuming process, used mainly by larger businesses. For a review engagement report, the accountant performs more in-depth checks and cross-checks. No matter which type of statement you have prepared, don't skimp by choosing the cheapest accountant. You get what you pay for.

With a compilation report, although accountants perform certain checks, they cannot guarantee that the accounting is correct. Bank accounts may be reconciled and all information processed, but the information may not be correctly allocated or information may be missing. If you are buying a business, contact the accountant who prepared the statements to verify the accuracy of the books and records. If the person preparing the books does not have an accounting background, errors are sure to occur.

You will find the word "unaudited" on each statement page. This means that the accountant has not performed a full audit of the books. Audited statements are usually required for nonprofit organizations or businesses that have gone public on the stock exchange. They are costly and not necessary for the average business.

2. Balance sheet

A balance sheet reflects the value of the business at a given month-end date: its assets, liabilities, and the current equity in the business, as well as how much profit (or loss) the company is making (or losing). It reflects the ending balances at the completion of the fiscal period for which the statement was prepared.

Accounting can be prepared two ways: the cash method, which records only transactions made by the statement date, or the accrual method, which takes into account all transactions for the fiscal period, including uncollected or unpaid accounts.

3. Statement of retained earnings

Applicable only to incorporated businesses, this page is an ongoing record of the business's profits or losses for both the period in question and since inception. It shows the opening balance for the period and adds or subtracts the current profits or losses, reflecting a new closing balance. These figures are a similar calculation to the equity section of an unincorporated business.

4. Statement of income and expenses

This statement reflects all sales and other income the business has generated for the period, less all expenses. The "bottom line" indicates the net profit or loss the company has incurred for the fiscal year to date. An example is given in Figure 3.4 of this chapter.

5. Notes to financial statements

At the end of the financial statements, the accountant provides details as to how certain figures were calculated. These include how inventory was costed, when the business was incorporated, the rates of depreciation used, the terms of loans and shareholder loans, and any other information that the IRS or banks may need to see.

6. Statement of changes in financial position

A statement of changes in financial position is only prepared for some incorporated businesses. Banks like this type of information. It details where the money came from during the year (profits or loans) and how the money was used (to finance a loss, pay back loans, or purchase assets). It shows the working capital of the business and whether it has increased or decreased during the year.

Accounting Terms and Definitions

During your entrepreneurial career, you will hear many new words and terms. Now is the time to learn what they mean. The terms are explained here, in the same order as they appear on a typical financial statement.

Balance sheet terms

Assets: *Everything the business owns.* These include bank accounts, inventory, accounts receivable, equipment, buildings, vehicles, computers, deposits, and investments. Assets are broken down on the balance sheet into current assets and fixed assets.

Current assets: *Any asset the company owns that could be turned into cash within one year.* These are listed in order with the most current, cash in the bank, first.

Cash at bank: *The total cash in all bank accounts.* Each account is reconciled (balanced) with the bank statement or bank book to the cent. When you read the statements, all bank accounts will be grouped together as one total. If the balance is overdrawn, it will show farther down as a liability.

Accounts receivable: *Uncollected debts owing to the business.* This amount should be balanced to a client list of monies due, called a "receivables list" or an "aged analysis." The age of the debt is separated into current, thirty, sixty, ninety days, and over. This list should be prepared monthly and used to help you collect outstanding accounts.

Prepaid expenses and deposits: *Expenses paid ahead of the statement date and/or funds or deposits in trust.* Examples of prepaid expenses include the last month's rent on a lease, a deposit on utility services and annual insurance policies. A policy paid in July with a December business year-end has six months of the policy prepaid, which is an expense for the next fiscal period. Prepaid expenses also include equipment maintenance contracts, vehicle and shop insurance, and property taxes. Your accountant will calculate these figures for you.

Inventory: *The value at cost of unsold materials or products.* This includes manufacturing raw materials, goods purchased for redistribution, or finished goods. An inventory evaluation must be taken when a statement is prepared. Old, obsolete, or slow-moving products should be devalued in price at year-end and included in this figure. Assets or consumables, such as stationery, are not considered inventory because they are not resold.

Work in progress: *Partially completed contracts, services, or manufactured products not yet billed to clients.* The value of the work to date is estimated and classified as "work in progress" instead of being called "accounts receivable."

Fixed assets: *An asset owned and utilized by the business.* These consist of equipment or similar items with a singular value of over $100. Smaller items, for example, a calculator, are overhead expenses. Fixed assets are listed at purchase cost, not appraised value. They include furniture, fittings, computers, cellular phones, buildings, vehicles, manufacturing equipment, land, machinery, telephone systems, and leasehold improvements.

Leasehold improvements: *A permanent addition to a structure.* These are assets that remain in the building if a company closes or moves, and include new carpeting, lighting, shelves, or renovations to a building. (See the following definitions for depreciation and amortization to see what happens then.)

Accumulated depreciation: *An allowance made for the wear and tear on a capital item (asset).* Each type of fixed asset has a defined rate of depreciation, determined by the IRS. Ask your accountant to explain the various rates and methods because initially it can be confusing. Your accountant will depreciate your assets for you and the current year's depreciation shows on the income and expense statement. Accumulated capital cost allowance is the total depreciation claimed since the asset was purchased.

Amortization: *The allowance for wear and tear on certain fixed assets.* Leasehold improvements are a good example. If you signed a five-year lease and spent $10,000 on improving a building, your accountant would depreciate these leasehold improvements over a five-year period, or at a rate of $2,000 a year. The balance sheet shows the amount of amortization claimed since the improvements were made.

Net book value: *The difference between the purchase price of an asset less accumulated depreciation.* For example, if equipment is shown at a value of $40,000 and accumulated depreciation is $35,400, the net book value is $4,600. This tells you that the equipment has been around for a long time. Net book value reflects an asset's true value.

Incorporation fees: *Fees paid to incorporate a business.* This cost is shown on the balance sheet as an asset and is amortized, starting in the first year, over a period of sixty months. The amortized amount becomes an operating expense.

Goodwill: *The intangible dollar value paid for a business.* If a person purchased the business before you, they probably paid a certain amount for goodwill, and in turn will charge you a goodwill sum. It is amortized over a period of years.

Total assets: *The sum of current, fixed, and other assets, less accumulated capital cost allowance.* This amount reflects the book value of all assets at the end of the accounting period.

Liabilities: *The total of all debts owing by the business.* These are broken down into current liabilities and long-term liabilities.

Current liabilities: *Debts owed by the business that are due and payable within one year.* These include bank overdrafts, short-term loans, supplier accounts (accounts payable), federal and state taxes payable, employee payroll deductions due to various agencies, and Workers' compensation.

Equity: *The amount of money the business owes the owner.* In a proprietorship, this is the capital put in by the owner less money taken out, plus or minus profits or losses. In an incorporated company, equity consists of the shares issued, plus or minus profits and losses. This section reflects "the bottom line" and overall performance of the business

Long-term liabilities: A debt due and payable over a period of years. Examples are equipment loans, bank loans, mortgages, loans from friends, and shareholders' loans. The principal portion due for each loan within one year is recorded under current liabilities. The remaining balance shows under long-term liabilities. Your accountant calculates these balances for you.

QUICK TIP

Limit Long-Term Liabilities: As tempting as it is to borrow from whoever and wherever you can, long-term debt is a noose around your neck, just like a home mortgage. Explore all avenues of financing before you sign on the dotted line. If you need to borrow large amounts of money, perhaps you should rethink your venture.

The balance sheet equation: *Total assets equal the total of liabilities plus equity.* This is the magic of double-entry bookkeeping—it really works. Figure 3.3 shows a simple transaction.

Figure 3.3: **A SIMPLE BALANCE SHEET EQUATION**

Andrew invested $50,000 to start a mobile gymnasium business. He used $20,000 of his own money and borrowed $30,000 from the bank to purchase a vehicle.

His current asset is cash in the bank	$15,000	=	ASSET
His fixed asset is automotive equipment	$35,000	=	ASSET
His long-term liability is a bank loan	$30,000	+	LIABILITY
His capital is his equity	$20,000	+	EQUITY
(Or shareholder's loan if incorporated)			

Balance sheet equation:
Assets ($50,000) = Liabilities ($30,000) + Equity ($20,000)

Cash Flow: *The movement of money in and out of a business.* A business with "poor cash flow" will have trouble paying its bills. "Planning your cash flow" means projecting when and how the money will come into the business and where and when it will be spent. A "healthy cash flow" means a business is operating at peak efficiency and has enough money to pay its liabilities.

Working capital: *The difference between the dollar value of current assets and current liabilities.* A bank will always look at a business' working capital when considering a loan application. The theory is that if you turned all your current assets into cash and paid off all your current bills, a healthy company should have some cash left over. In many cases, the equation seems to work the other way. Here is an example of healthy working capital:

Current assets:	$27,942
Less current liabilities:	$15,355
Working capital:	$12,587

An example of a business not experiencing a healthy working capital situation would be to reverse the above asset and liability figures.

Statement of income and expenses terms

A statement of income and expenses graphically illustrates how a business operates over a given period. It is usually broken down into three or four sections and gives management valuable information. It shows all income, cost of sales, gross and net profits, and overhead expenses. Using a furniture store as an example, a statement of income and expenses is given in Figure 3.4.

Income (sales or revenue): *The total of all revenue sources earned from a business.* Income is mainly derived from sales but also includes interest earned from bank accounts, royalties, and commissions. It does not include funds from loans, and can be broken down into various categories to help you further analyze sales.

Cost of sales: *The actual costs incurred to generate a sale before operating overhead.* Each business incurs different sales costs dependent on the type of business. They can be broken down into cost of sales and then direct sales costs. Cost of sales usually applies to a business that carries inventory. This calculation is the cost of manufacturing, distributing, or retailing a product. A service business, such as consulting, usually incurs overhead costs only, although some service businesses—such as housepainter or car mechanic—will carry a certain amount of inventory.

Direct or sales costs: *The expenses incurred to sell a product.* These expenses can be separated from normal cost of sales to analyze expenses applicable to selling products. This is useful as it helps you better monitor your profit margins.

QUICK Tip

Gross Profit: *The difference between the selling price and the cost of sales.* This is a vital area to monitor because it is the gross profit that pays for the overhead expenses and your wages. It is expressed as a percentage of sales on a financial statement and should be consistent with your expected profit margins. A slight reduction in profit percentages can represent substantial dollars.

Overhead expenses: *Costs incurred to sustain the business operation.* These expenses include items such as rent, telephones, and insurance. Some costs do not change whether sales are made or not. Some increase or decrease depending on sales volume, such as advertising. They are listed in alphabetical order on a financial statement.

Net profit/(loss): *The profit (or loss) after all expenses and before corporate or personal taxes.* Often referred to as the "bottom line," this is the profit that the business generated after all costs were incurred. An incorporated business or a proprietorship pays tax on this amount. Figure 3.4 shows an example of a furniture store's income and expense statement and a description and analysis of the results.

Figure 3.4: STATEMENT OF INCOME AND EXPENSES FOR JUDY'S HOME FURNISHINGS INC.

Revenue:		
By furniture sales	$ 62,000	
By bedding sales	45,000	
By small item sales	18,000	
	$125,000	
Cost of sales:		
Opening inventory	$ 12,000	(Furniture in inventory at beginning of period)
Purchases	50,000	(All furniture purchased for the period)
Freight in	1,000	(Freight costs to deliver furniture to store)
Customs & duty	5,000	(Import, customs, and brokerage charges)
	68,000	
Less closing inventory	(9,000)	(Cost price of unsold inventory at end of period)
Total cost of sales:	$ 59,000	
Gross profit: (53%)	**$ 66,000**	(Cost of sales subtracted from sales)

(Gross profit is calculated by dividing $66,000 into $125,000 as a percentage. This is the gross profit on retail, not cost price.)

Direct sales costs:		
Wages—sales staff	$ 25,000	(Wages paid to sales staff)
Discounts	1,000	(Discounts given on sales)
Damaged goods	500	(Damaged furniture written off)
Delivery expense	3,000	(Delivery costs to clients)
Total direct costs:	$ 29,500	
Gross profit: (29%)	**$ 36,500**	(Direct costs subtracted from gross profit)
Overhead expenses:		
Accounting fees	$ 500	(Cost to prepare statement)
Advertising	2,000	(Newspapers, flyers, magazine advertising)
Bad debts	200	(Uncollectible accounts receivables)
Bank charges	500	(Monthly bank and credit card fees)
Depreciation	2,500	(Allowance for wear and tear of assets)
Employee payroll costs	2,800	(Employer portion of payroll deductions)
Fees, licenses, taxes	300	(Licenses due to organizations & property taxes)
Interest, loans	1,500	(Loan interest for period)
Legal fees	400	(Legal fees, excluding incorporation)
Management salaries	15,000	(Shareholders' salaries, incorporated company)
Office stationery	1,500	(Printing, coffee, and office supplies)
Office salaries	7,000	(Clerical wages)

Promotion	1,200	(Client gifts, incentives, open houses, etc.)
Rent	5,000	(Monthly rent)
Repairs & maintenance	700	(Store repairs, general maintenance)
Shop supplies	500	(Odds and ends, small tools)
Telephone, cell, computer	800	(Line rentals, long distance, Internet, cellular)
Utilities	1,200	(Light, heat, and water)
Workers' compensation	800	(Workers' compensation)
Total overhead	$ 44,400	
Net profit/(loss):	**$ ($7,900)**	**Loss**

Analysis of a statement of income and expenses It appears that Judy's Home Furnishings Inc. has a few problems. The gross profit margin is healthy at $66,000 or 53 percent after cost of sales, but when sales wages and overhead costs are deducted, there is no profit left. Wages total $47,000, or 37.6 percent of costs. The total cost of sales is $88,500, or 71 percent of sales. Add on all wages, and cost of sales plus wages equals $110,500. This leaves a measly 11.6 percent of sales, or $14,500 to cover the overhead costs. This store employs four people—two sales staff, the owner, and a bookkeeper. Either the wages are too high or the sales are too low. Perhaps staff hours should be reduced or a better marketing strategy implemented.

The other overhead costs are not far out of line. Marketing is necessary, and as a general rule, four to seven percent of sales should be allocated to promotion, and $2,000 represents only 1.6 percent of sales. Other overhead costs could be slightly trimmed but the main problem appears to be high wages that are not supported by sufficient sales. Some astute financial management is needed here to reverse the bottom line.

How to Analyze a Financial Statement

Learn how to read financial statements and practice interpreting the various pictures that financial statements paint. Practice using the Complete Computer Care Center's case study on the next page. Read the statements in Figure 3.5 on page 75 and see what they tell you. Write down your observations before reading the analysis.

CASE STUDY: Complete Computer Care Center

Marcel started Complete Computer Care Center, a home-based computer sales and service business. At the end of his second year, he took his books to his accountant to have the year-end prepared. When he started his business, Marcel's idea was to educate and service clients in all facets of computer technology, including designing the right system to suit their needs, purchasing and installation, software education, consulting, problem-solving, and equipment servicing.

He purchased his equipment from a reputable supplier who extended good warranties. Because the industry was so competitive, he knew that his gross margins on equipment were not much over 10 percent. But with the busy lifestyle that many of his small business clients led, he hoped to encourage them to hire him to solve all their problems, from installing the new system and software to networking and upgrading their systems with new technology—such as firewalls, new anti-virus software, and scanners. Using technology, Marcel could fix many clients' problems by connecting to their computers from his office, saving unnecessary traveling time and costs.

Marcel purchased the latest computer equipment for himself and this year he borrowed money from the bank to buy a used van. His father lent him $15,000 to start the business, which was not due until he had completed four years in business. He purchased some new systems for resale near the end of the year, as they were "a steal" and he knew he could make a better profit on them. He always kept some equipment in inventory.

It was a competitive field and Marcel found that he was busy reading and educating himself to keep up with the latest technological advances. He attended an expensive conference and actively promoted his business through both networking and various marketing strategies. Marcel's hourly billing rate for consulting and service calls was $95, a reasonable industry billing charge. He paid a bookkeeper to prepare his books every three months and subcontracted out some of the work that he could not handle. He had a new webpage designed and kept it high on the search engines. He was married with a lovely wife and had a second child on the way. Life was hectic. At the end of the year, Figure 3.5 shows how his financial statements looked. What do you observe from these figures?

Figure 3.5: **ANALYZING COMPLETE COMPUTER CARE CENTER'S FINANCIAL STATEMENTS**

Complete Computer Care Center
Balance Sheet
December 31, XXXX (Unaudited)

ASSETS		
Current assets:		
Cash at bank	$ 3,237	
Accounts receivable	7,310	
Inventories	18,247	
Prepayments & deposits	310	29,104
Fixed assets:		
Computer equipment	25,500	
Office furniture	3,170	
Automotive equipment	15,750	
	44,420	
Less accumulated depreciation	(13,263)	
		31,157
Total assets:		**$60,261**
LIABILITIES		
Current liabilities:		
Accounts payable	$28,862	
State & federal taxes	3,198	
Current portion bank loan	3,150	35,210
Long-term liabilities:		
Bank loan	14,400	
Loan, R. Matthews	15,000	29,400
		64,610
EQUITY		
Balance beginning of period	$ 1,290	
Contributed capital for period	1,210	
	2,500	
Net profit for period	7,757	
	10,257	
Less draws for period	(14,606)	(4,349)
Total liabilities and equity:		**$60,261**

Complete Computer Care Center
Statement of Income and Expenses
December 31, XXXX
(Unaudited)

Revenue:		
By computer sales	$ 82,250	
By parts and small items	22,978	
By consulting	10,341	
By service repairs	39,021	154,590
Cost of sales:		
Opening inventory	7,830	
Purchases	104,175	
Freight in	2,790	
	114,795	
Less closing inventory	(18,247)	
		96,548
Gross profit: (37.5%)		**$58,042**
Overhead expenditure:		
Accounting fees	1,800	
Advertising	3,120	
Bad debts	1,170	
Bank & credit card charges	2,635	
Computer supplies	3,470	
Depreciation	11,090	
Discounts	1,020	
Education, books, seminars	3,130	
Fees, licenses, taxes	980	
Insurance	760	
Internet & website	3,210	
Loan interest	1,230	
Office supplies	910	
Promotion & marketing	2,310	
Rent & taxes	2,110	
Repairs & maintenance	790	
Small tools & shop supplies	910	
Subcontract labor	2,100	
Telephones	1,280	
Travel & accommodation	1,210	
Utilities	710	
Vehicle–gas	1,630	
Vehicle–repairs & maintenance	2,710	50,285
Net profit for period:		**$ 7,757**

How did Marcel manage?

When Marcel sat down with his accountant to review his financial statements, here are some of the observations that the accountant made and discussed with him. Did you identify any of these points?

The balance sheet story

Current assets: With little in the bank and $7,310 still to be collected from accounts receivable, Marcel's inventory is tying up much of his cash flow. On reviewing the age of the receivables, some were well over ninety days. Marcel found it difficult to call clients and ask for money, so his accounts payable were mounting up. Some of the accounts could become bad debts if he doesn't diligently pursue his collections.

Fixed assets: Because most of his assets depreciate at an accelerated rate, their net book value has dropped from $44,420 to $31,157 in two years. Depreciation is a large expense this year, accounting for $11,090.

Current liabilities: Marcel's accounts payable are high because of his large inventory purchase. He also hasn't paid all his tax liabilities for the year; some are quite late, so he must quickly find $3,198. Together, he has $32,060 to pay, and little in the bank. His focus must be to sell as much inventory as possible and collect his unpaid accounts.

Long-term liabilities: His bank loan still has over four years to be paid off, but the monthly loan payment must be made to ensure that he maintains a good credit rating. There is nothing to pay on his father's loan for another two years.

Equity: Marcel's equity in the business started at $1,290 this year, as he suffered a loss in his first year of start-up, which is subtracted from his equity portion. He didn't put much into the business and only made $7,757 profit. However, he took out $14,606 from the business, double the amount of profit he made. This affects his cash flow and is one reason why his bills are piling up.

Working capital: Current assets are $29,104 and current liabilities $35,210. This affirms that Marcel is definitely experiencing a cash flow problem. With both the business overhead and a family to support, it's time to take a close look at how he is operating the business and how he could become more cost- and time-efficient.

The income and expenses statement story

Revenue: The annual revenue of $154,590 looks healthy for a one-person business, but if you analyze the equipment and parts sales, they constitute $105,228, or 68 percent of his income, which only generated an approximately 10 percent profit of $10,500. His consulting and service revenue totals $49,362, which represents 520 billable hours. If you divide that by 50 weeks, he is only billing 10.4 hours a week, or two hours a day—not enough considering the time that he really puts into the business. His concept of "sell them a system and service them forever" is a good one, but perhaps he should work harder to build up his service clientele and then focus on selling new systems when he is generating more billable hours.

Cost of sales: Marcel didn't factor in a freight cost for some of the systems, and by working on such a small gross profit margin, his profit on computer sales was reduced from $11,410 to $8,688, or 8.26 percent. His gross profit looks high at 37.5 percent, but that is because his consulting and service work is included in the figures. Considering the time spent talking with clients, pricing systems, submitting quotations, picking up and delivering—including a free hour for set-up—Marcel is losing money as a systems supplier.

Overhead: Employing a bookkeeper to do the accounting is probably a wise move because accounting is not Marcel's forte; however, using subcontractors for work he doesn't have time for is not so wise. Ignoring collections cost him $1,170 in bad debts, and offering credit card payment options incurred big bank charges. The discounts could be discontinued; most people don't expect them on service accounts.

To keep up with changing technology, success in this industry requires that Marcel spend time and money on books, certification, and education. It is a cost of doing business. Perhaps the expensive trip to the conference could have been foregone for education closer to home. Most of the other costs are within reason for a small business, as long as Marcel's marketing and advertising are producing the desired results.

Summary: The net profit isn't enough to support Marcel, even adding back the depreciation, which is not a cash expense. He won't be paying any income taxes this year, which is not a healthy sign. It is better to pay taxes on profit earned, particularly as his self-employment taxes are calculated on this amount and help to provide for future retirement. Marcel needs to seriously rethink how he will focus his business in the coming year, as his cash flow is in a precarious position. His best bet is to revisit, reevaluate, and revise his business plan—and listen closely to his accountant.

The five-minute financial test below will test your knowledge of this chapter and the meaning of some of the basic accounting terms. The answers are on the following page, so complete the exercise—without peeking. If you get them all right, buy yourself a small, tax-deductible treat.

The Five-Minute Financial Test

Test your knowledge of basic accounting terminology by filling the blanks.

1. A computer system is classified as an ____________________
2. An unpaid bill for stationery is called ____________________
3. A five-year bank loan is called a ____________________
4. The difference between sales and cost of sales is called ________ ____________________
5. Accumulated depreciation is ____________________
6. In a proprietorship, a loss is ________________ from equity
7. Purchases, freight, and duty are all part of ________________
8. Advertising, telephone, and shop supplies are called ________ ____________________
9. Current assets and current liabilities are payable within ________ ____________________
10. In a proprietorship, money contributed by the owner is called ____________________
11. Capital is calculated by subtracting ________________ from ____________________
12. Unpaid sales invoices due by clients are called ________________ ____________________
13. The unpaid taxes charged on sales invoices are called __________ ____________________
14. The annual allowance made for the wear and tear of assets is called ____________________
15. Net book value is the cost of an asset less ________________

Answers to the five-minute financial test

1. Asset
2. Accounts payable
3. Long-term liability
4. Gross profit
5. The amount of depreciation of an asset since purchase
6. Deducted
7. Cost of sales
8. Overhead expenses
9. Twelve months
10. Capital
11. Current liabilities from current assets
12. Accounts receivable
13. Current liabilities
14. Depreciation
15. Depreciation

What Is the Next Step?

Now that you have a better understanding of business and accounting terminology, the next step is to start researching the market to see if your business idea will work for you. Until you complete this process, you can't be sure that there is a niche or need to take your concept and turn it into a viable, income-generating business.

Chapter 4

How Do You Research the Market?

You have an idea, but will it fly?
Research will confirm your piece of the pie.

- **Does your idea have market potential?**
- **Will your business solve clients' problems?**
- **My top ten home-based businesses**
- **What do you research?**
- **Where do you find research material?**

Does Your Idea Have Market Potential?

At some point in our lives, many of us have thought of a brilliant business idea. The successful ones are those who take their golden idea and thoroughly research the market. Now it's time to take your dreams and ideas and discover how practically they can be applied to a business. The first step is to identify a *need* and a *niche* in the marketplace. Remember those two words—"need" and "niche." Don't aim for a huge slice of the pie. The next step is to see whether a small slice of the market will support your business idea and your lifestyle.

How many times have you heard people say, "I have the greatest idea for a business! This is going to be a winner!" The vision of being their own boss and the dough rolling in blinds many would-be entrepreneurs as they plunge quickly and fruitlessly into a money-losing venture.

Don't Skip the Research: Researching a new business' potential is one vital area where many people fall down, cutting the process short in their haste to get started. Doing your homework can be tedious and takes weeks—even months, depending on the size and complexity of the business. But long-term, the efforts are well worth it. Your new business will have greater longevity and success if you know your exact place in the market and the competition that you face.

Keeping up with technology and changing marketing techniques are huge challenges. Those who cater toward long-term future trends will have an excellent starting point. Those who drift into something in an unorganized manner will drop out quickly.

Will Your Business Solve Clients' Problems?

A business should offer solutions to people's problems. You are not selling a service or a product, you are selling a solution. Change is constant, so factor it into your plans. The most valuable commodity these days is time. People are too busy and stressed out. Technological knowledge is a necessity.

How can your business cater to solving these problems? What niche can you fill?

Take Your Business to the Customer: Think how you could simplify stressed-out home-based workers if you brought your business to them or filled a need that isn't being filled. For example, people are now setting up in business as professional declutterers and organizers. They recognize the growing needs of busy people. Many large companies now cater to this overworked market. Home-based business is a growing and permanent long-term trend. Could your business service this market?

An ever-increasing number of people are working from home. They are isolated, coping with multiple tasks, plus juggling work and family. How could you help them? The top home-based businesses in North America are nearly all related to services that small business people need, such as business and financial consulting, Internet and computer services, marketing and advertising, graphics, writing, and sales.

My Top Ten Home-Based Businesses

As a professional who works long hours in a home office, if the business doesn't come to my home, much of the work is achieved using technology, including remote computer repairs or emailing graphic files. Having personally used all these services, here are my top ten businesses for busy home-based people:

1. Computer and equipment servicing, repairs, and cleaning
2. Software program education
3. Office services for editing, data entry, and research
4. Gofer (errands, after-school child care, and chauffeur)
5. Personal fitness coach
6. Home delivery shopping service

7. Declutterer, organizer, house cleaner
8. Mobile automotive mechanic and car detailer
9. Hairdressing and beauty needs
10. Personal chef and meal delivery service

As this list implies, maintaining a healthy computer system and knowing how to use the software is imperative for most businesses these days. Time is wasted on mundane office chores and running errands. The busy person has no time for cleaning, cooking, and shopping. Keeping fit should be a priority. If the boss isn't healthy, then the family and business won't be either. These types of businesses are all service-oriented and don't take a lot of money to get started.

What Do You Research?

You are not just starting or buying a business, you are determining how to generate enough profit to pay you a decent wage and build a healthy business over time. You need to be sure that when those doors open, your business will meet all your expectations. Your market research should explore the following areas:

1. The current and future markets
2. Consumer trends
3. The local market
4. National and international markets
5. Industry knowledge
6. The competition

1. The current and future markets

Your business must withstand the ever-changing consumer and market trends. As the world and technology change, so new businesses are born and old ones die. Look at the new businesses that have evolved recently, including home air filtration systems, Web design, Internet mail-order, digital printing, recycling, bottled water, and computer consulting, to name a few. A few products that have died—or are dying—include LP records, typewriters, audio tapes, and carbon paper.

***CASE STUDY:* Paying Attention to Detail**

For many years, Mark had been intrigued with the idea of starting a car detailing business. At age twenty-seven, he met someone who had started a mobile business, and his idea finally clicked. He would fill a need by starting a mobile car detailing business, bringing his service to the homes of busy workers. He spent $500 buying supplies and jumped right in. Then he was accepted by a government-funded self-employment program. Here he learned to research, market, prepare a business plan, and develop his business and entrepreneurial skills. He worked hard at learning and applying his new skills to the business.

A true entrepreneur, Mark pays attention to the little details. He follows up with clients, uses a referral program, sends thank-you cards with discount coupons, leaves candies with his name in the vehicles, and stresses service to the max. He maintains a database with well over two hundred clients.

Mark did everything right and was honored by winning the program's annual New Entrepreneur of the Year award. By paying attention to the small details while keeping the big picture in mind, Mark is on his way to a successful career as a young entrepreneur.

***QUICK* Tip**

Keep on Reading: The business magazine *Red Herring* (www.redherring.com) predicts the top ten business start-ups of the future, and most are in these technology sectors—biotechnology, energy, semiconductors, hardware, software, wireless, and communications. In 2003, one of *Red Herring*'s top ten trends was financial planning, which obviously reflects the financial concerns of millions of baby boomers. Obviously, our world will continue to become an even more complex place to do business. Keep informed of future trends through books and the Internet, especially as related to your field.

The extent of your study will be determined by whether you intend to trade locally, nationally, or internationally. Answer the questions in Figure 4.1 to start.

Figure 4.1: RESEARCHING YOUR FUTURE MARKET

As you research your new business, be sure to address these important issues.

	Yes	No
1. Will this business be viable within the next five to ten years?	☐	☐
2. Has the history of this industry been stable?	☐	☐
3. Is this industry growing?	☐	☐
4. Is there export potential in the future?	☐	☐
5. Are imported products cheaper and of comparable quality?	☐	☐
6. Is this a short-lived business subject to consumer trends?	☐	☐
7. Could this business be diversified?	☐	☐
8. Can this business offer services/products that others don't?	☐	☐
9. Is this business seasonal?	☐	☐
10. Is there enough cash flow to maintain a sufficient inventory?	☐	☐
11. Will this business be subject to major changes in the next five years?	☐	☐
12. Am I flexible enough to adapt to constant change?	☐	☐

2. Consumer trends

Consumers drive the market, and their needs are constantly changing. For example, take two traditional industries, vacuums and sewing machines. We still need clean houses and our clothes need sewing, so the need for these products has not changed. What has changed are consumers' priorities. Working moms spend less time cleaning, or they hire someone. Products have changed to reflect society's new needs, such as home cleaning equipment that eliminates allergens. Many vacuum dealers have diversified into home air filtration systems due to the significant increase in allergies and worsening air quality.

Where moms used to sew their families' clothes, we have now become throwaway society. My ninety-five-year-old mom still darns, knits, and sews. I either throw the holey socks or ripped clothing away or take the clothes to her to fix. There's no time for sewing now, yet in my past life, I sewed and knitted. Children are rarely taught the art of sewing now as moms are too busy, yet future trends will gear toward catering to the baby boomers who will have both the time and more disposable income.

Health and fitness has become a huge current and no doubt future trend. Companies are catering to the fact that obesity and lack of fitness in both adults and children has become a global concern. Even McDonald's has introduced a line of healthy alternatives, realizing that a large portion of their market is families concerned about their weight and diet. Fitness centers and personal trainers are now integral to many people's lives. These global trends are also an important part of your research.

Current and future trends Listed here are many trends that will impact the future. Can your business accommodate, cater to, or withstand these trends?

- The huge increase in baby boomers with more disposable income
- Baby boomers who are caring for their aged parents
- Lack of facilities and long-term care for aging seniors
- The environment—chemicals, global warming, pollution, conservation, recycling, endangered species
- The large swing toward self-employment and home-based businesses
- Lack of time to perform basic chores, such as shopping and house cleaning
- Healthier diets—natural foods, less fat, vegetarian meals
- Exercise and fitness
- Housing—multiunit dwellings, downsizing of homes, and numbers of children
- Technology—communications, Internet, computer reliance
- Increased desire and necessity for knowledge and education
- Immigration—changing populations
- Youth—fewer job opportunities
- The huge influence of the media
- The need to be entertained
- Less income as job markets change

- Downsizing of businesses
- The Internet—bringing the world into the average home
- Vitamins, alternative medicines, therapies, and remedies
- International economies—their changing structure and currency values
- Cocooning—September 11 created a universal awareness of home and family
- The increased popularity of home improvements and decorating
- The younger generation's need for everything—*now*

3. The local market

The majority of small businesses are service businesses that serve their local community. Thorough local research is important, as there can be a lot of hidden competition, namely the many unlicensed home-based businesses that do not openly promote their services yet are still taking a nibble at your slice of the pie. Your city or county office will have some very helpful information, as will chambers of commerce. The city or county office can usually give you a list of the licensed businesses in your field, and from this you can deduce which ones are housed in commercial premises and which ones are home-based.

Chambers of commerce Well acquainted with their business sector, your local chamber of commerce is a valuable research source. They are in business to help the businesses in their community and can help you with a variety of pertinent information that will shorten your research process. Although each chamber may slightly differ in services offered, most should offer similar to the following:

- Referrals to reputable realtors for leasing commercial space
- Referrals to reputable goods and services businesses
- Printed information on the demographics of the town and its residents
- Information on local regulations
- Discount packages of coupons for business services
- Business start-up pamphlets and books
- Business library
- Online membership directory
- Membership business directory for review

Local government offices Your local government office is also a mine of research information and will supply you with the following resources:

- Zoning regulations for businesses
- Signage regulations
- Home-based business regulation information
- Business license directory
- Environmental laws and policies
- Local demographics—population, age, male/female ratio, marital status, household sizes, labor force by industry, languages spoken, schooling, businesses in your area
- Applicable local regulations and applications for new commercial building permits
- Other licenses you may require

Be a Super Sleuth: Peruse the businesses for sale classifieds and call ones similar to yours. Try to find out why they are selling, whether their business is successful, and how long they have been in business. If you can find an old Yellow Pages (check with your local public library), call businesses in your field and see if they are still operating. You will be surprised how many were listed two years ago that are not listed now. Talk to ones who are still in business or visit their premises to "snoop out" the reason for their success.

Researching your community Take a community tour to gather the following information:

- The number of competitors successfully trading in your area
- The accessibility of your potential location
- Where people prefer to shop
- The quiet shopping areas and what type of stores trade there
- How your competitors advertise in the local paper
- What competition is listed in the local Yellow Pages
- Leasing costs of suitable vacant buildings with parking accessibility

4. National and international markets

If you are looking to trade across the country, you can learn more about the national market by consulting statistical agencies, such as Federal Statistics (www.fedstats.com), and by researching on the Internet. The search engine Google is an excellent source for locating websites. (See the appendix for information on useful websites.) Contact national associations in your field and visit their websites. Attend as many industry-related trade shows as possible for new information and to weigh up the competition.

Exporting If you are considering manufacturing and exporting, there is government help available. The federal government is keen to boost export sales, and a sound idea and business plan may qualify you for a loan. Marketing internationally requires knowledge in:

1. Current and future market trends
2. Customs procedures, regulations, and paperwork
3. Transportation choices and costs
4. Financial transactions in foreign countries
5. Methods of distribution
6. Locating distributors, manufacturing representatives, buyers, and sales agents
7. Packaging and labeling requirements

Visit an international trade show. You will be exposed to the most current information available, be able to study your competition in depth, and research your business potential. Without the latest information, you could be reinventing the wheel.

Resources The SBA has an excellent publication for small businesses looking to export that details all the ins and outs of exporting. It is available to download online at www.sba.gov/managing/marketing/exportguide.html. The guide has provisions for you to answer some important questions and is loaded with resources and contact information for just about every agency you may need to deal with. It even includes international calling codes.

Figure 4.2: **PRODUCT EVALUATION CHECKLIST**

Consider the following questions when evaluating a product you may want to sell.

	Yes	No
1. Are the products well established in the marketplace?	☐	☐
2. Are you aware of their seasonal selling cycles?	☐	☐
3. Are products regularly upgraded or changed?	☐	☐
4. Could you be caught unexpectedly with obsolete inventory?	☐	☐
5. Do the manufacturers offer satisfactory warranties?	☐	☐
6. Are replacement parts readily available?	☐	☐
7. Are the products competitively priced?	☐	☐
8. Are they UL (United Laboratories Inc.) approved?	☐	☐
9. Are buying trends increasing?	☐	☐
10. Are you satisfied with the quality?	☐	☐
11. Are the products comparable to those of the competition?	☐	☐
12. Do you know the age groups that buy these products?	☐	☐
13. Do you know the products' life expectancy?	☐	☐
14. Could they become obsolete due to changing technology?	☐	☐

5. Industry knowledge

The old saying "we learn by our mistakes" will not do your reputation any good if it applies to your lack of expertise. Know your industry inside out so that if problems arise, or a customer asks technical questions, you are knowledgeable enough to resolve these problems and answer their questions competently and confidently.

Product knowledge If your business sells products, one way to expand your knowledge is to contact the manufacturers or a local distributor. They are usually happy to send you information and answer your questions. Figure 4.2 lists some relevant questions to answer.

Your research may determine that your costs or prices will be too high compared to the competition, or that over the last five years, demand for the products is declining due to technological changes and shifts in consumer trends. In another five years, the demand may become substantially less. Products may appear of good quality but not be something that you would feel confident selling. Perhaps the manufacturers' warranties are inadequate or replacement parts are expensive and difficult to secure.

Service knowledge Apart from needing the expertise and the ability to communicate well with people, your service business must offer you some longevity. Be prepared to change as technology changes. For example, in fifteen years, accounting has progressed from handwritten ledgers requiring many hours, even days to prepare, to software programs that can post hundreds of entries in seconds. Although highly efficient, accountants had to find more customers to increase their reduced billing hours.

In your research, be sure you can answer yes to the questions in Figure 4.3:

Figure 4.3: SERVICE BUSINESS CHECKLIST

Before you start a service business, use this checklist in the research stages.

	Yes	No
1. Do you have thorough industry knowledge?	☐	☐
2. Are you prepared to keep up-to-date through education?	☐	☐
3. Is your service currently in demand?	☐	☐
4. Will it be needed in the next five to ten years?	☐	☐
5. Can you price your rates competitively without price-cutting?	☐	☐
6. Can your ideal customer afford your service?	☐	☐
7. Do you know your competition within a ten-mile radius?	☐	☐
8. Do you know your geographic boundary?	☐	☐
9. Do you understand your liability should something go wrong?	☐	☐
10. Are you aware of potential industry changes in the near future?	☐	☐
11. Are you prepared to change with industry trends?	☐	☐

6. The competition

Competition is a fact of life, so your business needs an edge to succeed. You may have an excellent idea, but ask yourself, "How much of the market can I expect to capture?" Know as much as possible about your competitors and their marketing strategies. Answer two important questions:

WHAT IS MY EDGE?

1. What can I offer that the competition can't?
2. What does the competition offer that I can't

Take a field trip The best way to research the competition is to take a field trip, armed with notepad and sharp pencil. Identify at least five main competitors, both large and small. Act as if you are interested in purchasing a product or using the service. Find answers to the questions outlined in Figure 4.4 on the next page.

Initially, you can research many of your competitors using the Internet. Consumers expect a "real" business to have a website, so the ones you find on the Internet are at least taking their business seriously. Their sites will give you some excellent background information. Making a physical assessment is the next step.

Figure 4.4: **CHECK OUT THE COMPETITION**

1. What appeals to you most on entering their premises?
2. How large an inventory do they carry?
3. How are products displayed, and are the displays eye-catching?
4. How many customers are in the store, browsing or buying?
5. What attracted the customers who are purchasing products?
6. Were staff friendly and helpful?
7. Are their prices in line with your industry?
8. Are your prices competitive with theirs?
9. Did you wait long to be helped?

continued

10. Was the salesperson knowledgeable?
11. Were they willing to bargain or undercut other competitors?
12. Were take-home brochures or literature available?
13. Do they offer any special services, such as free delivery?
14. Would they replace a faulty product immediately?
15. What could be improved, and how could you improve in these areas?
16. What age group are their customers?
17. What is their return policy or work guarantees?
18. Do they offer credit terms or credit card facilities?
19. What means of promotion do they use (e.g., coupons, flyers, free samples)?

Prepare a SWOT analysis

Your strength lies in knowing and assessing your competitors' strengths and weaknesses—and your own. Now it is time to analyze.

QUICK Tip

How can you utilize your strengths and overcome your weaknesses? Called a SWOT analysis, it stands for:

Strengths
Weaknesses
Opportunities
Threats

Draw up two lists, one for your SWOT analysis and one for your competitors. Now answer these questions:

- What are my strengths and how can I incorporate them into my business?
- What are my weaknesses and how can I overcome them?

- What are my opportunities and how can I utilize them in my business?
- What are my threats and how can I overcome them?
- What are my competitors' strengths and how will they affect my business?
- What are their weaknesses and how can I take advantage of them?
- What are their opportunities and how will they affect my business?
- What threats do they present to my business?

Alert!

Know Your Competitors Well: If you cannot research some of your main competitors due to distance, first check their website and then call and ask for information to be mailed. Ask as many of the questions in Figure 4.4 as possible.

With a clearer indication of your own strengths, weaknesses, opportunities, and threats, you are now better armed to plan your industry niche.

QUICK Tip

Know Your Competition: Build a profile of each main competitor outlining how they market, why customers shop there, their pricing and service policies, what areas need improving and how successfully you can compete with them. At the same time, you will probably glean ideas for promoting or improving your own business.

Perform a market survey

Now it's time to talk to consumers or potential clients. It's amazing how talking to people will shed new light on your business and affirm your direction. Many people skip this step, yet large and successful businesses would never even contemplate such behavior.

Design a questionnaire along the lines of Figure 4.5 and hit the streets to get your answers. The more people you talk to, the more confident you will feel. Interview as many targeted people as possible, so choose people who may use your business. Give the participant a little gift or a token of your appreciation, along with your contact information and a discount coupon for when you are open for business. A little thank-you goes a long way.

Figure 4.5: **SAMPLE CONSUMER MARKET SURVEY**

In order that we can offer the best possible service, please complete this short questionnaire. Thanks for your time and input!

1. Why would you use this type of business?
2. How often would you use these products or services?
3. What is the final factor in your buying decision—price or service?
4. What kind of service would you expect?
5. What type of after-sales service or guarantees do you expect?
6. What would you pay for a service/product such as this?
7. Have you heard of this type of business before?
8. Where did you hear about it?
9. Where would you look for this type of business?
10. What services would the ideal business provide to you?

Where Do You Find Research Material?

There is so much information available now about starting a business that there is no excuse not to be well informed. Here are some resources to help you.

1. United States Small Business Administration

The Small Business Administration offices found across the country are wonderful gold mines packed with gems of essential information for both new and growing entrepreneurs. Partnering with SBA lenders, SCORE Counselors, the Small Business Development Center, and women's business centers, there is not much you won't find there in the way of resources to help you.

CASE STUDY: The Ten-Question Eye-Opener

For three years I have taught Entrepreneurship Skills in the Equine Industry, an accredited fifteen-week course at a university college. The class usually consists mainly of young women who are crazy about horses and who dream of owning a horse-related business. Part of their business plan entails doing a market survey, similar to Figure 4.5, interviewing ten people. The results have been amazing. Many students have commented that talking to people gave them new ideas, confirmed and increased their enthusiasm, or made them realize that they needed a lot more homework on their idea. Some changed their business direction after doing the survey, realizing the impracticality of their original plan. Others realized that they wouldn't make a sufficient living. In all cases, the survey was a tremendous help in formulating their plans and in identifying areas needing reevaluation.

Information is provided about all government services, programs, and local, state, and federal regulations. Information on most pertinent small business topics are available online, including business plans, marketing, financing, payroll, licenses, permits, business law, taxes, self-employment taxes, and employer identification numbers. This information can be downloaded from their website. Visit your local office, browse their library, or talk to a business officer. Their website address is www.sba.gov.

2. Small Business Development Centers

With over a thousand locations in the United States, small business development centers are focused on their local community's economic development. Services include access to all business startup resources, tourism, local regulations, demographics and statistics, a variety of small business and special events information, including local, state, and federal loans programs. Many offer technical and international trade assistance. Find the office nearest you at www.sba.gov/sbdc/sbdcnear.html.

3. Fedstats

If you need demographic, trade, social, international, educational, or economic statistics, www.fedstats.gov is the site to visit. They provide information by sector, state, regionally, or nationally. Informative statistical online publications and links to all other federal agencies with statistical information make this site a one-stop stats shop. There are even specially prepared statistics available for schoolchildren of all ages to use.

4. Yellow Pages

What an information mine! You can research your competitors either online or in print by studying their advertisements and see how they advertise and what services they offer. Assess how many competitors are in your trading area and get some indication of their size.

5. Chambers of commerce

Your local chamber of commerce is in business to help businesses, both new and established. If you are serious about starting a business, join your local chamber so that you have better access to all their resources and information. Many supply business start-up kits, resource guides, business plan and cash flow information, and some even offer one-on-one consulting services.

Get Involved: As a member of a chamber of commerce, you'll have access to mailing lists, networking opportunities, seminars, a host of special discounts, and member-to-member benefits, monthly newsletters, and special events.

6. Local government offices

Visit your local office for community statistics, traffic counts, potential rezoning plans, new building applications, codes, regulations, and other business information.

7. The Internet

When doing research, nothing beats sitting in the comfort of your own home collecting information. There is virtually nothing you can't find on the Internet. It is a powerful, fast, cheap, and efficient research tool—in fact, for research, it is indispensable. Many informative small business websites can be found in the appendix.

8. Trade shows and seminars

Trade shows allow you to be inundated with the most up-to-date information on your industry, helping you make informed decisions. There are also entrepreneurial trade shows that demonstrate new products and franchises. This is an opportunity to assess new competitors in the market and also promising new businesses.

Network and Grow: Attend as many business-related seminars as possible. Not only will you learn new skills, you can network with other entrepreneurs and do business with them. Nothing beats a face-to-face meeting to start building relationships.

9. Publications

Use Internet listservs, newspapers, flyers, magazines, directories, and trade and financial papers to glean every ounce of information you need. Subscribe to journals and newspapers specifically aimed at your type of business or borrow them from your local library.

What Is the Next Step?

Once you have confirmed your niche in the market and feel confident that you have a viable business idea, you may need the services of a lawyer for signing a lease, a partnership agreement, or an employee contract or for purchasing a business. Few of us understand legalese or all that fine print. Some unfortunate people don't use a lawyer and get burned. So next we'll take a look at why you need legal agreements and what a lawyer can do for you.

Figure 4.6: MARKET RESEARCH RESOURCE CHECKLIST

Use this checklist to ensure that you leave no stone unturned in gathering your market research information.

Resource	Researched
U.S. Small Business Administration	☐
Local Small Business Development Center	☐
Fedstats	☐
Yellow Pages	☐
Chamber of commerce	☐
Local government office	☐
The Internet	☐
Industry trade shows	☐
Seminars or conferences	☐
Industry newspapers and magazines	☐
Local and national newspapers	☐

Useful telephone numbers and websites:

____

____

____

____

____

____

____

____

Chapter 5

Why Do You Need a Lawyer?

To save any future fighting,
get it all in writing.

- **What does a lawyer do?**
- **How do you find the right lawyer?**
- **What is a buy-sell agreement?**
- **What if legal problems arise?**
- **What do all those legal terms mean?**

What Does a Lawyer Do?

Lawyers are in business to protect your rights and to work for you. No matter how small your business, there are numerous areas where you should consult with a lawyer. Few people understand the fine print on contracts and legal documents, yet once you sign on the dotted line, you have contracted to adhere to specific terms, and these agreements can be upheld in court. People often don't understand the content of a contract but sign it anyway.

Many people have lost money on smiles, verbal agreements, and handshakes. Generally, a contract does not have to be in writing to be binding on the parties. The problem with verbal agreements is proving the contents of the contract once a dispute arises. Although it is human nature to want to trust people, get everything in writing anyway. The most common areas where a lawyer can help you follow:

1. Buy-sell agreements
2. Setting up a partnership, corporation, or LLC
3. Building and capital equipment leases
4. Royalty agreements
5. Agent and distributorship agreements
6. Franchise agreements
7. Disputes with clients
8. Corporate affairs

1. Buy-sell agreements

If you are buying an existing business, have a lawyer review the vendor's agreement, which can be one-sided, with little protection for the buyer. A buy-sell agreement sets out the terms of both the purchase and the sale, setting parameters for both parties (explained later in this chapter).

2. Setting up a partnership, corporation, or LLC

Although a partner may seem ideal when starting a business, the percentage of partnerships that succeed is low. (See Chapter 8 for a discussion of partnerships.) A partnership agreement protects both parties by setting down mutual guidelines, parameters, responsibilities, and duties.

An agreement will define the shared areas of management that need to be clarified, such as net profits and losses, the injection and withdrawing of capital, interest on capital investments, management duties, banking authorizations, accounting records, salaries, termination or sale, death, disputes, and arbitration. Spending the money on a thorough agreement can help prevent bickering and be in place should the time come when the partnership dissolves.

Plan for the Future: Your agreement should set out the terms and conditions for the business reverting to the other partner. There are many unforeseen reasons why a partnership may dissolve, including ill health. Decide whether the buyout clause will include a value on intangible assets, such as goodwill or trademarks.

3. Building and capital equipment leases

You have probably already seen—or signed—a lease agreement and noticed but did not read the pages of fine print. When you sign a rental lease, you are accepting full responsibility to pay for that leased space or equipment for the term of the lease. It is a contractual agreement to adhere to all the terms and conditions until the lease expires. Don't assume, as many people do, that it is a "standard" lease. Have a lawyer review and explain it all to you before you sign. See Chapter 6 for more information about leases.

Plan Ahead for Succession: Buyouts on a partner's death may be funded with life insurance premiums paid by the business. The decedent's estate is paid in cash from insurance proceeds and the surviving partner takes over the business at no additional cost.

CASE STUDY: The Lease That Wasn't

Gordon, Robin, and their spouses became partners in a new catering business. Robin professed to be conversant in legal and accounting matters, and so took responsibility for the "legal mumbo-jumbo," while Gordon focused on getting the operation going. The business thrived, and more money was invested into leasehold fixtures and equipment.

After a year of operation, the building was suddenly foreclosed on. The lease they had signed was in fact only a sublease on which the payments were not being made. In order to save money, Robin had not taken the trouble to have the lease agreement checked by a lawyer. The business was closed down and much of the equipment seized. The partners had borrowed against their home mortgages for the business, and they were left with little, except huge bills and business losses. The stress caused Robin's marriage to break up. This could have all been prevented by a visit to a lawyer. Don't "save money" by doing it yourself. Spend time and money with a professional. They are here to protect your interests.

4. Royalty agreements

Your business may involve income from royalties, such as publication of a book or selling the rights of a product to another company. Usually, you are selling a license to another party for them to manufacture and sell the product in return for a percentage of the income generated when it is sold. If you are dealing with international intellectual property rights, such as books, use a foreign rights agent and a lawyer.

Professional Help Equals Profit: Royalties can range from 10 to 15 percent of the final sale price of the item. However, when you deal with foreign countries, royalty structures vary significantly from country to country. Work with an agent who has a solid reputation.

Be careful what rights you sign away with these agreements and be sure that your product will be manufactured and marketed to your satisfaction. Rights can encompass printed, manufacturing, electronic, national, and world rights. Where possible, include a timeline for the length of the agreement and a performance clause. If you agree to give exclusive rights, the timeline should be short or you should be guaranteed a minimum return.

5. Agent and distributorship agreements

Some businesses may involve the sale of products or services through an agent—for example, authors, actors, and professional speakers. You may also engage an agent to distribute your products or services, or you may act as an agent or distributor for other businesses. The agent or distributor earns an income by selling the commodity and receives a fee or a commission, which is a percentage of the sale price. Generally, agents' fees range from 15 percent upward.

Both parties have certain rights and responsibilities, which should be clearly defined in an agreement. Some agents require exclusivity, so think about including a performance clause and ensure that the agreement can be readily rescinded if either party is not satisfied with the other. Use a lawyer to draft and/or review these agreements before signing.

6. Franchise agreements

There are a myriad of franchises opening, operating, and closing, and their agreements are pages of legalese that are often difficult to understand. Some set out stringent terms and conditions and appear to benefit the franchiser more than the franchisee. Don't even try to wade through them by yourself. Seek legal advice and interpretation.

7. Disputes with clients

You hope it never happens—a client decides to sue you for incompetency or damages caused through your services or products. Your first protection against this common occurrence is a good liability insurance policy, discussed in Chapter 6. Your next move is to consult a lawyer to decide on the best form of resolution. From the initial discussion with an unhappy client to your meeting with a lawyer, keep your cool and document all conversations.

8. Corporate affairs

A lawyer can act on your behalf in corporate matters such as:

- Employment contracts with management staff
- Wrongful dismissal claims
- Patents and trademarks
- Collections
- Intellectual property rights
- Taxation disputes

How Do You Find the Right Lawyer?

Know your needs

The more people you talk to about finding a lawyer, the more stories you will hear about both good and bad experiences. What works for one person won't necessarily work for another. Perhaps the best advice is don't ask your friends for a referral to "a good lawyer." If the relationship doesn't work out, you may not be friends for long.

Law practices come in all shapes and sizes. Usually, a law firm will focus on one area, such as divorce, immigration, or corporate law. You need a lawyer who specializes in business law. If you owned a Mercedes, you'd prefer to use a mechanic familiar with Mercedes, not just a general mechanic. Use the same principle when lawyer-shopping.

Lawyers are often active chamber of commerce members and your local chamber staff get to know many of the professionals in the community. Ask if they can recommend a corporate lawyer with expertise in the area you require. As with any referral, ask about the services the lawyer performed for them.

Prepare for your consultation

Use the initial consultation to establish whether you feel comfortable with the lawyer. Prepare yourself by listing the potential topics you want to discuss, including the fee structure, whether your request can be processed in your desired time frame, and whether the lawyer can provide you with references. After your consultation, decide whether this lawyer meets all your criteria. Remember—you are paying good money for someone's services. It is your right to pick and choose whom you hire, so if you feel the need, interview three or four before choosing one.

Here is a useful website that should help you:

QUICK Tip

Go One-Stop Surfing: The American Bar Association has a resource-crammed site loaded with information on every conceivable legal subject. The ABA offers viewable publications, links to lawyers across the United States, referrals, legal aid information, a lawyer locator, legal research, and too much to list here. Visit http://w3.abanet.org/ home.cfm.

As you formulate your business plan, use Figure 5.1 on page 108 to remind you of areas where you may need a lawyer. This will help in both planning your budget and your first consultation.

What Is a Buy-Sell Agreement?

A buy-sell agreement is drawn up between two parties when a business is sold to protect you both. When you engage a lawyer to review an agreement, they will perform many searches and checks to ensure that what you think you are buying is in fact what you are getting. Some vendors make verbal promises that they have no intention of keeping. They tend to play down the negatives of the business and sometimes forget to mention important factors.

Get Everything in Writing: If you consider verbal offers and promises made by the vendor important to your purchase, ensure that these points are all documented in the agreement, no matter how trivial they may appear, and no matter how sincere the vendor appears to be.

If a vendor promises to train you full time for a month, get it in writing. If the vendor suggested that the business should generate a certain annual sales volume, get that in writing too. Then, if you are doing everything right and the business fails to meet certain expectations, you have a signed document and legal recourse. A buy-sell agreement sets out the full terms of the purchase, the goods and services to be purchased, payment conditions, and all other conditions that you might not think to consider. See the example in Figure 5.2 at the end of this chapter.

Figure 5.1: **DO YOU NEED A LAWYER CHECKLIST**

Enlist the services of a lawyer if you are considering any of the following activities:

1. To review a buy-sell agreement on purchasing a business ☐
2. To set up a partnership, corporation, or LLC ☐
3. To review a lease for a building ☐
4. To review a lease for a vehicle or equipment ☐
5. To review a royalty agreement ☐
6. To prepare or review an agent/distributorship agreement ☐
7. To review a franchise agreement ☐
8. To advise on or prepare an employment contract ☐
9. To advise on or register patents and trademarks ☐
10. To advise on intellectual property rights and contracts ☐
11. To advise on collections procedures ☐
12. To advise on general corporate matters ☐

A lawyer will thoroughly investigate and advise you on the following areas before letting you enter into an agreement. These are particularly important if you are buying an established business or any business where assets are part of the purchase price.

QUICK Tip

Know What You Are Signing: Some vendors will prepare their own agreements, expecting you to eagerly sign on the dotted line. If a vendor or his or her lawyer has prepared an agreement, ask your lawyer to review it. If you prepare your own agreement, have it checked by a lawyer. It doesn't matter how small the business, an agreement will protect you, particularly if the deal turns sour.

1. Searches

First, a lawyer will conduct the following searches:

- A search to determine that the company is in good standing and the true identity of the individuals who own or control the business
- A check with state and local authorities regarding licensing, taxes, and zoning
- Searches through special registries, for example, real estate titles, liens, and encumbrances usually may be checked with the county auditor; liens on equipment, fixtures, and inventory ("security interests") may be checked with the state agency designated by statute
- A check that there are no infringements of registered patent trademarks or copyrights, or infringements of any laws, statutes, or other regulations.

2. Tax considerations

Taxes have an important bearing on the purchase of an existing company, and your lawyer will investigate on your behalf:

- **Assets:** If assets are a large portion of the purchase price, you must know their tax position and whether they have already been depreciated.
- **Tax history:** There should be representations and warranties regarding any previous problems with the tax authorities. There may be tax benefits and previous losses to consider in the purchase price.

- **Taxes payable:** When a business is sold, taxes are usually payable on the sale of the assets.
- **Other:** Other tax issues might include whether the vendor or purchaser is filing taxes and remittances for that particular year, or on any land, or on a particular asset that is being transferred for sale.

3. Incorporated businesses

With the purchase of an incorporated business, you usually purchase the shares of the company at a certain value, and the assets and the liabilities of the business remain at book value. Your lawyer will research the following:

- Representations and warranties regarding the shares
- Representations whether it is a reporting company or not
- Where the company is registered, where it does business, and when and where the last annual report was filed
- How many authorized or common shares the company has issued, and how many shares are validly issued and outstanding
- Whether the vendor has authority under the terms of the memorandum and articles of the company to sell shares or capitals, as well as a list of directors and officers of the company.

4. Noncompetition

How would you feel if after nine months of purchasing your business, the vendor opened a similar business close to you? It has been done. The vendor could be forced into opening another business to survive and will start where they have the expertise and business contacts.

A noncompetition clause will prevent this, usually by prohibiting the vendor from participating in, setting up, or operating a business similar to the one you have purchased within the next two to five years within a given geographical boundary (anywhere from a few-mile radius to state or nationwide). This comforting clause should be standard in most agreements.

5. Exclusivity

If this business involves handling an exclusive product line or service, include an exclusivity clause to prevent the vendor from selling the same product, right, or service to other people later. An exclusive product or service makes a business more financially viable to the purchaser. Without this clause, you are leaving yourself wide open—it's been done before.

6. Records and documentation

Certain items belong to and should remain with the business after the sale; specifically, all company records and documentation. These include client lists, sales, marketing and costing information, accounting records, files, working papers, supplier information, lists of information sources, correspondence, and all business records required for the day-to-day operation. Unfortunately, nothing can prevent the vendor from keeping copies of records of client contact information, and computers make it so easy. But your agreement can legally prevent the vendor from using the information.

7. Licenses and rights

Your lawyer will ensure that any licenses, area, or other business rights, designs, or trademarks being purchased with the business are noted in the agreement. If the business is limited to a specified geographic area, such as with dealerships or franchises, clearly identify this area with a map in an appendix.

Understand Agreements: In one case, a new dealership did not honor the promises of certain area rights written into their distributorship agreement. But the agreement was not clearly worded and ultimately, the disappointed distributor had little recourse. He had to sit back and watch the dealership owners blatantly encroach into his territory, often using leads that the new dealer had generated through paid advertising.

8. Risk of loss

It is the vendor's responsibility to insure the assets until you have purchased the business. If there is any damage to the assets before you take possession, it is the vendor's responsibility to compensate for damages. Clearly stipulate who is responsible for maintaining insurance and whether the purchaser has an obligation to maintain certain insurance policies.

QUICK Tip

Dazzle 'Em with Documents: Practice shows that the person with the most detailed documentation has a better chance of winning a court case. A judge can only base his or her opinion on the evidence presented.

9. Other considerations

Following are some other considerations that may apply to your purchase:

- **Employees:** If the business already has employees, obtain a vendor's statement detailing the number of employees and whether they have a collective agreement. There may be obligations to long-term employees, which require extensive notice on termination. Unpaid retirement plan contributions, employee vacation pay, sales bonus plans, or incentive schemes at the takeover date must also be considered. How will these projected future expenses be accommodated in the buy-sell agreement?

- **Company debts:** Your lawyer should research the company's debts or contractual obligations.

- **Financial assistance:** If the vendor is offering financial assistance in the form of a loan to the purchaser, two issues could be relevant:
  - a) Does the vendor have the right to accelerate or call the entire loan due, and if so, on what grounds?
  - b) Under what circumstances does the vendor have the right to repossess the business or its assets?

- **Support documentation:** Enclose a list of documents to be transferred at closing, especially if there are corporate records, business licenses or noncompetition agreements, resignations of the previous directors of the company, and transfers of title. Appendices to the agreement may include a list of property being transferred, leases, licenses, types of insurance coverage, contracts, and financial statements.

- **General provisions:** At the end of the agreement, there is a section of general provisions that includes a statement that both the vendor's and purchaser's liability remain in force after the agreement has been closed. This clause is inserted for future protection.

Another provision should state that "This agreement contains the whole agreement between the vendor and the purchaser, and this supersedes all other previous agreements; there are no representations other than those contained in this agreement, and the purchasers or vendors have relied on these representations."

What If Legal Problems Arise?

Once your agreement is signed, dated and the takeover date completed, the business is yours. If a serious problem arises that cannot be resolved, seek your lawyer's advice. If the agreement has been broken and settlement cannot be reached, the court will make a ruling based on the agreement and the events.

Cases are built around evidence—not hearsay (i.e., any statements quoted by a third party). For statements to be admitted as evidence, the person must be called as a witness. Written statements and usually audio tapes are not acceptable evidence.

Document Details: Keep a log of events, phone calls, meetings, and statements made by vendors and their associates. If the need arises, these people can be called to the stand to testify. Your documentation will allow for thorough questioning and a better chance of winning your case.

If the business is being adversely affected by this disagreement, document as much information as possible. Compensation may be awarded for loss of profits. Your agreement will be written proof of a contract between the parties involved. Without it, you do not have grounds for a court case.

What Do All Those Legal Terms Mean?

The legal profession speaks its own unique language in most contracts and agreements. A glossary of common legal terminology follows to help you better understand all the legal mumbo jumbo:

Assign: To give someone else your property or rights under a contract
Assurance: A positive declaration
Authorize: To commission or allow
Case: A disagreement filed in court
Consideration: Payment for something given, including money, services or promises
Contract: A written (or sometimes verbal) agreement that can be enforced
Covenant: A promise or pledge constituting part of a contract
Deed: A document in which an owner transfers title to real estate
Default: Failure to act or meet one's obligations
Encumbrance: An impediment, usually a loan or mortgage on a property
Hereafter: In the future
Herein: In this place
Hereinafter: Below
Heretofore: Formerly, once
Herewith: With this
Indemnify: To protect someone or hold them harmless
Lien: A hold on another person's property until an outstanding debt is paid
Memorandum: Notes or records made for future business use
Misrepresent: Falsify or distort facts
Statute: A written law
Vendor: Seller
Vested: Placing of the right to
Warranties: Guarantees, pledges, or assurances

Figure 5.2 gives an example of a simple buy-sell agreement, outlining the sale of a gift shop. This is only a sample agreement to demonstrate which areas legal agreements might cover. Consult a lawyer when having your legal agreement prepared and listen to his or her advice.

What Is the Next Step?

Once you understand the legal aspects of your business, you should start preparing a business plan, but first you must research start-up expenses. You won't get too far without knowing exactly what you need and how much it costs. Sometimes, it's surprisingly expensive, particularly if you are leasing commercial premises, so next we'll explore basic start-up costs.

Figure 5.2: **A SIMPLE BUY-SELL AGREEMENT**

THIS AGREEMENT made the ***Twenty-ninth*** Day of ***July, 2005***

BETWEEN:

Peter James Turnbull, of ***1084 South Drive, Summerville*** in the County of ***Peaceland***, in the State of Illinois, USA.

(Hereinafter called the "Vendor")

OF THE FIRST PART

AND:

Sarah Elizabeth Scott, of ***19775 - 26th Avenue, Preston*** in the County of ***Westville***, in the State of Illinois, USA.

(Hereinafter called the "Purchaser")

OF THE SECOND PART

WHEREAS:

a. The Vendor carries on the business of selling retail gifts to the general public under the business name "Artsy and Crafty," (hereinafter called the "Business") and operates the said business in Willowdale Mall, in Westville, in the State of Illinois, and in connection therewith owns certain records, supplies, and other assets at the aforesaid address.

b. The Vendor has agreed to sell the Business and the said assets and the Purchaser has agreed to buy the same on the terms and conditions hereinafter set forth.

continued

PURCHASE AND SALE

1. In consideration of the terms and conditions of this Agreement and based on the warranties and representations herein contained, the Vendor agrees to sell and the Purchaser agrees to purchase all the property, rights, undertakings and assets as listed in Appendix A (except as hereinafter provided), belonging to or used in the Business, as a going concern, including but without limiting the following:

   (a) The goodwill of the Business, together with all inventories, trademarks, designs, licenses, permits and other rights used in connection with the Business, and all records, documentation, correspondence, and other property related to the Business.

   (b) The Vendor agrees to provide one month's full-time training to the Purchaser at no additional cost.

   (c) The Vendor shall assign the lease to the Purchaser.

   (All of which property, undertakings, and assets are hereinafter called the "Assets")

VENDOR'S REPRESENTATIONS

2. The Vendor represents, warrants, and agrees that:

   (a) The Vendor has the power, authority, and capacity to enter into this Agreement and to carry out the transactions contemplated hereby, all of which have been duly and validly authorized.

   (b) The completion of the transactions contemplated hereby will not constitute a breach by the Vendor of any statute, bylaw, or regulation or of any contract or Agreement to which the Vendor is a party or by which it is bound or which would result in the creation of any lien, encumbrance, or other charge on any of the Assets.

   (c) The Vendor has good and marketable title to the Assets, free and clear of all liens, mortgages, encumbrances, equities or claims of every kind and nature whatsoever.

   (d) The vendor is not in violation of and has received no notice in violation of any term or condition of any statute, bylaw, or regulation to its Business.

   (e) The Vendor has no indebtedness to any person, firm, or corporation which might, by operation of law or other else, hereafter constitute a lien, charge, or encumbrance upon any of the Assets.

PURCHASE PRICE AND PAYMENT

3. The Purchase price payable by the Purchaser to the Vendor for the Assets (the "Purchase Price") will be One Hundred and Twenty-Five Thousand Dollars ($125,000.00).
4. The Purchase Price shall be paid as follows:
   (a) Twenty-five Thousand Dollars ($25,000.00) shall be paid directly to the Vendor's Attorney upon execution of this Agreement, as a deposit in trust.
   (b Fifty Thousand Dollars ($50,000.00) shall be paid to the Vendor's Attorney on the date of closing, which shall be no later than August 1, 2005.
   (c) Fifty Thousand Dollars ($50,000.00) shall be paid to the Vendor's Attorney in trust in monthly installments of $2,083.33 for a period of Twenty-Four (24) months, plus interest of Nine Percent (9%) per annum, payable in one check each year on the Thirty-First of August, 2006 and 2007.
5. Upon execution of this Agreement, the Purchaser shall deliver to the Vendor:
   (a) A certified check or bank draft in the amount of Twenty-Five Thousand Dollars ($25,000.00).
   (b) A certified check or bank draft in the amount of Fifty Thousand Dollars ($50,000.00), dated August 1, 2005, to be held in trust by the Vendor's Attorney.
   (c) The balance shall be paid under the terms of a Promissory Note payable in thirty-six (36) equal installments with interest at 9 percent per annum, secured by a UCC-1 Security Agreement and Financing Statement in a form acceptable to Seller.

VENDOR'S COVENANTS

6. The Vendor will:
   (a) Take or cause to be taken all proper steps, actions, and proceedings on its part to enable it to vest a good marketable title in the Purchaser to the Assets, free and clear of all liens, mortgages, encumbrances, equities, or claims of every nature and kind whatsoever and shall deliver, upon date of execution, such bills of sale, transfer, assignments, and consents (including consents by Creditors of the Vendor under, or other evidence in compliance with, the Bulk Sales Act, if required), and consents to transfer of licenses, leases, contracts, and rights as the Attorney for the Purchaser may require;

continued

(b) To deliver possession of the Assets to the Purchaser on execution of this Agreement;

(c) From the date of execution of this Agreement to the date of closing, maintain in force policies of insurance heretofore maintained, and obtain and maintain such additional policies of insurance as may be required to insure the Assets, in the amount against such perils as are customary in other similar businesses;

(d) From the date of execution of this Agreement to the date of closing, take good care of the Assets and take all reasonable care to protect and safeguard all Assets;

(e) Execute and do all such further acts, deeds, things, and assurances as may be requisite in the opinion of the Attorney for the Purchaser for more perfectly and absolutely assigning, transferring, assuring to, and vesting in the Purchaser titles to the Assets, free and clear of all liens, mortgages, encumbrances, equities, and claims of any nature and kind whatsoever;

(f) Vendor shall not from the date of execution of this Agreement to date of closing, sell, consume, dispose of or transfer possession of any of the Assets except in the ordinary course of business;

(g) Vendor shall not from the date of execution of this Agreement, and for a further period of Five (5) years, own or operate a business involved in the wholesale or retail selling of arts, crafts, and similar items, within a Ten (10) mile/Sixteen (16) kilometer radius of the Willowdale Mall in Westville, Illinois.

PURCHASER'S CONDITIONS

7. Notwithstanding anything herein contained, the obligation of the Purchaser to complete the purchase hereunder shall be subject to the following conditions:

(a) The representations and warranties of the Vendor contained in this Agreement shall be true on and as of the date of execution.

(b) All of the covenants and Agreements of the Vendor to be performed on or before the date of execution pursuant to the terms and conditions of this Agreement shall have been duly performed.

(c) No substantial loss or destruction of or damage to any of the Assets shall have occurred on or before the date of execution.

(d) The Purchaser shall have received from her Attorney an opinion to the effect that a good and valid title to the will vest in the Purchaser, free and clear of all liens, encumbrances, equities, or claims of every nature or kind whatsoever.

The foregoing conditions are for the sole and exclusive benefit of the Purchaser and may be waived in whole or in part by the Purchaser.

VENDOR'S CONDITIONS

8. The obligation of the Vendor to complete the sale under this Agreement shall be subject to the condition that on the date of execution the Purchaser pay to the Vendor all monies due to be paid to the Vendor under this Agreement.

POST-EXECUTION AGREEMENT

9. If the Purchaser shall fail to make all or any part of any payment to be made pursuant to paragraphs 5(a), (b), and (c) herein, and such default shall continue for a period of seven (7) days, the Vendor may, by notice in writing to the Purchaser, declare the full balance owing under paragraphs 5 (a), (b), and (c) immediately due and payable.
10. If the Purchaser shall fail to pay the balance owing, as demanded in writing by the Vendor pursuant to paragraph 9 herein, and such further default shall continue for a further period of seven (7) days, then the Vendor's Attorney is hereby authorized by each party hereto to take all necessary steps to recover the promised funds.

GENERAL PROVISIONS

11. All transactions in the Business, on or after the date of closing, shall be for the account of the Purchaser.
12. The Assets shall be at the risk of the Vendor up to the date of closing of this Agreement and shall be at the risk of the Purchaser on or after the date of closing of this Agreement.
13. All representations, warranties, covenants, and Agreements of the parties contained herein shall survive the execution date of this Agreement and the payment of the Purchase Price.
14. The Vendor shall indemnify and save the Purchaser harmless from all loss, damage, cost, actions, and suits arising out of or in connection with any breach of misrepresentation, warranty, covenant, agreement, or condition contained in this Agreement.
15. If prior to the date of closing, there shall have been any loss or damage to any of the Assets, and the Vendor shall be entitled to receive monies as a result of such damage or loss, the Purchase Price shall be reduced by an amount equal to that portion of the Purchase Price allocated to the asset totally destroyed, or if the asset is only damaged or partially destroyed, the reduction in the Purchase Price shall equal the amount of the insurance paid to the Vendor with respect hereto.

continued

16. Time shall be of essence in this Agreement.
17. The purchase and sale of Assets herein contemplated shall take effect as of and no later than the opening of business on the ***Twenty-ninth*** Day of ***July,*** 2005, which shall be 'the date of closing'.
18. Any notice required or permitted to be given hereunder may be effectively given by prepaid post addressed to the Vendor at:

    1084 South Drive, Sommerville, Illinois, 61798

    and prepaid post addressed to the Purchaser at:

    19775 - 26th Avenue, Preston, Illinois, 60942

And if given aforesaid, any notice shall be deemed to have been given seventy-two (72) hours following such posting.

19. This Agreement shall enure to the benefit of and be binding upon the respective successors and assigns of the parties hereto, **PROVIDED THAT** this Agreement shall not be assigned by the Purchaser without the Vendor's consent, which consent shall not be unreasonably withheld.
20. Both the Vendor's liabilities and the Purchaser's liabilities as contained herein shall remain in force after the execution of this agreement.
21. This Agreement contains the whole Agreement between the Vendor and the Purchaser, and this Agreement supersedes all other previous Agreements. Both the Vendor and the Purchaser state that there are no representations other than those contained in this Agreement.

IN WITNESS WHERE OF the parties hereto have hereunto set their hands and seals on the day and year first above written.

SIGNED, SEALED AND DELIVERED
by the Vendor in the presence of:

Mary Jane Whitehead

NAME

5751 Central Road, Oaklands, IL

ADDRESS

Peter James Turnbull

SIGNED, SEALED AND DELIVERED
by the Purchaser in the presence of:

Russell Brian Smithers
NAME

19834 Oak Street, Preston, IL
ADDRESS

Sarah Elizabeth Scott

APPENDIX A
LISTING OF ASSETS, ARTSY AND CRAFTY GIFT SHOP

ITEM	PURCHASE PRICE
Two Electronic Cash Registers, "Cashall" brand	$ 4,200.00
Six six-foot counters with shelves underneath	2,700.00
300 feet glass wall shelving	2,500.00
Crystal chandelier	800.00
Persian display rug	750.00
Carpets, lighting fixtures	4,100.00
Coldasair refrigerator	400.00
Quickcook Microwave oven	250.00
Coffee pot, cups and cutlery, miscellaneous plates	50.00
Kitchen table with four chairs	100.00
12 Brass display stands, various sizes	1,200.00
Lateral four-drawer filing cabinet	400.00
Pentium Computer, hard drive, keyboard, Laser printer, 17" flat screen monitor	2,400.00
Computer desk, adding machine & miscellaneous stationery	750.00
Inventory as listed on Appendix "B" at cost (to be adjusted at date of takeover by Purchaser)	65,400.00
One month full-time training by Vendor	.00
Goodwill value	39,000.00
TOTAL PURCHASE PRICE:	**$125,000.00**

Chapter 6

What Start-Up Expenses Will You Incur?

It's a brand-new business, so much to do. Let's buy everything sparkling new!

- **What type of building should you lease?**
- **What communications systems should you use?**
- **What office and computer equipment do you need?**
- **What office supplies do you need?**
- **What insurance policies might you need?**
- **What is risk management?**
- **Step-by-step start-up checklists**

What Type of Building Should You Lease?

Oh, the excitement of getting everything ready for your new business! There is so much to do and so much to buy, and of course, you want to create a professional image. It's fun to shop for new equipment and stationery or plan the design of your new retail store. But slow down...it is so easy to make hasty and expensive decisions at this stage. This is the beauty of preparing a business plan—if you first research all costs, you can then tailor them to suit your budget, one of the largest expenses being the leasing and outfitting of a building.

Without serious homework, many people mistakenly consider only price, ignoring other factors vital to the smooth long-term operation of the business, including the following.

1. Size and growth

As most of us are not clairvoyants, choosing the right-sized building is difficult. Lease charges are based on square footage, with added costs for taxes and amenities. Costs dramatically increase with the addition of just a few hundred square feet, so don't let size be the deciding factor; consider these other important components listed in this chapter before you race out and sign a lease.

QUICK Tip

First Plan on Paper: Make a scale drawing of your ideal building, allowing room for equipment and machinery or retail shelf space, work and bench space, storage facilities, vehicles, lunchroom, washrooms, and office space. This should indicate the required minimum square footage to comfortably house your operation.

Budget permitting, allow for a 20 percent increase in growth in the first two years. If the budget is tight, you may have to limit this luxury, keeping in mind that if the business is successful, you may have to make other arrangements.

2. Industrial locations

Manufacturing and distribution premises require research in the following areas:

- **Utilities:** Research the cost of extra plumbing or electrical work and the monthly utilities charges before the lease is signed. Your utility company can give you monthly readouts from the preceding year. Buildings can use considerable power during colder months because they are not economically heated or insulated. You may want to consider a more effective heating method. Don't forget to budget for a deposit on utilities.
- **Warehouse or storage space:** Consider the building's accessibility and maneuverability in relationship to its usage and the equipment or products you are housing. You may need racking or shelving to store inventory. Some real bargains can be found at liquidation centers. If you are shipping and receiving large products, you need adequate dock and loading facilities. Maximize your efficiency by having the right equipment to do the job, otherwise you are practicing false economy.
- **Ventilation:** Windows may not supply enough ventilation during summer, making working conditions oppressive, particularly upstairs. This affects employees' productivity, as will extreme cold. You may have to install air conditioning.
- **Security:** Deadbolts are necessary on exterior doors, bars on windows, and a monitored alarm system is essential.

CASE STUDY: Raising the Rooftop

I once worked for a satellite distributorship (before the days of cable TV) that leased a large upper floor of a building because the rent was cheap. No one thought about the logistics of moving or housing the rather large satellite dishes, which, even when broken down into pieces, were too wide to pass through the stairwell. A roof hatch was built and the dishes had to be lifted up to the roof and then lowered into the building. Apart from the inconvenience, the roof hatch was difficult to secure and the building was broken into several times.

3. Business and retail locations

Perhaps the biggest mistake made when leasing a retail location is to look for cheap rent. If a retail location is wrong for your business, you are almost signing a death warrant when you sign the lease. Be prepared to pay higher rent for a prime location. Costs are usually indicative of a location's visibility and viability. Here's how to avoid some common mistakes that will cause you future grief:

- Research should pinpoint the competition in the area, so don't lease a building close to them. You'll waste money on advertising trying to attract customers.
- Customers need easy accessibility. We live life in the fast lane, so ensure there is ample parking or they will go elsewhere.
- Don't lease a "cheap" retail building in an industrial area, as people visiting industrial areas are on business and not in the mood for retail shopping.
- Moving a business when it has outgrown its premises is costly, so look for a location that will suit your needs for the first five years. Your first two years will not generate enough profit to finance a move, which usually involves extensive, nonrecoverable renovation costs.
- Save time physically hunting for the ideal location by using the Internet to locate realtors and potential premises in your desired area.
- If you lease space in a shopping mall, be prepared to pay a percentage of gross sales to the mall managers toward their communal advertising costs. This can eat a huge hole in your profit margin.

QUICK Tip

Study the Customer: Study the patterns of walk- and drive-by traffic. Note people's reactions as they walk past other stores. If a store attracts their attention, find out why. Drive past your potential location. Is it visible to customers? Note stores and businesses that catch your eye. What attracted your attention? A field trip will give you ideas for displays, color schemes, and effective marketing techniques.

4. Signing a lease

A lease is a legal and binding agreement between the landlord (the lessor) and the renter (the lessee) for the term of the lease. Because a lease is a complex agreement, have your lawyer explain it to you before signing.

During negotiations, estimate how long you will need the building and ask for "first right of refusal," which gives you the first option to renew the lease. Any terms and conditions agreed on by the landlord should be documented in the lease, as verbal agreements can be forgotten. For example, when a three-year lease is signed, it must stipulate if and when there will be any rent increases. Usually, you will pay the first and last month's rent in advance, so include this in your projections. The last month's rent is held in trust—and should be interest-bearing—until the lease expires.

Property taxes and shared janitorial, maintenance, and strata fees should be included in the cost of the lease. Ask about these extras and budget for them. You are responsible for the monthly rent for the term of the lease, so include a subletting clause as a backup. Most landlords are cooperative and prefer contented, prompt-paying tenants. Talk to your lawyer before signing the lease.

5. Building renovations

Plan your cash flow by dividing renovation costs into priorities: renovations that must be immediately completed, those that can wait a few months, and those that can be deferred until the profits start rolling in. Give your business a chance to get started before spending working capital on major cosmetic facelifts to someone else's building. Get three quotes and look for quality work that comes with a guarantee.

Renovate and Reduce Your Rent: Landlords are often happy to negotiate. A building may need repairs or painting, and some landlords will trade a few months' rent in return for these improvements. A note of caution: installing permanent fixtures is like throwing money out the window, particularly in a short-term lease, as most fixtures cannot be removed after you leave. Clarify this issue with your landlord before making any expensive decisions.

6. Exterior signs

Unless your business is home-based (where only small exterior signs are allowed by most cities or counties) you need signage, a costly addition to your budget. Both your local government office and landlord should be consulted as regulations often restrict exterior signs, and your landlord may require signs that conform to certain specifications.

Before deciding, drive around and look for signs that catch your eye. Start with the basics—you can always add more later. Flashing neon signs can be expensive, depending on their type and size, and come with a monthly rental contract. Portable flashing signs are highly visible and eye-catching, particularly for advertising a special event or sale. Vinyl banners are reasonably priced and can also be used in trade shows. As this is a competitive industry, once you know what you want, obtain at least three quotes before making a decision.

What Communications Systems Should You Use?

Consumers have become impatient, demanding answers and service *now*. They are also sick of unanswered voice mails. Therefore, it is in your best interest to be available to clients. As technology becomes more complex, the cost of keeping in touch has become a major expense. Because technology is changing so rapidly, it is difficult to advise new businesses, but here are some basic requirements.

1. Telephones

There is an abundance of sophisticated telephones available, so choose one to suit your needs. If you move around in your business, you might carry a cellular or cordless telephone to ensure that you do not miss calls. Call display and call alert services allow you to identify first and second callers.

Telephone lines If you do not require a listing in the Yellow Pages, home-based businesses can operate efficiently using a residential line. Many phone companies offer special SOHO packages. If you also use a cellular phone, this number can be used to advertise in the Yellow Pages and save yourself the cost of a business line. For a business requiring more than one telephone, phone systems can be leased or purchased. They are expensive, so plan carefully before ordering.

Different ringing tones using different numbers on the same residential line can be used for either a fax or family line. The ring tone for each number is distinctly different. If you use your residential line for Internet access, an incoming call under the call-waiting service may terminate your connection. You can disable call waiting—consult your telephone company for advice. If you do not use high-speed Internet access or a fax modem, a home-based system should include two residential lines—one for day-to-day business and one for the fax and Internet. Voice mail, call waiting, a cellular phone, or a pager may also be necessary.

Add-on services There are numerous bundles and packages available from your telephone company, including that much-hated voice mail. As we can't always be available to answer the telephone, voice mail is a necessary evil, ensuring that clients can reach you. Other options are available, but may be rarely used and add significantly to your monthly account.

Return Calls Promptly: Any business communication should be professional, including your voice mail message. "Bill is not available, leave a message after the beep" doesn't cut it in business. Leave a positive, courteous message that informs callers that their call is important to you and that you will return it promptly. If you are going out of town or will be unavailable for a while, change your voice mail message to let callers know that you are unavailable for a certain period and, when possible, leave an emergency contact number.

Long distance If you regularly call long distance, there are some cheap rates available—often up to half what you would pay through your regular phone service. If you move only your long-distance calling to another company, some companies will increase the cost of your package, so ask before making a choice. Choose a long-distance package that will allow cheap rates during business hours, and check with your provider every few months, as they often change rates without letting their customers know.

2. Fax machines

Sending emails with attachments has quickly replaced the need for a fax machine; in fact, these days, most incoming faxes are junk mail. If you use a fax modem, you have the ability to view and delete faxes before printing. In most cases, a scanner can eliminate the need to fax original documents. Fax capacity is now an integral part of many printer/scanners (see the section on computer equipment later in this chapter), so evaluate your need for a stand-alone fax carefully—they cost anywhere from $100 and up.

3. Cellular phones

They are attached to everyone's ears and have become an integral piece of business equipment. Cell phones have so many options that most people could never hope to understand how to fully use them. If you are regularly away from your business, you need one to check messages (or emails) and for call forwarding. Another toy that quickly racks up the charges, be aware of expensive roaming long-distance costs when you are out of the normal reception area. Or, if you truly need it, get a roaming-free national plan. If you talk on a cell phone a lot or while you are driving, purchase an in-ear microphone to use for hands-free conversations.

Shop and Save: It's a competitive business, so shop around. Many companies offer free phones if you sign contracts, with attractive offers such as the first 150 minutes and upward free for as low as $20 a month. You will also pay a monthly access fee of a few dollars, plus taxes.

Before you commit, remember that if your business doesn't succeed, you will be stuck with the phone. Buyout lease costs are approximately $20 a month for each unused month. Some businesses use a pager service (as cheap as $10 a month) coupled with a cell phone for situations when one can't answer the phone.

CASE STUDY: Stuck with the Bills But No Phone

Perry's landscaping business was quickly growing, and he realized the need for a salesperson to help with the quoting, marketing, and selling. He hired what appeared to be Mr. Right, who insisted he needed a cell phone. When the first bill came in, Mr. Right had obviously been making mountains of personal calls. After discovering other indiscretions, Perry fired him. The season was coming to a close, so Perry didn't rehire, but still had to pay for the phone. Early into the next season, he severely injured his back and had to close the business. He found a "friend" to sublease the phone, but she didn't pay the bills and moved out of town—with the phone. Poor Perry was stuck with months of unpaid bills, a two-and-a-half-year lease buyout, and no phone.

4. Internet access and email

Nowadays, it seems that if you don't have a dot-com or at least an email address, you aren't considered a real business. There are many books on this subject, but here are some factors to consider before hooking up.

Internet access There are two choices for Internet service, slow- or high-speed. A dial-up service requires a separate telephone line to keep the business line free. The connection time can take fifteen to thirty seconds using a modem in your computer. Many telephone companies include the cost of dial-up access in their phone packages. High-speed access, either through your local cable or telephone company, is instant and usually dependable but comes at a higher cost. Monthly charges are approximately $30 with unlimited usage and may cost more if you network other computers. After changing from dial-up to high-speed cable, I am absolutely sold. The extra cost is more than negated by the time and frustration saved. If you travel frequently, a laptop with wireless capabilities becomes a necessity. With Wi-Fi hotspots available in so many locations, you never need to be out of touch.

Website A website acts as a 24/7 silent advertisement. You can design one yourself or spend tens of thousands of dollars; bells and whistles run the full gamut. An ideal site offers your product or service information, a corporate profile, and consumer information. If you are considering a website to complement your marketing, study others in similar businesses and talk to people who have good sites to see what type of traffic they draw and what they are spending to achieve their results.

If you design your own site, ensure that it is professional or you will turn potential customers away. You will have to register your domain name as either a .com, .net, or .org, to name a few, with an annual fee of approximately $75. Monthly hosting fees range from $10 and up, plus the cost of updating, which can range from $50 to $95 an hour. If you regularly submit your name to search engines, this too is an added cost. Know why you want a site and what you expect from it and allow plenty of time to have the right one designed for you. Consult with three different Web design companies before making a final decision.

What Office and Computer Equipment Do You Need?

Office equipment

Certain furniture and equipment are standard business requirements. If you don't have anything, starting from scratch can be expensive. Shop around at the various used furniture and larger office stores or through a buy-and-sell classified newspaper. The larger stores have online and printed catalogs to use as a guideline. If you are setting up an office where clients come to visit, make it comfortable, tidy, professional, and inviting. Figure 6.1 outlines some of the basic costs.

Computer equipment

To be competitive, a business needs a computer system that encompasses accounting, word processing, some graphic abilities, a database and Internet access for research, email, and marketing. A small service business might escape the traumas of becoming computer-literate, but progressive companies will ensure they are plugged in and online. The new millennium is all about knowledge, information, and fast communication. If you don't understand computers, part of your business education should be to attend evening classes so you can learn what your computer can do for your business. Consult an expert so that you purchase what you really need and no more.

Figure 6.1: THE COST OF FURNISHING YOUR OFFICE

	Low end	High end
Office desk	$70	$750
Computer workstation	65	600
Chair for desk/computer	50	800
Four-drawer vertical file cabinet	130	650
Four-drawer lateral cabinet	320	900
Hanging file folder frames (six)	10	25
Fax machine	100	500
Adding machine with tape	20	190
Bookshelf or storage unit	20	260
Guest chairs	25	400
Total outlay:	**$810**	**$5,075**

(This list does not include a computer system—that is extra.)

Basic system requirements

It seems that the moment you buy a state-of-the-art computer system with peripherals, it becomes obsolete. The trick is to buy one that remains efficient for at least three years; only the software may need upgrading. The market is extremely volatile. One computer expert recently informed me that prices on new products decrease by an average of 5 percent a month. The cost of a system can range from $1,500 to $6,000. Depending on your needs, a system should include the following:

- **Hard drive:** A Pentium 4, 80GB hard drive with 512MB RAM memory should handle most businesses' needs for a few years but will set you back $1,800. Smaller hard drives are cheaper but may need upgrading or replacing sooner. This amount includes a CD-ROM drive, but add a CD-ROM writer for copying files or downloading Internet information. DVD drives are also available.
- **Monitor:** A fifteen-inch screen is bad for your eyes if you spend copious time at the screen. Opt for a seventeen-inch (flat screen, $150). LCD liquid crystal flat screens are now available up to twenty-one inches or more in size. They are expensive (up to $2,300) but save the eyes and free up desk space.
- **Scanner:** An inexpensive and useful tool for preparing marketing information, copying pictures and graphics and scanning original documents, a scanner can range in price from $100 to $750.
- **Keyboard and mouse:** Be kind to your hands and use an ergonomic keyboard and mouse. Wireless models are available for $60 and up for the two, or keyboard ($20) and mouse ($30) and up.
- **Printer:** A quality laser printer is an essential and worthwhile investment for professional presentations. They cost at least $200, with toner cartridges costing up to $100 (about 2,500 copies, dependent on the brand). Inkjet color printers are cheap to buy ($50 to $750) but expensive to operate because of the cost of the ink cartridges. Only buy one if color copies are essential to your business.
- **Multifunctional printers/copiers:** For many small businesses, buying a multifunctional black and white printer is the most economical way to go. These machines are a space-saving combination of printer, copier, stand-alone fax, PC fax, and scanner. Their prices range from $230 to $850. Some models eventually require a drum replacement at cost of up to $175.
- **Extras:** There will always be extras you need to complete your system, such as a good-quality power surge bar ($20), a firewall ($40), a networking adapter for more than one computer ($15), a modem ($30), extra cables ($20), and a Zip drive plus disk for backup ($130), so include these in your budget.

- **Software:** Your computer will likely come with a Windows operating system, and which version you use will depend on your needs. If you install Microsoft's Office Suite, it will talk a universal language to people who send you documents by email and has enough programs to satisfy most basic office needs. Some users prefer Corel WordPerfect Office Suite, which I use, so if you use Corel, install Microsoft Word as well for receiving email word documents. Use a good antivirus program immediately; Norton is excellent ($50), easy to use and can be programmed to do a daily virus scan and automatic live updates.
- **Accounting software:** If you process a volume of monthly sales invoices, use accounting software such as Simply Accounting, Mind Your Own Business, or QuickBooks. These programs are designed to handle accounts payable, accounts receivable, invoicing, inventory, and payroll. With a well-designed accounting system (consult your accountant for advice here), you have instant access to accounting records. Sales information can tell you how much each product is selling in dollar value. These figures are helpful when reordering inventory or comparing product profits. Applicable state and federal tax figures are also instantly available.

If you use an accounts receivable system, accounting software maintains a separate record for each client and gives you an instant "aged analysis" showing the age of all outstanding accounts and how much is owed. This information is invaluable for monitoring potential bad debts and for collection purposes.

Don't Cook the Books: If you don't understand figures, either take an in-depth bookkeeping course, use an accounting service, or hire a part-time bookkeeper. An accounting program does not make you a competent accountant. The old saying "garbage in, garbage out" holds true when you don't understand why you debit or credit an account. Financial information will be incorrect, and it is expensive to have an accountant repair the damage.

What Office Supplies Do You Need?

Brand yourself first

Before ordering office stationery, your first step is to "brand" yourself by deciding on a corporate theme, which then appears on all correspondence and marketing materials. Branding consists of four main elements, which are discussed in detail in Chapter 10:

1. Logo
2. Slogan
3. Mission statement
4. Corporate design and color theme

QUICK Tip

Use a Graphic Artist: Your branding should appear on all stationery, signs, and marketing materials—even shipping labels—so you are promoting your business image at all times. Budget to have a graphic artist design a logo and corporate theme that clearly reflects who you are and what you do. Many people design their own and the result is unprofessional, discouraging potential clients.

Office supplies

Budget $200 to $500 for suspension files, file folders, stapler and staples, three-hole punch, paper clips, pins, envelopes, stamps, bulldog clips, pens, pencils, highlighters, rulers, adding machine tape, notepads, laser or photocopier paper, pens, correction fluid, daybook, self-inking or rubber stamps, self-stick notes, and extra toner and file trays, to name just the basics.

Sales invoices

Where retail stores use cash register tapes and credit card receipts to record sales, all other businesses need sales invoices for recording each transaction. It is an IRS tax auditing requirement that invoices are numbered and a numerical copy maintained in accounting records. An extra copy for clients'

CASE STUDIES: Helping Themselves to the Profits

One small business employed three salespeople who decided they would help themselves to inventory, sell it, and pocket the funds. The business didn't have stringent inventory control or accounting checks in place. The salespeople took a bunch of invoices with them on the road "in case they made a sale along the way"—which they did. They gave deals if the purchasers paid cash and the money went into their own pockets. Eventually the financial figures reflected an unaccountable loss, and a numerical invoice and strict inventory check was undertaken. The missing invoice numbers were tracked down to the three salespeople who claimed that they either lost them in the car or canceled them and tore them up. Nothing could be proven and they were never charged with theft, which amounted to nearly $50,000. This theft caused the company to eventually close its doors.

files can be a valuable reference, so decide on two- or three-part invoices printed on NCR (carbonless) paper. If you cancel an invoice, mark it void and keep all copies in the numerical file. Have a printer drill two or three holes for filing in binders. Some invoicing options are:

- **Prenumbered invoice books** stamped with your name on the top can be purchased at a stationery store. It's not consistent with a professional image but it works for some, particularly contractors who write invoices for customers while on the job. Where loose invoices get lost, a book keeps them in one place.
- **Custom-designed invoices** with the help of a printer and graphic artist can reflect a professional, corporate theme. An economic ordering quantity is usually five hundred or more.
- **Designing your own invoices** (with professional advice) and taking a good copy of the master to an instant printing service can work. Some businesses print their invoices straight onto letterhead and then copy them for extra file records.

- **Computer-generated invoices** may be an option if you use a software program for billing. Research the national forms companies for designs that are compatible with your program.

Letterhead, envelopes, and business cards

To maintain your corporate theme, have a simple letterhead designed and avoid using too many colors or large fonts. Stationery costs vary depending on paper stock, logos, colors used, and quantities ordered. A neat, well-written letter has more impact on the reader than a badly worded one presented on embossed letterhead with gold printing. If you keep to one color, printing costs are lower. A textured and colored paper stock, such as cream or parchment, can present a professional image at an affordable cost. Printed envelopes are costly—you could use an adhesive address label that doubles as a shipping address label.

When you order stationery, the shorter the print run, the higher per sheet cost, so get a quote in quantities of five hundred and a thousand. However, don't order a thousand letterhead just because it's cheap; you may have enough stock to last for twenty years. Some people print their own business cards, and as there is a lot of competition in the printing and office supply industry, it pays to shop around. Digital printing now allows for more customized, print-on-demand short runs, so explore this option.

What Types of Insurance Might You Need?

Business and liability insurance

Most people don't think twice about the price of insuring their vehicle, yet many business owners neglect incorporating a comprehensive insurance strategy that includes insuring their most valuable asset—themselves. There is a myriad of policies and coverage available, so let's demystify the most important ones.

Property insurance Businesses in a commercial building need adequate fire, theft, and damage coverage, just as you would insure your home. With fire, water, or sewer damage or vandalism, buildings and equipment can be replaced, but not the cost of reconstructing files, documents, and accounting records.

A commercial policy can be designed to suit all of these needs, including broken windows and glass, employee theft, business interruption, contractor's equipment, fleet insurance, and even kidnapping and ransom. Some areas you may not be aware of that are protected in a policy are temperature change, computer fraud, and peak season inventory insurance. Policy price is dependent on your individual business requirements.

CASE STUDY: Upping the Ante

Working as a consulting controller for a personnel agency employing temporary staff, I reviewed their insurance policies. I discovered that the computer equipment was woefully underinsured, as was the employee theft coverage at only $5,000. On my recommendation, the equipment insurance was upgraded and employee theft coverage increased to $25,000. An employee later stole $500 while on assignment, and after I completed my contract, another employee embezzled nearly $10,000. Had the policy not been upgraded, the business would have suffered a substantial loss.

Liability insurance Professionals should insure for "errors and omissions" and professional liability. Special policies are available for doctors, accountants and lawyers. We all hear about clients suing businesses for malpractice, faulty products and liability through accidents, so ensure you have adequate coverage. Ask your insurance agent to help you establish a comprehensive policy. Many companies bundle both property and liability insurance into a Business Owner's Policy (BOP).

Also discuss "care, custody and control inclusion." Without coverage, even if an employee is working on a client's problem and it is under your control, you are not covered against potential damages caused by your employee. If you cannot get this coverage, know the risks when you send people onto a job. For example, if your employee steam-cleaned a $3,000 couch and damaged the upholstery, your business will get sued. Without "care, custody and control" coverage, the insurance company will not cover you. Not only will you have the damages to pay, but also the legal costs.

Home-based businesses Home-based business insurance is a rider added to your existing home policy and is restrictive in its coverage. These policies insure equipment and inventory to a limited value in the home, but usually do not include client liability. Although a cheap option, if a client comes to your house, trips over the dog and breaks a leg, you are not covered if you are sued. The Independent Insurance Agents of America (IIAA) advise against these riders unless minimal risk is involved.

A better suggestion is a home office policy, as it includes some business liability and lost income coverage plus normal homeowner's inclusions. A step between home and full business insurance, there is limited coverage for loss of business records, property contained off-site and breakdown of equipment. Visit http://info.insure.com/business/homebizoffice.html for more information.

Personal insurance

Not only are you the most important asset to your business, you are even more important to your family. Ensure that you are well insured and their needs well covered. Here are some policy types and benefits to consider.

Life insurance Life insurance has three primary purposes: to provide cash for dependents to settle your debts; to supplement the family income; and for estate and retirement planning. Seek professional advice for the latter, as it usually involves purchasing permanent insurance, such as universal life policies. These policies have considerable benefits. If your policy is convertible, you can convert to a universal life policy without a medical assessment.

To provide sufficient cash for family and business purposes when calculating how much insurance you need for the family, consider how long your dependents will need extra money. This depends on your spouse's ability to earn an income and your financial obligations. For example, a single person starting a business may only need enough to pay off the company debts, while a family person with a spouse who stays home will need $1,000,000 or more to pay off personal debts, provide for the family, and possibly plan for retirement, depending on the spouse's age and earning potential.

Your insurance agent can prepare a financial needs analysis to help determine the amount you need. Factor in inflation when doing this calculation.

At 3 percent inflation, a need to supplement income by $25,000 will grow to $50,000 in twenty-four years. The amount of insurance required for the business will depend on several factors:

- If family members are involved in the business, how easy will it be for them to find another similar-paying job if the business fails?
- If family members can take over the business, coverage is required to bridge the time required to recover and get the business going again. In addition, the bank will probably like to see any loans paid out.
- If the business has to be sold, the chance of realizing its true value is remote. Creditors can attack life insurance intended for the family if one spouse has signed personal guarantees, which is common. For example, if you have a lease or bank loan that is guaranteed by the surviving spouse, the landlord and bank can come after the life insurance proceeds.
- If the business is a partnership or corporation, it is important that there is insurance in place to enable the surviving partners or shareholders to buy out the surviving spouse's interest. Seek advice on who should own the insurance, as there are significant tax implications if the insurance is corporate or personally owned.

Term insurance Term insurance is affordable and comes in one- to thirty-year terms. Premiums are guaranteed for that period of time and automatically renew at a higher, set rate for the next term.

Shop around to Renew: Do not automatically renew if your health is good, as the renewal rates can be 25 to 100 percent more than the premiums if you shop around for a new policy. The assumption is that you only renew if you are too sick to get a new policy.

Term insurance meets the need for cash as you build your business and provides for your family's needs. The most cost-effective term insurance is a guaranteed renewable and convertible ten-year term. Much of the competition is focused on this type, which consequently has the lowest premiums. There are also preferred and regular rates. A thirty-five-year-old can purchase $500,000 for about $18 a month at regular rates, where the preferred rates would be approximately $14. For more information visit www.lifeinsurancequote.com where you can obtain instant, online quote.

Disability insurance If you suffer a serious accident, injury, or illness that prevents you from working for an extended period of time, the financial risks to your business and family are significant. Current and future income stops while business and personal expenses continue. Workers' compensation pays a percentage of your income, but only 8 percent of disabilities are usually covered, as accidents often occur off the job or illness is involved, and payments will likely fall short of what you will need. One of the leading causes of divorce is long-term illnesses and the associated financial stress.

Provide some protection with a good disability insurance policy. Although it is designed to protect your income, if you are starting out, there is no income to protect. Consequently, you will only qualify for a minimal amount—possibly $1,000 a month or less. There are policies available for whatever amount you want up to $3,000 or more monthly, but the company performs an income test at time of claim, reviews your actual income, and pays approximately 66 percent.

Plan Well Ahead: One possibility is to purchase a personal disability policy based on your income at least one year before you plan to start a business. Most applications query your intention to leave the current company within a year. A "yes" answer and you don't get the insurance. Ensure that the policy covers you if you change jobs and that the coverage is underwritten when you take out the policy. This means they will pay what you have purchased and will not do another income check at time of claim.

Talk to an expert and ask how you will be paid if you can do part of your job, or as you regain your health. There are usually residual or partial disability payments but benefits vary. Further, do you want to wait thirty, sixty, or ninety days before payments start? The premiums are about twice the cost for thirty days as compared to ninety days. Some disability policies cover your "out of pocket" business expenses; you can add this rider regardless of how much income you have.

Critical illness insurance A new insurance called "critical illness coverage" pays a lump sum of $50,000 or more thirty days after you are diagnosed with a life-threatening illness, such as heart attack, stroke, or cancer. Many people recover from these critical illnesses but not until they have experienced considerable emotional and physical health problems, causing significant financial stress. The premiums are lower than for disability insurance and the amount you purchase is not as limited. Many business owners return to work within three months from most injuries or simple illnesses and would not collect much on a disability insurance policy. Critical illnesses keep them off the job much longer and the money is paid out after thirty days. For more information, visit www.critical-illness-insurance.com.

Plan an exit strategy

As the business increases in value, consider either disability buyout insurance or critical illness insurance on each partner or shareholder. Few businesses can carry an ill partner for an extended period of time—you need an exit strategy. Set out the conditions in a shareholder or partnership agreement and ensure that the decision to trigger the funds rests with the insurance company. If you have insurance owned and paid for by your company, check the tax implications with your accountant. Use a well-recognized, experienced insurance professional.

What Is Risk Management?

Starting a business involves taking certain risks, some so remote that it is not necessary to plan for their occurrence. Other risks may concern you, but are too costly to protect yourself against. Others are affordable to insure against.

CASE STUDY: Paying through the Roof

John, a small, unincorporated contractor, hired a subcontracting company to replace the roof of a condominium he was contracted to repair. A freak storm caused $200,000 damage to the condominiums on the top floors. The subcontractor who performed the work did not have insurance to cover this damage, so the insurance company that paid for the repairs successfully sued John for the $200,000. He liquidated his savings and never quite recovered financially from this experience.

The risk in this case study could have been eliminated in three ways. First, John should have checked that the subcontractor had the necessary insurance; if not, he could have ensured that his liability insurance included subcontractors; or, if he had invested in segregated rather than mutual funds, they would have been creditor-protected, and the insurance company would not have had access to them. Segregated funds are similar to mutual funds but are sold through insurance companies. Proceed with caution because the amount of the creditor protection depends on which state you reside in.

Figure 6.2 outlines some common business risks, their significance, and what can be done to protect yourself against these situations. If you choose not to cover these risks, then you are assuming the risk and ensuing financial consequences yourself. Consider the assessment of the risk and then explore the cost to insure against it. Remember: don't be cheap by under-insuring yourself, your partner, the business assets, and potential business risks.

Step-By-Step Start-Up Checklists

As you establish each start-up cost for your new business, use the checklist in Figure 6.3 as a guide to the overall cost. Then transfer these figures to the appropriate places in your business plan.

Figure 6.4 is a checklist in order of priority of the steps you should take when setting up your business. Use it to keep track of where you are and don't miss any important steps. If your business is home-based, some of these steps will not apply to you.

Figure 6.2: HOW TO REDUCE BUSINESS RISK

Risk	Significance	What you can do
Business failure	Unlikely but would have serious financial consequences: • Property, home, investments • Mutual fund investments	Incorporate • Transfer ownership to others • Transfer to segregated funds
Theft, fire liability, water damage	Low risks that a good business insurance policy will cover.	Consult an experienced insurance broker for a comprehensive policy.
Employee on-the-job accident	What is your liability if you hire someone who is then injured on the job?	Without workers' compensation, you may be personally liable for medical and future income costs.
Death	Highly unlikely yet still a possibility.	Term or life insurance to provide for debts and family.
Disability or illness	A real risk. Long hours and stress take their toll.	Disability and/or critical illness insurance.
Key employee or partner is injured or dies	Some employees or partners are critical to your overall business success.	Obtain life, disability, or critical illness insurance on them. Insurance can provide a lump sum to buy out a partner if disabled for over a year.

Figure 6.3: ESTIMATED BUSINESS START-UP COSTS

Type of Expense	Estimated Cost
1. Consultations with accountant	$________
2. Consultations with lawyer	________
3. Lawyer's fees to prepare buy-sell agreement	________
4. Purchase price of business	________
5. Incorporation fees	________
6. Business plan preparation	________
7. Loan application and financing fees	________
8. First and last month's rent	________
9. Renovations to office space	________
10. Utility deposits	________
11. City or county business license	________
12. Other licenses	________
13. Telephone, fax line, and Internet installations	________
14. Cellular phone purchase and access fee	________
15. Interior and exterior signs	________
16. Computer system	________
17. Printing and stationery	________
18. Office furniture and equipment	________
19. Marketing costs	________
20. Office supplies and miscellaneous	________
21. Business and life/disability insurance	________
22. Other: ______________________________	________
TOTAL:	$________

Figure 6.4: BUSINESS START-UP CHECKLIST

Step Procedure	Check
1. Decide which type of business is right for me	☐
2. Research the market and the competition	☐
3. Take vendor's proposal to accountant for review	☐
4. Visit city or county clerk to review codes and regulations	☐
5. Research other licensing requirements	☐
6. Contact lawyer to review/prepare buy-sell agreement	☐
7. Prepare business plan and projections	☐
8. Find suitable location for business	☐
9. Research costs of all renovations to office	☐
10. Contact lawyer to have lease reviewed	☐
11. Talk to bank manager about financing requirements	☐
12. Register business name	☐
13. Have incorporation papers prepared	☐
14. Call telephone company for phone requirements	☐
15. Order cellular phone (you will need all your phone numbers so that stationery can be ordered)	☐
16. Apply for necessary business licenses	☐
17. Open business accounts and credit card applications	☐
18. Apply for business registration	☐
19. Apply for state sales tax registration	☐
20. Apply for payroll registration and information	☐
21. Register with workers' compensation insurance	☐

continued

Step Procedure	Check
22. Prepare marketing and advertising campaign	☐
23. Research computer requirements and prices	☐
24. Talk to accountant about accounting system	☐
25. Get quotes on exterior and interior sign work	☐
26. Get quotes on printing requirements	☐
27. Contact insurance broker	☐
Other: ______________________	☐
______________________	☐
______________________	☐
______________________	☐
______________________	☐
______________________	☐
______________________	☐
______________________	☐
______________________	☐
______________________	☐

What Is the Next Step?

You have a great idea, it's been well researched, and you know your approximate start-up costs. Things are looking good, so now it's time to start putting together a formal business plan to see how viable this idea really is. Where will you borrow money? How much will you need? Will your ideas transfer into a viable business concern? Now is the time to put all those ideas on paper, document your research, and do some serious number crunching. The following chapter walks you through the various components of a business plan.

Chapter 7

What Is a Business Plan?

Success doesn't just happen—it usually takes thorough planning, and of course, money always helps.

- **Why do you need a business plan?**
- **Where do you find help with business plans?**
- **What is in a business plan?**
- **How do you prepare projections?**
- **Who will lend you money?**
- **Doing it right: Your business plan checklists**

Why Do You Need a Business Plan?

You have probably discovered by now that there is more to starting a business than you first thought. There is so much to learn and gather that it can become quite overwhelming. Have you assessed whether you are an entrepreneur at heart and ready for the challenge? Do you have a good indication of the type of business you want? This next step will test your theories and indicate whether to proceed further.

A business plan is a necessary tool for all businesses. Just as a home is not built without blueprints or a movie made without a script, you don't start a business without a sound and workable blueprint. You now take the information you have gathered and put those ideas formally onto paper.

No Plan, No Money: Without a business plan, banks or investors will not entertain the thought of financing your business. It is your only foot in the door, so make sure it shines.

You will learn how much you need to borrow, whether you can afford to borrow, your break-even point, and whether the business can afford to pay you a satisfactory wage. People often prepare a plan and start crunching numbers, only to discover that their idea needs reworking or is not financially viable. It is better to discover this on paper rather than after you've started.

Where Do You Find Help With Business Plans?

With the Internet, sample plans can be freely downloaded and used as a reference. Most banks and large accounting companies have publications or CD-ROMs to help you. As well, try the following resources:

- **Small Business Administration:** Before you start your business plan, make an appointment with your local Small Business Administration center to discuss what type of information your business plan should

contain. This will save you a great deal of time and energy and start you in the right direction. They also have loads of resources.
Website: www.sba.gov.

- ***Entrepreneur* Magazine:** Everything you need to know about business plans, including articles, sample plans, and loads of links to nationwide resources.
  Website: www.entrepreneur.com.
- **Center for Business Planning:** Offers samples of winning business plans, software, resources, links, and helpful articles.
  Website: www.businessplans.org
- **Small Business Development Center:** Offers nearly thirty industry-specific business plans, a virtual business plan tour, software and loads of information.
  Website: www.sbdcnet.utsa.edu.SBIC/bplans.htm
- **Planware:** Offers free downloadable business planning software, a sixty-five page guide, financial and strategic planners and free online advice.
  Website: www.planware.org/busplan.htm
- **BPlans.com:** This site offers over 250 plans, many of them industry specific, and is a mine of information and resources.
  Website: www.bplans.com

Get Professional Advice: Enlist a consultant or accountant's help in compiling the business plan's information into the correct format, and have him or her review it after both the first and final drafts. Putting it all together can be challenging. A bank would prefer to see that you have involved a professional—it helps to validate the contents.

Expect to spend anywhere from two weeks to a few months in completing research and putting the plan together. Some people hire a consultant or accountant to prepare their whole plan, which isn't a good idea, because *you* need to have answers to all the questions to operate your business successfully—and to satisfy a lender or investor.

What Is in a Business Plan?

Follow a plan format that ensures you research all the important areas of your business, and if it is being used for lending or investment purposes, that you have provided all the information that lenders need. Your first task is to decide why you are preparing this plan. Answer these questions:

- Why am I preparing this plan?
- Who else will be reading it?
- Why will they be reading it?
- What do they need to know?

QUICK Tip

Know Your Goals and Objectives: By knowing why you are preparing this plan, you can save time and effort by focusing on the important areas. Business plans often contain filler information that is not pertinent. Look at sample plans from the sites mentioned earlier to get an idea. If you need to borrow funds, ask the lending institution exactly what is required.

The size of the final document will be dependent on the size and complexity of your business and whether you are looking for outside funding. The end result should be professionally presented, with typewritten pages and a table of contents, and securely bound. Include the following sections

1. Executive summary

The executive summary should be no longer than two pages. Prepare it after the plan is complete, as it summarizes the whole plan in a nutshell. Make it dynamic and exciting to generate the reader's interest. Loans officers or investors have read copious plans and tend to skip through them if they get bored.

2. The company

Introduce the business in more detail, outlining your type of business, giving its history (if you are purchasing an existing business) or an outline of the new business's products or services. With an existing business, highlight any recent special achievements. This section should be broken down into the following subsections:

a) **General business overview:** A description of the business, where it fits into the marketplace, what needs it will fill, and how it will fill those needs. Describe the markets that will use your business and include any business history.
b) **Company structure:** Outline the corporate structure of the business. Include a list of shareholders or partners and incorporation information.
c) **Location:** Describe the location, its benefits, amenities, and accessibility to customer traffic. Include freight routes if it's a manufacturing or wholesale business, traffic statistics if available from your local county, and area demographics and growth rate. Detail parking and zoning information, the cost and terms of the lease, taxes, and utilities. List any foreseeable disadvantages to your location and explain why you chose it. Detail office space, storage, and operational facilities. List any renovations or alterations that need to be completed.

QUICK Tip

Cover All Bases: Lenders look for sound managerial experience in the key areas of sales and marketing, accounting, and technical operations. A gap in any one area will count as a strike against the business. Ensure you have covered all these bases in your plan. Competent managers are a strong indication that the business will be in good hands.

d) **Key personnel:** Include a brief profile of all key partners or employees, their duties and experience, and include their résumés in the appendix.

Highlight their education, expertise, business qualifications, and history, and supply references if available.

e) **Goals and objectives:** Outline your goals and objectives, both long- and short-term. Many people neglect this area, failing to think past the start-up stage. Your goals and objectives should be explained in more detail in other sections of your plan and be considered when preparing financial figures.
f) **Strengths and weaknesses:** Blow your horn and detail the business's strengths. Stress where and why you excel in these areas, whether it be great customer service, pricing, or a strong distribution base. Don't include marketing strengths and weaknesses—this will be covered in the marketing section. Discuss your weaknesses and how you plan to overcome them.
g) **Mission and vision statements:** A mission statement describes your company philosophy in a few sentences. A vision statement describes how you see your company in the future. Think carefully about each one. Study other mission statements and design one that is uniquely yours. A mission statement shows your commitment to the business and its customers and gives you a written promise to uphold.

3. Products and services

Your business is all about selling services or products, so ensure that what you are offering is marketable and profitable. Use the following headings to detail this information.

a) **Product description:** Describe your products or services, their benefits, and how they fill a need in the marketplace. Show your advantage over the competition and the volume you can output. Describe your business's developmental stage. List potential or current contracts. Refer to any letters of intent from prospective clients and include these in the appendix.
b) **Cost of sales:** The basis of your business is profit margins. Show what products sell for and provide the costs of raw materials, freight, packaging, wages, and so on. Note the expected gross profit margins and whether they will change if you diversify or expand. Clearly explain how the manufacturing or distribution process will operate, remembering that a lender may not be familiar with your type of business.

c) **Future projections:** If you plan future expansion, research, or development, include this information. List any potential threats or opportunities.
d) **Legal concerns:** If your business entails legal considerations such as patents, copyrights, trademarks or special licenses, include relevant information.

4. Marketing strategies

Refer to both market research (Chapter 4) and how you plan to market your business (Chapter 10). As marketing is a key component to the success of your business, prepare this section in depth. Include the following topics.

a) **Market research:** Break this section down into the following subsections:

- An analysis of today's market and trends
- Past and future industry, global, and consumer trends
- Your target market, its size, and demographics
- Your ideal consumer profile
- Your projected share of the market
- Geographic boundaries and seasonal trends
- Customer service policies
- Strengths and weaknesses
- Market survey results

Show You Did Your Homework: Include a summary of your market survey results including how many people you contacted, the questions you asked, and their responses. Note if you have changed your strategy based on these results. Convert answers into percentages, for example, "75 percent of respondents said they would use my service at least four times a year."

b) **The competition:** Both you and the lender must understand the strength of your competitors. Research and address the following topics:

- The current competition, their size, and market share
- Future competition
- The strengths and weaknesses of the competition
- How you can overcome their strengths and capitalize on their weaknesses
- Your strengths and weaknesses (use the SWOT analysis in Chapter 4)
- Your edge over the competition and your cost to stay competitive

c) **Marketing and sales strategies:** Part of your business plan will be a marketing plan, which details how you will find potential customers. A sound marketing plan includes a mix of methods, including using various media, promotional methods and one-on-one techniques. Address these topics:

- Promotional and media methods you will use
- Special services or policies
- The target market these methods will reach
- The effectiveness of each method
- The frequency of use
- How you will sell your products/service (agents, representatives, staff)
- Incentive or sales bonus schemes
- The reach of your sales force

5. Operational information

Plan how you will operate your business, from overhead costs to distribution channels. Include the following information:

a) **Overhead costs:** Explain your estimated overhead costs and demonstrate a break-even point. If future plans involve expansion, reflect these costs. A detailed explanation of these costs will be included in your projections, so don't go into great detail here.
b) **Suppliers:** List your major suppliers, their terms of credit, and their product availability. Note whether you have to sign any personal guarantees to obtain credit from them.
c) **Quality control:** Describe your policies on quality control, any relevant hazards or environmental risks, and how you propose to overcome these

obstacles. Mention any specific safety procedures relevant to your operation.

d) **Distribution:** Outline how your products will be distributed or delivered and any competitive advantages to your methods.

e) **Employees:** List the staff positions along with their job descriptions, areas of responsibility, and expected salaries.

f) **Assets and equipment:** Note any equipment on hand or to be purchased, its value or cost, and its life expectancy.

g) **Insurance policies:** List the various insurance policies you will take out, including liability, theft and fire, workers' compensation, and key management and employee insurance.

h) **Licenses and permits:** List any licenses or permits that your business requires to operate and their cost.

6. Financial information

The viability of your new venture will culminate when you prepare projections of income, expenses, and cash flow, and when you review how much money you may require. Even if you are not borrowing money, projections and cash flows facilitate making many future decisions.

If you are attempting to borrow money, the financial section should include the following:

a) **Projections of income and expenses:** Projections are a month-by-month estimation of sales and expenses, including start-up costs, itemized in the month the revenue was earned and the costs were incurred. Prepare the first year in months, and by quarters or annually for the following two to five years. The bottom line reflects profits or losses.

Back up the Numbers: Include notes in your business plan to substantiate the numbers—it's easy to create figures out of thin air. Be conservative with revenues and practical with expenses.

b) **Cash flow forecasts:** The projections should be accompanied by cash flow forecasts for the corresponding periods. A cash flow forecast differs from projections, as it estimates when revenues will be received and when expenses will be paid, and includes income from loans and other sources. Samples can be found later in this chapter.
c) **Financial statements:** Banks require a projected balance sheet and, if you are purchasing a business, past financial statements for the last two to four years.
d) **Capital expenses:** Include a list of capital spending, such as asset purchases or building renovations. When a lender considers a proposal, these values help determine how a loan will be used and secured.
e) **Net worth statement:** Lenders require personal statements of net worth from owners, partners, or shareholders. Loans are often personally secured, and this statement lists your personal assets, liabilities, and net worth. Net worth statements also indicate the stability of the key management players.

7. Funding requirements

This section is devoted to the sum you need to borrow, how you expect to repay it, and over what time period. Your projections and cash flow forecasts should have indicated how much the business needs and can afford to repay. The total monthly loan payment shows on the cash flow forecast and loan interest only on the projections. You should explain how you intend to secure the loan and with what assets. If you are looking for an investment partner, note the share of the company available in return for their investment and what else you intend to offer them.

Outline the following:

- When you need the money and how much
- The type of loan you are applying for
- The desired terms of repayment
- A breakdown of how you will use the funds
- Future funding requirements, if any

CASE STUDY: Planning for Success

Mary Jane Stenberg had no concept of a business plan until she participated in a nine-month, part-time business growth program. Her fledgling company, Stenberg and Associates, provides employment training for a variety of career opportunities. After two years in business, she already employed five people. Mary Jane paid bills and drew a salary, but her dreams were to expand—yet she didn't know how to start.

Now, eight years later, she heads a highly successful business with two locations offering fourteen training programs and employing thirty-seven people. How did she grow her business so rapidly and successfully? Mary Jane attributes her success to always using a business plan before making any decisions.

"I followed the business plan I had learned to prepare during the course, and used the template for other things, such as expansion," she explains. "I learned so much. Whenever I wanted to get larger, I revisited and revised my plan. You have to have your plan and abide by it, but don't be afraid to change it."

Many owners forget to use a business plan once they are operational, so remember this success story and use one to start—and grow—your business.

8. Appendix

Include *copies* of any documents that back up and strengthen the information in your business plan, including:

- Up-to-date financial statements from the business you are purchasing
- Personal statements of net worth
- Letters of reference and letters of intent
- Product pictures or relevant newspaper articles

- Résumés of key employees or partners
- Incorporation or business registration papers
- Cash flow and projection forecasts
- Permits, licenses, trademarks, or patents
- Market surveys
- Equipment and asset appraisals
- Partnership or employee agreements
- Insurance policies and leases

How Do You Prepare Projections?

Let's work through the numbers with Phenomenal Flowers Inc. Following are examples of three months of a twelve-month income and expense projection, a corresponding cash flow forecast, and reconciliation of the two. Jasmine is the owner of Phenomenal Flowers Inc. and wants to borrow $12,500 from the bank to open a retail outlet. She prepared draft projections and discussed the results with her accountant.

Projections of sales and expenses

Figure 7.1 demonstrates the projected (estimated) sales and expenses for the store. Jasmine made the following assumptions:

- The gross profit margin after purchases and wastage is 45 percent of retail price.
- One full-time employee is paid $1,800 a month.
- Start-up expenses include consulting with an accountant, insurance policies, renovations and repairs to the store, marketing, advertising, phone line installation, and office supplies.
- The employee will use Jasmine's van for deliveries.
- If the business starts in March, it can capitalize on Easter in April and Mother's Day in May.
- Jasmine doesn't expect a steady customer base for six to twelve months.
- The doubling of sales from March to April will transpire from her grand opening advertising.
- Repairs and maintenance will be paid on completion of the work.

Figure 7.1: **PROJECTIONS OF SALES AND EXPENSES**

PHENOMENAL FLOWERS INC.
Twelve Months Projected Sales and Expenses

Description	**March**	**April**	**May**
Sales	$ 4,500	$ 9,000	$12,150
Cost of sales:			
Purchases	2,350	4,600	6,300
Wastage	125	350	380
	2,475	4,950	6,680
Gross profit	**2,025**	**4,050**	**5,470**
Overhead expenses:			
Accounting fees	1,500	200	200
Advertising	775	750	850
Bank charges	65	65	70
Fees, licenses & taxes	230	45	0
Insurance	2,400	0	0
Loan interest	100	100	100
Office supplies	923	180	90
Promotion/marketing	400	500	450
Rent	1,250	1,250	1,250
Repairs & maintenance	1,780	200	100
Telephone	410	125	125
Utilities	300	300	300
Vehicle–gas	100	100	100
Vehicle–repairs & maintenance	130	130	130
Workers' Compensation	65	65	65
Wages	1,800	1,800	1,800
	12,228	5,810	5,630
Profit/(loss)	**(10,203)**	**(1,760)**	**(160)**
Accumulated	**($10,203)**	**($11,963)**	**($12,123)**

Cash flow forecast

In preparing the cash flow forecast (Figure 7.2 on the following page), Jasmine assumed the following:

- The bank would loan her $12,500 on an unsecured line of credit, which she wants to pay off quickly. She would put $5,000 into the business.

Figure 7.2: **CASH FLOW FORECAST**

PHENOMENAL FLOWERS INC.
Twelve Months Cash Flow Projections

Description	March	April	May
Cash receipts in:			
Cash sales	$ 2,700	$ 5,400	$ 7,290
Receivables–30 days	0	900	1,800
Receivables–60 days	0	0	900
Loan proceeds	12,500	0	0
Total cash:	**15,200**	**6,300**	**9,990**
Cash disbursed:			
Cost of sales	0	2,475	4,950
Accounting fees	0	1,500	200
Advertising	0	775	750
Bank charges	65	65	70
Fees, licenses & taxes	230	45	0
Insurance	2,400	0	0
Loan interest	0	100	100
Loan principal	0	700	700
Office expenses	300	473	180
Promotion/marketing	400	500	450
Rent & taxes	1,250	1,250	1,250
Repairs & maintenance	1,780	200	100
Telephone	0	410	125
Utilities	0	300	300
Vehicle–gas	100	100	100
Vehicle–repairs & maintenance	130	130	130
Workers' Compensation	0	0	195
Wages	1,800	1,800	1,800
	8,455	10,823	11,400
Surplus/(deficit):	**6,745**	**(4,523)**	**(1,410)**
Opening balance:	5,000	11,745	7,222
+ cash receipts	15,200	6,300	9,990
– cash disbursed	8,455	10,823	11,400
Closing balance	**$11,745**	**$ 7,222**	**$ 5,812**

- Half of her sales would be on account, receiving half in thirty days and half in sixty days.
- Her floral supplies would be paid for by cash at the auctions, which she would charge to her Visa and pay off the monthly balances in thirty days.
- Smaller trade accounts would be paid in thirty days.
- Bank charges, loan interest, rent, and utilities would be paid when due.
- Repairs, renovations, marketing, and insurance would be paid immediately.

Reconciliation

To understand how the projections relate to the cash flow, Figure 7.3 shows the outstanding monies due to and by the business at the end of the three-month period. This figure agrees with the projected sales and expense statement.

Figure 7.3: RECONCILIATION OF CASH FLOW WITH PROJECTIONS

PHENOMENAL FLOWERS INC.
Reconciliation of Sales Projections with Cash Flow

Accounts receivable balance due:	$ 6,660
Less accounts payable balance due:	7,095
Shortfall:	435
Loan due:	12,500
Contributed capital:	5,000
Current debts:	17,935
Less cash on hand after three months:	(5,812)
Reconciliation with loss:	**(12,123)**
Less loan principal repaid: (Non-operational cost)	$ 1,400

What her accountant noticed

Jasmine's accountant was somewhat concerned with the projections. Month three reflects the store's break-even point, yet until Christmas, the retail floral trade is relatively quiet. With the business heading into summer, no amount of marketing is going to bring in customers when they are on vacation. With the store costing $5,630 in monthly overhead, how are the sales going to be sustained to pay the bills?

Jasmine may have to consider hiring a part-time employee and not taking wages from the business for up to a year. She should reduce her loan principal payments to the standard three percent of the outstanding balance, plus interest, and reduce her marketing costs over the summer, saving the marketing push until later in the year. These measures would reduce overhead to approximately $4,000 and help with cash flow, but the store still has to generate $9,000 a month in sales to break even. Jasmine's accountant felt that the bank would not give her a loan based on these projections and advised her against opening the store until she could devise a more profitable solution—or business.

Who Will Lend You Money?

If you have a viable business plan, the ability to repay, and, most important, security for the loan, you have the right formula. Deciding what type of money to borrow and from whom is the next hurdle. Many businesses do not require large sums to get them started, and often, people can't get a small loan from the bank, so they look elsewhere. Be aware of the pros and cons of nontraditional financing before you make your decision. With all potential lenders, consider the ten tips for borrowing in Figure 7.4 on the next page.

Traditional financing options

You have a sound business plan and are ready to approach a lending institution for financing. The following are your traditional options. Explore these options before shopping for dangerous money.

1. Small business loans Banks offer a variety of loans, although start-up loans can be difficult to obtain unless you meet their lending criteria, which is based on the three Cs: cash flow, credit, and collateral. They prefer to lend for purchase of hard assets, but as each loan is different, talk to your bank manager to familiarize yourself with what they offer.

Figure 7.4: TEN TIPS FOR BORROWING

1. Don't approach a lender for "working capital." Loans are usually given for tangible assets that can be secured.
2. Don't expect a lender to finance your whole venture. The owner is expected to invest money, at least one-third of the start-up cost.
3. When you call for an appointment, ask what information will be needed so you are well prepared.
4. Dress smartly. Jeans and sneakers are out. Don't chew gum.
5. Research the various government-funded grants and loans before deciding on a lender.
6. Have an experienced third party critique your business plan before presenting it to a lender.
7. Have the approval of your spouse or partner before committing to financial obligations.
8. If you are initially turned down, take the lender's advice and rework your plan.
9. Discuss with your accountant whom you should approach for money and what type of loan may best suit your requirements.
10. In your interview, be a good listener. Don't try to hold the floor and convince the lender how great you are. He or she can tell this by your manner, presentation, and business plan.

The Small Business Administration offers start-up business loans that are administered either through banks or other approved lending institutions. They include:

- **Microloan, a 7(m) Loan Program:** These short-term loans of up to $35,000 can be used for working capital, inventory, asset, or supply purchases. The loan is made to a guaranteed intermediary, who then loans the funds to you.
- **Basic 7(a) Loan Guaranty Program:** Administered through commercial lending institutions, this popular loan helps small businesses that may not qualify through normal lending channels. It can be used for a

variety of business needs, with a loan maturity period of up to ten to twenty-five years.

2. Bank unsecured lines of credit For loans under $25,000, a line of credit is a source of reasonably priced financing. Interest rates fluctuate, based on current rates, and are usually two percent higher than a mortgage. A line of credit is usually repaid at a minimum of three percent of the loan, so on $25,000 you have to pay at least $750 a month. This option can work if you are sure the business can meet the monthly payments.

3. Bank secured lines of credit This is riskier financing because banks require security, usually in the form of a mortgage on your home. The upside is that while you are getting established, you have the option of paying only the monthly interest. The downside is that you are threatening the security of your family if the business doesn't perform as projected. Unless you are 100 percent sure that the business will be profitable in a short time frame, think carefully before putting your home on the line.

CASE STUDY: Nice Mortgage—No Business

Dennis, a new entrepreneur, remortgaged his home to open a retail furniture store. Thinking that he knew everything about running a store because he had competently managed one for many years, he leased a cheap building, completed renovations and advertising, and opened the doors. Dennis forgot one very important start-up step—his business license. When the zoning officer visited, he told Dennis that he was contravening the regulations because the property was not zoned for retail sales. He fought hard, but the county would not budge, and he had to close the store.

Dennis couldn't raise enough capital to move to another location. He returned his inventory, lost a 15 percent restocking fee of $7,500, and the last month's rent on the lease. He also suffered the cost of all the renovations, advertising, and signage. The final loss amounted to nearly $30,000. He will now be paying off his mortgage for the next twenty years.

4. Alternative lending sources There is a myriad of loan providers offering funding to help small businesses get off the ground. Lending institutions in different states offer varying terms, loans, and conditions for start-up, young entrepreneurs, and minorities. Your business may qualify for a government grant or a farm or rural loan.

Surf Safely: If you are searching for financing on the Internet, which most people do once traditional sources have turned down their application, be very careful of which company you deal with. Easy money comes at a price. If you are not sure about the legitimacy or best practices of a company, discuss it with your local SBA office and Better Business Bureau.

A loan calculator is a handy tool for when you are preparing projections and funding information. Visit www.bankrate.com. You can quickly calculate your loan repayments based on the amount, term, and interest rate to include in your cash flow and projected expenses.

QUICK Tip

Visit Your Local SBA: Small Business Administration offices and Small Business Development Centers are in business to help both start-up and growing businesses. Offices are located across the country and online at www.sba.gov. Talk to a business officer in your town, as they are conversant with all the available state and federal loans programs.

An informative site with loads of solid business start-up advice, loan and financing information, articles, a business loan glossary, and links can be found at www.businesstown.com/finance/money.asp.

"Risky" financing alternatives

When traditional financing is not an option, some eager entrepreneurs seek riskier financing. This route may be destined for failure because if traditional financing is denied, there is usually a good reason—this is a warning to revisit the business plan and the whole business idea. Here are some options to consider and the risks involved.

1. Family or friends It's easy to approach parents or family for a loan, but not so easy explaining to them why you can't repay them. Before you consider this option, clarify how they would feel should the business not be profitable and the loan not paid back as per the agreed terms. The benefit to these loans is that family can be flexible if repayments are late, and loans can be interest-free or low interest. If the loan could jeopardize family relationships, perhaps it isn't advisable.

The same principle applies to friends. What do you value the most, your business or your friendship? There is no better way to ruin a good friendship than by not repaying debts. Don't ask friends to guarantee a loan for you either. This also ruins friendships. I once guaranteed a small loan for a friend who didn't honor some payments. I made the payments but it caused the demise of a long-time relationship.

2. Second or increased home mortgages Similar to a secured line of credit, an increased or second mortgage is risky financing for a new business. It's a long-term battle to regain home equity if the business doesn't succeed. You will be left with a large mortgage payment, business debts, and the possibility of the bank foreclosing on your home. Many marriages have dissolved for this reason. Business is a gamble, even when you have a good poker hand.

3. Credit cards For short-term financing, credit cards come in handy—but at what price? They give you a false sense of security because they allow you to make minimum monthly payments. At the same time, high interest rates compound at an alarming rate.

4. Redeeming traditional IRAs It's difficult enough to save for an IRA, and even more difficult to put the money back once it is withdrawn. There are also tax consequences, so discuss this with your accountant. Redeem them only if you are *sure* that you can replace them within sixty days. An extra tax burden is the last thing you need in your first year of business.

Freeze Liabilities: Many businesses use credit cards to pay for supplies and start-up costs, so if you have to use them, keep strict control over your spending habits. Use them as a thirty-day, interest-free, short-term business loan. Pay off the full balance each month. Collect points but not interest charges. If you have trouble controlling your plastic purchases, cut up your cards or freeze them in a block of ice—it's called freezing your liabilities.

5. Finance companies and brokers Finance companies and brokers are often willing to lend money with fewer security requirements than a bank demands, but you may pay exorbitant interest rates. Some people have obtained second mortgages from finance companies, ultimately paying just interest without reducing the principal amount. Proceed with caution and preferably, avoid this type of financing altogether.

CASE STUDY: The Eternal Loan

Terry and Marianna were in dire straits with their business. Terry spent freely while Marianna lay awake worrying about the mounting debts. Their home was mortgaged to the hilt; the bank would not lend them more. Terry finally persuaded Marianna that with a second mortgage for $50,000, the bills could be paid off. The monthly payments would only be $400. In a moment of weakness, Marianna agreed. They signed with a broker for a two-year-term loan, paying interest only of $9,000. Terry didn't change his spending habits and at the end of two years, they still owed $50,000.

6. Venture capital and loans Venture capital is money obtained through investors who, in return for their investment, expect a share of your business and usually a say in its management. Expect to spend time looking for this type of financing. Venture capitalists usually only consider investing amounts from $100,000 and up. An excellent site for more venture capital information is www.vfinance.com.

Doing It Right: Your Business Plan Checklists

As you prepare your business plan, use the checklist in Figure 7.5 to review your progress through the various stages.

Figure 7.5: **BUSINESS PLAN CHECKLIST**

Ensure that you have completed all the following tasks when creating your business plan.

1. Before starting my plan:

- ☐ I have looked at sample plans to use as resources.
- ☐ I know why and for whom I am preparing this plan.
- ☐ I have clear and defined goals and objectives.
- ☐ I asked the lending institution what they need.

2. I have researched and documented the company with regard to the:

- ☐ General business overview
- ☐ Company structure
- ☐ Location
- ☐ Key personnel
- ☐ Goals and objectives
- ☐ Strengths and weaknesses
- ☐ Mission and vision statements

3. I have researched and documented the products and services:

- ☐ Product/service description
- ☐ Cost of sales
- ☐ Future projections
- ☐ Legal concerns

4. I have researched and documented the marketing strategies:

- ☐ The competition
- ☐ Marketing strengths and weaknesses
- ☐ Marketing and sales strategies

5. I have researched and documented the operational information:

- ☐ Overhead costs
- ☐ Suppliers
- ☐ Quality control
- ☐ Distribution
- ☐ Employees
- ☐ Assets and equipment
- ☐ Insurance policies
- ☐ Licenses and permits

6. I have researched and documented the financial information:

- ☐ Projections of income and expenses
- ☐ Cash flow forecasts
- ☐ Financial statements
- ☐ List of capital expenses
- ☐ Net worth statements

7. I have researched and documented the funding requirements:

- ☐ How much, terms, type of loan, use of funds

8. I have provided an executive summary:

- ☐ Synopsis of all of the above

continued

9. I have provided an appendix:

- ☐ Included all relevant documents

10. Now that the first draft is completed, I have:

- ☐ Typed my plan neatly
- ☐ Discussed it with my accountant
- ☐ Made suggested revisions
- ☐ Completed the final draft
- ☐ Shown it to my accountant
- ☐ Had it proofread and edited, made corrections
- ☐ Shown it to an experienced person for critiquing
- ☐ Completed the final copy (at last)
- ☐ Made an appointment to present it to the lender

What Is the Next Step?

A business plan is a true blueprint for your business. The next important step is determining the corporate structure of your business. Many people start as proprietorships and later incorporate. Others incorporate when they didn't need to. Looking at the pros and cons of both, you can decide—with the help of your accountant—which best suits your needs.

Chapter 8

Should You Incorporate Your Business?

If you plan for success and plan to grow, incorporation may be the route to go.

- **What is a proprietorship or partnership?**
- **Is a partnership a good idea?**
- **What is an incorporated business?**
- **How do proprietorships and corporations differ?**
- **Comparing balance sheet differences**
- **Should you incorporate your business?**

What Is a Proprietorship or Partnership?

Because starting a business is an expensive proposition, most start-ups—approximately two-thirds—tend to be proprietorships or partnerships. While this route is initially cheaper, those businesses seriously planning for growth should consider the benefits of incorporation.

QUICK Tip

Keep It Simple: For a small business consisting of only the owner and where the business has limited liability and net income, a proprietorship is the simplest and cheapest way to start.

A sole proprietorship is a business owned by one person. A partnership is owned by two or more people. Anyone can set up, register a name, and become a proprietorship. You are considered self-employed, not an employee of the company, as with an incorporated business.

What are the advantages of a proprietorship?

For small businesses that do not intend to have offices outside the state or aspirations of large profit, a proprietorship can be ideal. The advantages are:

1. **Less paperwork:** Once the name registration and business license are obtained, you are a legal entity. All businesses are required to keep proper accounting records, but a proprietorship doesn't have to have a full financial statement prepared at year-end. Therefore, accounting and record keeping is relatively simple.
2. **Tax benefit to business losses:** It's not uncommon to experience losses in the first year or two, and these losses can be used to reduce income from other sources. You are personally taxed on the net profit from a proprietorship, so if a loss cannot be used in the first year, it can be carried forward to the following year and be deducted from taxable self-employed net income.
3. **Easy to wind down:** If you choose not to continue with the business, it is simple tax-wise to close the business. Seek your accountant's advice.

4. Incorporation can be a future option: When the business grows to the point that incorporating is sensible, it is not difficult. The assets of the proprietorship are rolled over into the newly incorporated company, and depending on the time of the year, you may have to file both a proprietorship and an incorporated company tax return.

What are the disadvantages of a proprietorship?

In their haste to save money at start-up, some people regret their decision later on. Take into consideration:

1. No name protection: Even once you have registered your fictious business name, there is no protection from another person registering your name as an incorporated business. Your thriving, well-known business name is vulnerable to being stolen.

2. Liability: Because you are self-employed, you are the business, and therefore responsible for all the business debts. If you suffer cash flow problems, the financial security of your home and family are at risk. If the business fails and you are left owing a great deal of money, your only option may be to declare bankruptcy, which would totally devastate the family unit. It takes years of hard work to rebuild; many families end up shattered because the business failure ultimately results in the parents' divorce. You also leave yourself wide open for a variety of liability lawsuits.

3. Less flexibility: Corporations have more flexibility in tax planning than proprietorships. Because you are taxed on the profit you make, many proprietors make the mistake of looking for "write-offs" or doing cash-under-the-table transactions, both detrimental to growth. There is more flexibility to utilizing profits in an incorporated structure.

4. More difficult to borrow money: Because traditionally proprietorships don't show much taxable profit due to both size and "write-off" practices, it is often difficult to borrow money from the bank without substantial personal guarantees. Banks prefer to do business with incorporated companies.

5. Lack of credibility: Some clients prefer to do business with a company that has "Inc." or "LLC" after its name. Proprietorships often have that "mom and pop" or fly-by-night connotation. The consumers' concept may be that an incorporated business is a "real" one.

Protect Your Profit: Once a business is consistently netting over $45,000 a year and growing, incorporation is a wise choice. There are fewer opportunities to distribute profits widely in a proprietorship.

Is it advantageous to incorporate?

The advantages to being incorporated compared to being a proprietorship are entirely dependent on your type and size of business and the corporate structure you choose. Discuss the many options with a lawyer and accountant, as some structures suit some businesses better than others. Options include a C corporation, a Limited Liability Company (LLC), a limited partnership and an S corporation, which is allowed federally but not recognized in some states. This is why you pay professionals such big bucks; they protect your interests.

CASE STUDY: What's in a Name?

Anthony became well respected and well known in the graphics industry. His proprietorship, Cutting Edge Graphic Creations, had been in business four years. He considered incorporation but had not found the time to do the paperwork.

He received a call asking if this was the Cutting Edge Graphic Inc., and he informed the prospective client of the correct name. The caller apologized, said he had the wrong company, and hung up. Anthony's curiosity was piqued. He found no business in the phone book under that name, then asked the directory operator if there was a new listing and there was—Cutting Edge Graphic Inc. There was nothing Anthony could do. He realized that by delaying incorporation, he would now be confused with another business and potentially lose clients to them.

Use a Partnership Agreement: As discussed in Chapter 5, protect both partners by having a lawyer draw up a partnership agreement. Unfortunately, few partnerships weather long-term relationships without financial and emotional stress to both parties. A written agreement can reduce these stresses should the relationship dissolve.

Is a Partnership a Good Idea?

A partnership can bring a combination of talent and experience to enhance your business—two heads are usually better than one.

How do you choose a partner?

For example, if you are impulsive and creative, seek a partner who is level-headed and practical to help keep your feet on the ground. Choose your partner as carefully as you would choose a spouse. You will spend copious time together, and just as you and your spouse no doubt agree to disagree at times, so will the partnership experience disagreements. Seek a partner who has the following:

1. **Business experience:** Your partner should have experience in areas that you don't. There's little use having two salespeople alone. Between both of you, the technical, management, and marketing roles should be filled. Clearly define job roles and responsibilities in the partnership agreement.
2. **Money:** Deals such as "you put in the money, I'll put in the time" usually don't work. Both partners should contribute equally to the business. Without the financial commitment, a partner may not be sufficiently motivated to make the business succeed, and the lack of commitment could lead to arguments over who isn't doing or paying enough. You've probably had similar arguments with your spouse.

3. Compatibility: Partners must be emotionally compatible, able to communicate honestly and openly, and express their feelings when they don't agree. Don't "marry" for money or brains alone.

What are the advantages of a partnership?

A proprietorship can be a lonely experience. It's rather like being single—it suits some people but not others. Working together with the right partner has these advantages:

1. Reduces isolation, increases contacts: Proprietors often complain about being isolated from others. With a partnership, you have someone to brainstorm with and to complain to. A partner will bring networking contacts, information, and ideas. You have someone to lean on and to share the workload with—most beneficial when errands need doing, clients need visiting, or an emergency arises.

2. Shared financial responsibility: You are not left shouldering the full responsibility of raising start-up and working capital. Partners share not only profits, but also equal financial responsibilities. The combined assets and two incomes are more desirable to banks if you are seeking financing.

3. Expertise: A proprietor has sixty different jobs to do, quite a load to carry by yourself. A partner brings experience and expertise in areas different from your own. As you work together, you will learn from each other and broaden your own skill set.

What are the disadvantages of a partnership?

Think about it—you will be working together for up to twelve hours a day, sixty hours a week, and fifty weeks of the year. It almost sounds like a life sentence. While many husband-wife partnerships are successful, bringing a stranger into your business does have its downside. The main disadvantages are:

1. Lack of long-term compatibility: In all the years spent in business accounting and consulting, I have seen few partnerships succeed. The usual reason is incompatibility—partners are often chosen for the wrong reason. Choose carefully and have the protection of an agreement in place.

2. Financial problems: Money problems always cause arguments, and constant arguing between partners invariably leads to one threatening to walk out (just like a bad marriage scene). If a satisfactory resolution can't be reached, the conflict usually terminates what could have been a successful business venture.

3. Uneven workload: It's important to equally share the workload to avoid conflict over who is doing the most work. You must work together as a team. Think about how you feel when your spouse or partner doesn't carry the load at home. A business is no different.

What Is an Incorporated Business?

An incorporated business is a separate legal entity. Directors and officers purchase shares in the business and are responsible for its operation. You can incorporate a one-person business, and many people do. The company has a president, and if more than one person is involved, a secretary, treasurer, and directors who can vote on corporate policies.

The company owns all the assets and liabilities, and in some cases is responsible for debts incurred. This is called "limited liability" because it limits the directors' personal liabilities. Incorporation allows for better tax planning and use of profits. If you think incorporation is right for your business, consult with your accountant after completing Figure 8.2 at the end of this chapter.

QUICK Tip

Be Prepared to Do Your Homework: Because there are so many factors to consider before incorporating, take time to research both your options and the ensuing ramifications. The website www.companiesinc.com offers an extensive learning center for incorporation information. The FAQ section answers questions that you may not have thought about.

What are the advantages of incorporating?

For a business planning to hire employees, incur larger trade debts, borrow money, trade nationally or internationally, and grow larger, incorporation is the best solution. Here's why:

1. Credibility: Incorporation demonstrates to lending institutions, suppliers, potential clients, and investors that you are serious about this business. Where a proprietor may have difficulty in obtaining a loan, a lending institution will look more favorably at an incorporated structure, particularly if there are multiple directors and officers involved.

2. Limited liability: Some trade debts of an incorporated company are not the directors and officer's responsibility should bankruptcy occur, unless personal guarantees have been signed. Many people incorporate for this reason. People have been known to walk away from one incorporated business and start another one the next day, sometimes repeatedly.

However, there are certain debts that directors and officers are responsible for, including any fiduciary monies, for example, state excise taxes, or activities of the business improperly authorized by its directors. Banks rarely lend money without some guaranteed security, and because people use incorporation to reduce their personal liability, more trade suppliers are asking for personal guarantees.

3. Growth and tax planning: Incorporation provides more room to plan future growth. You can add to shareholders, as the structure is already in place. As employees of an incorporated company, they can draw a regular salary, contribute to social security benefits and make tax deductions, and at year-end, they receive a W-2 statement for tax purposes. You can better manipulate profits and plan your tax situation. If the company is making profits, your accountant may consider paying out dividends, bonuses, or extra salaries to reduce profits.

4. Corporate tax benefits: Incorporation allows tax deductions and benefits for both you and your employees that are not available to an unincorporated business. These include business trip and entertainment expenses and even recreational facilities. Contributions to approved pension plans are not only tax deductible, they also earn investment income and grow tax free until retirement or until they are withdrawn. Your accountant will outline these benefits in more detail for you.

CASE STUDY: Not Taking Care of Business

Kenneth and Marie were married for many years with three children and successfully operated two retail appliance stores. They had two faithful employees who helped with each store, which made a small profit. The couple had a yen to travel the world, and decided to scale back to one store, managed by the employees.

Immersed in their travel adventure, Kenneth and Marie forgot about the store, except for drawing a healthy monthly wage. Meanwhile, back at the store, the wages being drawn by the travelers were depleting the cash flow. Tax commitments fell behind, as did trade supplier accounts. Ignoring the long-distance warnings from both their accountant and employees, they continued to travel.

Finally, the employees tired of the situation, as did the suppliers, who backed up their trucks and emptied the store of inventory. When the couple did return, there was no business left and they had to declare corporate bankruptcy. The stress caused the marriage to dissolve. Because they were responsible for the various fiduciary payments, they also had to declare personal bankruptcy, losing their property and most of their possessions.

Stay Healthy—and Save: Even a one-person incorporated business can deduct health insurance, so for a growing business, incorporating may well save you money while providing attractive taxable benefits.

5. Corporations have authority and longevity: Incorporated businesses have the authority to carry on a variety of transactions that sole proprietors often cannot and that inhibit the growth of a proprietorship or partnership. These entities continue to operate after the owners die, and grow and succeed more rapidly than unincorporated businesses.

Protect Your Name: Although your name is offered a certain protection by incorporating, if you want to protect it nationally, consider registering your name as a trademark. You may grow your business to the extent that others may want to capitalize on your name. Visit www.uspto.gov under "guides" for answers. The various fee structures are also detailed.

6. More financial investment opportunities: If you are looking for loans, investment partners, or venture capital to grow the business due to expansion, there are more options open to a business operating under an incorporated structure. Investors and lenders have more faith in capturing a healthy return on investment. A proprietorship may grow, but rarely to the extent than an incorporated business does.

What are the disadvantages of incorporating?

Once you have read the advantages and disadvantages of incorporating, think seriously about your future plans and whether you are mentally and financially ready for the challenges and opportunities that owning an incorporated business presents. For a business planning to achieve great success, it's obvious that the advantages far outweigh the disadvantages. However, an incorporated company is subject to stricter reporting procedures in both legal and accounting matters. Consider these:

1. Higher start-up costs: Incorporating a business does generate more paperwork. First, the incorporation papers have to be prepared. Once registered, your lawyer prepares share certificates and articles of incorporation. Policies and decisions should be recorded in the company minute book, and an annual general meeting held. An annual report must be filed in your state to list any changes in directors or officers.

A basic do-it-yourself incorporation can cost as little as $99 and upward. If you visit reputable websites such as www.companiesinc.com, package prices include a variety of services, with price dependent on the services you require. Each state charges a fee for incorporating, and these fees range from $80 to $260, and from $80 to $600 for a LLC.

2. Higher accounting costs, more paperwork: Maintain scrupulous accounting records and documentation because the books could be audited at any time. Because a formal financial statement must be prepared and filed with corporate tax returns, accounting costs are more expensive. Even if you prepare your own books during the year, the cost will be at least hundreds of dollars.

3. Payroll records are required: As an employee of the company, you must register with the IRS and state tax agencies to make regular payroll and benefit deductions from your salary and maintain accurate payroll records. At year-end, a W-2 statement of earnings needs to be prepared. Make timely remittances to the IRS and all tax agencies, as penalties and interest are charged on late filing. Because you are acting as a federal tax collector, the IRS's attitude is not too friendly if payments are late.

How Do Proprietorships and Incorporations Differ?

From an accounting perspective, the financial statements for proprietorships and incorporations vary, as certain transactions are recorded differently, as explained below.

1. Shareholder's loan and equity

Proprietorship: Money put into a business is called "capital." Money withdrawn reduces the proprietor's capital or equity.

Incorporation: Money put into a business is called a "shareholder's loan" and can be repaid as the company agrees. It is classified as a liability.

2. Profits, losses, and net earnings

Proprietorship: A proprietorship's profit or loss is added to or subtracted from the capital. The profit is called "net earnings" or "taxable income," and this is the sum a proprietor is personally taxed on.

Incorporation: The profit or loss is added to or subtracted from the retained earnings. A loss is referred to as a "deficit."

3. Wage structure

Proprietorship: "Wage" withdrawals by a proprietor are not considered a business expense, nor are they taxed. Withdrawals reduce the equity in the business.

Incorporation: The shareholders' salaries are a management wage and are a business expense. The company pays corporate taxes on the net profit after all wages.

4. Legal fees for incorporation

Proprietorship: Legal fees incurred in the business start-up are always considered an expense.

Incorporation: The cost of preparing the incorporation is usually shown under assets on the balance sheet and is amortized over sixty months.

5. Share issue

Proprietorship: No shares are issued.

Incorporation: A share structure is decided on by the directors and officers (with the help of their accountant and lawyer). Various share structures are available depending on the complexity of the business and its long-term goals. A certain number of shares are authorized for the business and a certain number issued to the shareholders, which are proportionate to their percentage of ownership of the business.

Shares are issued both with and without par value. There are different classes of shares, as well as voting, nonvoting, and preferred shares. Your advisor will suggest the best format for your business. Most small businesses use a simple structure, which appears on a balance sheet in the following format:

CAPITAL STOCK

Authorized:	10,000 Class A common shares with no par value
	10,000 Class B common shares with no par value
Issued:	500 Class A shares at $1 each
	500 Class B shares at $1 each

Comparing Balance Sheet Differences

Figure 8.1 demonstrates a balance sheet for Jason's Garden Service, shown as both an incorporated business and a proprietorship. Changes in format are highlighted in italics. You will notice quite a different format in the liabilities and equity section. As an incorporated company, Jason's capital investment is repayable in full as a shareholder's loan. Banks like to see that shareholders have a financial stake in their business, particularly when they are lending the company money.

With the loss of $9,960, Jason's equity in the proprietorship has been reduced from $22,053 to $10,749. The incorporated company's loss is greater, as Jason's management wage of $1,291 shows on the income statement as an expense. The incorporated company will continue to reflect the loss of $11,251 on the financial statements until future profits exceed the loss amount. This loss is not deducted from Jason's shareholders loan; it is a corporate loss.

Figure 8.1: **BALANCE SHEET COMPARISON**

JASON'S GARDEN SERVICE (INC.) BALANCE SHEET
DECEMBER 31, XXXX (Unaudited)

	Incorporated	Proprietorship
ASSETS		
Current assets:		
Cash at bank	$ 11,019	$11,019
Accounts receivable	3,551	3,551

Inventories	6,245	6,245
Prepayments & deposits	1,080	1,080
	21,895	21,895
Fixed assets:		
Automotive–trucks	85,000	85,000
Office equipment	1,550	1,550
Office furniture	850	850
	87,400	87,400
Less accumulated depreciation	(21,000)	(21,000)
	66,400	66,400
Other assets:		
Incorporation fees	***700***	0
TOTAL ASSETS:	***$88,995***	**$88,295**
LIABILITIES		
Current liabilities:		
Accounts payable	$ 5,520	$ 5,520
Sales tax payable	631	631
Withholdings payable	2,342	2,342
Current portion bank loan	9,000	9,00
	17,493	17,493
Long-term liabilities:		
Bank loan	32,000	32,000
Loan, R. Davies	28,000	28,000
Shareholder's loan	***22,653***	***0***
	82,653	**60,000**
TOTAL LIABILITIES:	***$100,146***	***$77,493***
EQUITY		
Capital stock:		
Authorized:		
10,000 Class A common voting shares with no par value		
Issued:		
100 Class A shares @ $1	***100***	0
Contributed capital for period:	0	***22,053***
Draws for period:	0	***(1,291)***
Profit/loss for period:	0	***(9,960)***
Retained earnings (deficit)	***(11,251)***	0
	(11,151)	***10,802***
TOTAL LIABILITIES & EQUITY:	**$88,995**	**$88,295**

Should You Incorporate Your Business?

Incorporating a business needs some serious consideration before you take this step. The questions in Figure 8.2 below will help you determine whether incorporation is right for your business.

What Is the Next Step?

Once you have decided on the structure of your business, the next step is to research and become familiar with the myriad of rules, regulations, red tape, laws, and legalities that are involved in operating a business. Armed with this knowledge, you can better plan your time frame and budget, and be mentally prepared to face the paperwork jungle.

Figure 8.2: **SHOULD I INCORPORATE MY BUSINESS?**

If you answer yes to more than three of these statements, consider incorporation as a suitable and safer method of structuring your new business.

	Yes	No
I have future plans to expand.	☐	☐
I will need to borrow funds for this expansion.	☐	☐
I will carry a large inventory, over $10,000.	☐	☐
I will incur accounts receivable.	☐	☐
I will incur accounts payable.	☐	☐
I will work with a partner.	☐	☐
My business is retail, wholesale, or manufacturing.	☐	☐
I need my personal finances to be well organized.	☐	☐
I will be susceptible to liability.	☐	☐
I will be hiring employees.	☐	☐
I plan to build the business and sell in a few years.	☐	☐
Sales will be over $100,000 a year.	☐	☐

Chapter 9

What Are You Required to Do by Law?

Dot your i's and cross all your t's.
Fill out all the forms in triplicate please.

- **Local government approval**
- **Name registration**
- **Incorporation and licenses**
- **Bank accounts**
- **State and local taxes**
- **Employer Identification Number, forms, and payroll**
- **Workers' compensation or state disability insurance**
- **Other licensing agencies**
- **Is business as simple as A-B-C and 1-2-3?**

Before you read this chapter, make a fresh pot of coffee to keep your brain cells alert. There is a right and a wrong way to proceed legally with your business, and a step in the wrong direction will create time delays and, possibly, major setbacks. To make things easier, here is the task sequence and some helpful hints. Additional resources are listed in the appendix.

Local Government Approval

Before you start your business, check with your local town, county, or city government office for operating regulations and zoning laws for information on environmental and other restrictions on home-based businesses. Be sure your business conforms with the many regulations, as you could be denied a business license.

Licensing and inspections

Before a license is issued, your premises may have to be inspected by some of the following departments, so know which apply before you start your business:

- Fire department
- Health department
- Local pollution control agency
- Zoning and building inspector
- Waste management
- Motor carrier or dealer licensing (if applicable)
- Trade or professional licensing

Home-based businesses

Today's home-based businesses are considered incubators for growing a thriving business. They also cater to a high percentage of people trying to juggle a job with family care. Many progressive local governments are realizing the need to review their regulations and to encourage small home businesses to succeed. Many people contravene the regulations and hide their operations from the community. This means there is less chance to market their businesses, so many don't succeed. Don't take any chances; familiarize yourself with and comply with local regulations.

QUICK Tip

Be a Leader: If your local regulations do not accommodate your home-based business, approach your local chamber of commerce to see if they can work with the local government to revise its regulations. The Greater Langley Chamber of Commerce did this through their Small Business Advancement Committee, which I chaired, and although it took two years, the regulations are so user-friendly that they are being used as a model for other municipalities and earned the chamber one of three national "Most Friendly Home-Based Business Community" awards in 2000. Home-based businesses in Langley can now hire employees, use more space, and, in certain areas, make structural changes to buildings.

Your local regulations may differ considerably from those of neighboring communities. Many local governments impose some or all of the following restrictions:

- The business should be contained to the residence, and no structural alterations or additions to the residence can be made for business purposes.
- Use of the residential space for business may be limited in size.
- There should be no evidence of the business being operated from the residence, such as exterior storage or exterior operation, and no sign identifying the business. (If you drive past the house, you shouldn't notice that a business is being operated.)
- The home-based business is restricted to office use only. No retail sales can be made from the premises, and clients may not visit the home to purchase goods.
- The business can be conducted by a resident or members of the family only. No one else can be employed by the business.
- Generating noise, electrical interference, reoccurring ground vibrations, and noxious emissions, odors, or vapors is prohibited.
- Commercial vehicle usage and residential deliveries may be restricted.
- The business may not generate special traffic beyond normal traffic volume.
- Some condominium zoning regulations and homeowner's associations forbid the operation of home-based businesses.

CASE STUDY: Selling Himself Short

Danny opened a small store on his property, selling hay, feed, and retail agricultural products. He didn't apply for a business license, thinking that selling agricultural products in an agricultural area wouldn't cause any problems. Someone reported him to the county—perhaps an envious rival or neighbor. Despite his best efforts to save the business, Danny did not succeed. He was selling retail products from his home that were not produced on the farm and had contravened the local home business regulations. Although he had invested a great deal of money, he was forced to close down.

Name Registration

Once you are sure your business conforms with local government regulations, next register your business name. If you are a sole proprietor, name registration is not necessary in all states but is a good idea. If you are incorporated, a limited liability company, a partnership, or limited partnership, name registration is usually automatic when you file the appropriate legal paperwork with your secretary of state.

1. What is a fictitious name?

If a sole proprietor wants to operate under a name other than their given name, they must register a fictitious name, sometimes with the state, but usually with the local county or city office. A fictitious name allows government agencies and customers to know who owns the business in case there are legal issues. It also prevents confusion between other businesses, as no two businesses can have the same fictitious name. If you do not hold an approved license, you cannot register a name that insinuates that you are a licensed operator.

2. How do you register your business name?

Most local government or secretary of state offices have online searchable databases where you can perform a search to ensure that the name you want is not chosen. Because each state differs in its requirements, first check with your county clerk. Once a name is secured, you can complete the necessary paperwork. Most states require that partnerships and sole proprietors file a fictitious owner affidavit with the county office.

QUICK Tip

Utilize Online Services: All states offer a variety of online services, ranging from name searches and reservations to registering all your business' government and legal requirements. Visit www.irs.gov/businesses under "Starting a Business" for links to all secretary of state offices.

Incorporation and Licenses

After addressing these issues, you may then proceed with incorporation, as explained in Chapter 8. Until your name is approved, don't order stationery. Incorporation approval can take from ten days to six weeks, depending on where you live. You need these papers for license approval and usually to open bank accounts. Once incorporated, the IRS can issue your Employer Identification Number, usually online or by fax.

Business Licenses

When your company name has been approved and the business is incorporated, you can apply for the appropriate business licenses and permits at your local city or county office, which are usually issued without delay. As other licenses may be required for your type of business, also check with the secretary of state and your Department of Revenue or equivalent agency.

Bank Accounts

Opening your business accounts may take a few days. Allow up to two weeks if you need Visa or MasterCard facilities. Pay for as many expenses as possible by check; it makes for easier bookkeeping because cash receipts can get lost and credit cards make for complex accounting. A check is a written record of each transaction and will suffice in an audit as proof of payment.

Order a two- or three-ring check binder and make sure the check stubs are large enough to record daily deposits, expense details, and computer codes. Use your personal checking account as little as possible—expenses can be forgotten and it appears unprofessional.

State and Local Taxes

Most states require that a sales tax be collected on goods purchased or imported for use or consumption. The tax is usually collected by the retail outlet or by the final vendor. Additional taxes are levied against hotel rooms, tobacco, and motor fuels. Local government taxes may also apply. Wholesale sales to other retailers or distributors are normally exempt from sales tax, as are out-of-state sales.

Federal excise taxes apply to the manufacture and sales of certain products and on certain types of businesses. A retail excise tax is imposed on some trucks, trailers tractors, and other vehicles used on public highways. There are environmental, communication, fuel, and air transportation taxes to be considered. For a full explanation, read IRS Publication 510. Taxes are due quarterly and are filed on a Form 720, 2290, or 730.

Employer Identification Number, Forms, and Payroll

If you are incorporated, a partnership, or a sole proprietor with employees, you need to register for a Federal Employer Identification Number (EIN) to pay a variety of taxes and payroll withholdings. This number identifies all your federal tax accounts, including income tax, estimated tax payments, excise taxes and employment taxes. For more information, contact the IRS or visit their website at www.irs.gov/businesses, register online, and order their Publication 583, "Starting a Business and Keeping Records."

What is the self-employment tax?

Sole proprietors and unincorporated partnerships who earn more than $400 net of expenses a year must pay self-employment tax, which provides coverage for Medicare, Social Security, and retirement, and survivor and some disability benefits. This is reported on Schedule 1040 and Schedule SE. The IRS Publication 533, "Self-Employment Tax," explains how to remit these taxes, along with your estimated federal income tax using Form 1040-ES vouchers.

What are your responsibilities as an employer?

Once you hire employees, the paperwork war and form-filling-out nightmare begins. There are many IRS guides available for download or through their service centers. If you are not sure whether to hire a person as a self-employed contractor, download Publication 15-A, "Employer's Supplemental Tax Guide."

There are various forms for you and your employees to complete when you hire them. It is your responsibility to deduct the correct amount of Social Security, Medicare, state workers, disability, and income tax withholdings, and to maintain proper payroll records. These must all be paid on time, as large penalties are imposed on overdue amounts.

What forms must be filled out?

On hiring an employee, you need to complete the following forms. If you hire young people under age eighteen, other restrictions and state paperwork may apply.

- **Form I-9, Employment Eligibility Verification:** Your employees must be able to legally work in the United States, so both employer and employee complete this form, available from the U.S. Citizen and Immigration Services (USCIS). Keep it in your files.
- **Form W-4, Employee's Withholding Allowance Certificate:** The employee completes this form so that the employer knows the correct amount of income tax to deduct from their wages. The IRS may require a copy under certain circumstances, so keep it on file.
- **Form W-5, Earned Income Credit Advance Payment Certificate:** Employees who qualify for an advance on earned income for qualifying children must complete this form. The employer must then advance the EIC payments to the employee.
- **Payroll records:** Each employee needs an individual payroll record with full name, address, social security number, starting date, and wages. Each payroll period, you record the daily hours worked, wages, and all deductions. Figure 9.1 on page 197 demonstrates an example of semi-monthly deductions.

Hiring school-age employees (under age eighteen) will often require additional state paperwork for releases from both the school and parents. Also, hazardous jobs are normally denied to underage employees.

Bank It: Some business owners have trouble paying sales taxes and various employees' withholdings. Pay federal (and in some states) wage deductions and employer contributions through the electronic deposit system. As some are paid quarterly or annually, it's easy to use up the money, so bank the various monies into a separate savings account so that you have it when you need it.

The forms don't stop there. There are some information returns used to compare payments you receive or make to certain companies or individuals with the amounts reported on their income tax return (of course, the two should agree). Four forms that fall into these parameters are:

- **Form W-2, Wage and Tax Statement:** This form, prepared annually for employees, is used to report all income, tips, allowances, bonuses, and all withholdings and deductions made to employees during the year.
- **Form 940, Annual Federal Unemployment Tax (FUTA):** This tax is on the first $7,000 of wages paid to each employee during the year. The percentage varies, either 6.2 or .08 percent, depending on whether the state has a qualifying unemployment program or if all state unemployment taxes were paid on time. It also applies to state unemployment exempted corporate officers/shareholders.
- **Form 1099-MISC, Miscellaneous Income:** Fill in this form if you paid an unincorporated subcontractor, lawyer, or independent businessperson such as your accountant; paid rent to someone other than your realtor; or gave a prize or award of $600 or more. There are other parameters for reporting miscellaneous income, so thoroughly read the instructions.
- **Form 8300, Report of Cash Payments Over $10,000 Received in a Trade or Business:** If you receive a business cash payment of more than $10,000 in total during a twelve-month period from one customer, you complete

this form within fifteen days of the payments exceeding $10,000. Publication 1544, "Reporting Cash Payments of Over $10,000 (Received in a Trade or Business)," will clarify this.

- **Form TD F 90-22.1, Report of Foreign Bank and Financial Accounts:** The IRS needs to know everything about your financial affairs. Much like the Form 8300, there is a fine of up to $10,000 if you do not report your foreign bank accounts by June 30.

Forms, Forms, Forms: You can see why your business needs an employee—so you can get on with the job while you pay them to fill in all these forms. There are more you must complete and file, so for a full list and links to them, plus a calendar of filing dates, visit www.irs.gov/businesses/small. If you feel overwhelmed with all this paperwork, get help! A bookkeeper working a few hours a month will do a lot to help ease your stress.

Figure 9.1: SAMPLE SEMIMONTHLY PAYROLL DEDUCTIONS

Gross semimonthly wage: $800.00

Federal:	Employee Medicare and Social Security (7.65 %)	61.20	
	Employer Medicare and Social Security (7.65 %)	61.20	
	Income tax withholding (single)	69.38	$191.78
State:	Income tax withholding (8 %)	12.62	
	Employee disability insurance (1.18 %)	9.44	
	Employer disability insurance (2.5 % estimated)	20.00	
	Employer unemployment (2.00 % estimated)	16.00	58.06
	Total remittance:		**$249.84**

How much does an employee really cost?

Hiring an employee is a big decision and a big expense; in fact, most employers agree that finding the right person is a headache. Be aware of all the costs involved when preparing projections. The hourly rate is just one part of the expense. Figure 9.2 gives an example of the cost of an employee earning $15 an hour over one month. Add benefits, parking, uniforms, sick time and downtime, and an employee becomes a costly expense.

Figure 9.2: THE REAL COST OF HIRING

40 hours a week x 4.33 weeks per month:	173.20 hours
173.2 hours x $15	$2,598.00
4 percent vacation pay	103.92
Federal employer deductions	198.74
State employer deductions	116.91
One statutory vacation	120.00
Workers' comp. (average rate of $3.50/$100)	90.94
Total monthly employee cost:	**$3,228.51**

The $15 an hour increases to $18.64 an hour, an additional $630.51per month, or 24.26 percent of $2,598.00. (The rates in these two examples are based on averages, as rates vary from state to state.)

What happens at year-end?

After the final pay period for the calendar year, each employee's payroll record is reconciled to your accounting records for the year and a W-2 Wage and Tax Statement is issued to each employee by January 31. A W-3 statement is then completed, which reports to the Social Security Administration all employee earnings and deductions for that year. This must be completed by February 28. Sometime later, the IRS will match the tax return reporting to these numbers. If you have not remitted your payments on time or did not pay enough, penalties are imposed, so take that as a reminder to not be lax with your paperwork.

How do I terminate an employee?

Before you terminate an employee, talk to a lawyer about any future consequences. Employees often file law suits against their employer after termination for a variety of reasons, including discrimination, defamation, wrongful dismissal, breach of employment contract, and unfair practices, to name a few. Become familiar with the state and federal labor laws and codes. Each state has a regulation on the payment due date of the last paycheck.

Get It in Writing: Wrongful dismissal cases and employee disputes with employers are common, so maintain a detailed file on each employee. Record details of conversations relating to job status, and if there are concerns with an employee, put them in writing to the employee so that you have a detailed paper trail should a legal problem arise.

Workers' Compensation or State Disability Insurance

All businesses hiring employees or subcontractors who are not independently covered by workers' compensation must register for workers' compensation insurance. If an injured employee has been found misclassified as an independent contractor, the employer has to pay all medical costs plus a myriad of penalties.

The cost and method of calculation varies from state to state and especially according to occupation. Coverage is based on either a percentage of wages paid or hours worked. In most states, private insurance companies provide coverage under the direction of a State Workers' Compensation statute. Compensation covers hospital, medical, retraining and wage replacement costs, and if an employee dies, can also cover survivor benefits.

In many states, sole proprietors, partners, and members of a limited liability company without employees are not required to take out coverage and are not covered by workers' compensation, but you can usually arrange for voluntary coverage. Where possible, insure yourself against work-related accidents or illness, because remember: You are your business. Coverage is mandatory if you employ one or more part- or full-time employees.

Cover All Angles: If you hire contractors, be sure they carry their own coverage and are registered with the state. If they have employees, be sure they carry an Employer Identification Number with the IRS, or that they have filed a self-employment tax return the previous year for similar work. Otherwise, it is your responsibility and in your best interests to provide coverage. The last thing a small business owner needs is to be sued for expensive medical claims.

Other Licensing Agencies

Depending on your type of business, you may also have to register with one of the following agencies:

- Department of Environmental Quality
- Department of Agriculture
- Department of Education
- Department of Transportation
- Department of Health

Other areas where you may need to contact a licensing agency include dealing with:

- Weights and measures
- Packaging and labeling
- Hazardous products
- Precious metals
- Textiles
- Foods
- Patents, copyright, industrial designs, and trademarks

Figure 9.3: **LEGAL REQUIREMENTS CHECKLIST**

To ensure that you do not miss an important step, follow this checklist to keep you on track. Check off and complete the issues that apply to you through the start-up stage.

	Apply	Done
My business can be legally operated within my community.	☐	☐
I am aware of all local government licensing requirements.	☐	☐
I have made appointments with these licensing agencies.	☐	☐
My home-based business conforms to local government regulations.	☐	☐
I have chosen a fictitious name and completed a name search for name registration.	☐	☐
I have registered my business or fictitious name.	☐	☐
I have consulted a professional for incorporation advice.	☐	☐
The incorporation papers are complete.	☐	☐
I have applied for a business license.	☐	☐
I have opened a business checking account.	☐	☐
I have applied for credit card facilities for customers.	☐	☐
I have opened a savings account for taxes and deductions.	☐	☐
I have registered with the state for collection of sales tax.	☐	☐
I have registered with the county/city for local taxes.	☐	☐
I have applied for an Employer Identification Number.	☐	☐
I have a Form 1030-ES for paying self-employment taxes.	☐	☐
I will be hiring employees or subcontractors.	☐	☐
I have purchased a payroll book or software.	☐	☐
I have included all costs of hiring in my projections.	☐	☐
I will have employees and need workers' compensation.	☐	☐
I have applied for workers' compensation insurance.	☐	☐
I will need licensing through other federal/state agencies.	☐	☐
I have applied for all applicable licenses.	☐	☐

Is Business as Simple as A-B-C and 1-2-3?

After all this mind-boggling information, it's time to have a little fun in the wonderful world of business, which should be a simple matter of earning a living—right? You sell a product or service, collect the money, and make a whopping profit—right?

Wrong. Don't think it will be that easy. Big Brother is working hard to create as many headaches and stumbling blocks as possible to test your entrepreneurial determination, strength, and patience.

Take, for example, that dense forest of numbers and acronyms to navigate. When you sell a product, you must collect the SST and remit it to the MRS, SCDR, IDR, or SDR, depending on your state. You must have an EIN for the IRS (Form SS-4), while employees need a SSN from the SSA (Form SS-5). When you pay your employees, you must either pay or deduct SID, SUT, SS, Medicare, and FIT, and probably SIT, some of which may be remitted electronically using the EFTPS. At year-end, you will pay or report FUTA, then prepare W-2s for employees and 1099s for independent contractors, so they can complete their 1040 or 1040EZ returns, including their EIC schedule and Forms 1 through to 9999.

The self-employed must pay SET, and all businesses must comply with the WCA and register for WCI. If you hire employees, fill out an I-9, W-4, and W-5. If incorporated, your accountant will prepare your year-end and fill out an 1120 or 1120-S return, with relevant schedules A through to Z. A partnership fills out a 1065. A LLC may fill out either a 1065, 1120, or 1120-S. return. If you are a sole proprietorship and home-based, you just need a simple Schedule C1040, Schedule SE, an 8829, and of course, a 4562 for depreciation. However, if you depreciate your home for the business, use the MACRS Percentage Table or Table A-7A in Appendix A of Publication 946.

The only way to keep track of all this paperwork efficiently is to purchase a PC, of which the depreciation is deductible on a 4562. The choice is whether to purchase a 400mhz Pentium 4 with a 1.8ghz, 80GB 7200 RPM IDE UDMA hard drive and an ASUS P4B -266 C-WOA motherboard, 512MB of RAM plus CD-ROM and burner, firewall, scanner and color printer, including a twenty-inch LCD monitor, or a 40GB Pentium 4 with 256MB of RAM, a laser printer, and ergonomic mouse—or should you purchase the whole zoo?

Should you buy IBM or Mac? Which programs will you need? Perhaps Windows NT? XP Pro OEM? Office Suite—or furnish the whole house? Don't forget your Zip drive backup, and 750MB disks, CD-ROM backup, or your floppy MF 2HD disks. And as this is written, the above will no doubt be obsolete information anyway.

When you've made all that lovely money, you should invest it wisely. The choices are many—MBFs, TBFs, mutual funds, IRAs, SEP-IRAs, 401Ks, Rollovers, RIAs, or CDs (not the music variety). Make sure your investments are FDIC insured. The decision seems simple in itself so don't waste too much time thinking about it. Right?

Now just think of your poor accountant when you bring in your year's paperwork. Before your GL, TB, and statements are prepared, he or she will probably take a few ASAs or a large nip of SC before tackling your piles of CRAP (Collections of Rubbishy Accounting Paperwork).

We live complex lives in a complex world, and even if you don't have a natural head for numbers or technical wizardry, you need to take time to learn the basics if you want to do better than just stay afloat.

What Is the Next Step?

You have a great idea, you did complete research, you started your business plan, and you know your approximate start-up costs. Things are looking good. But no business can succeed unless you understand how to market and plan a smart marketing campaign. It's the weak point for many businesses, so this next chapter will guide you through the basic steps of planning and implementing a winning marketing strategy.

Chapter 10

How Do You Market Your Business?

The idea is great, the plan is too.
Now how to tell the world about you?

- **What is a marketing plan?**
- **What are the four Ps of marketing?**
- **What is branding?**
- **Put your plan together**
- **How do you promote a business?**
- **Which advertising media should you use?**
- **How do you plan a marketing budget?**

What Is a Marketing Plan?

No matter how wonderful your concept, without a sound and aggressive marketing strategy, you will be lucky to get past first base. Ineffective marketing is common among the newly self-employed, as marketing takes a combination of skills that do not come readily to most people.

Marketing terminology

Some entrepreneurs make the mistake of thinking that marketing is just a matter of printing a few business cards; it's far more complex than that. Others confuse marketing with advertising or selling, so let's first define these terms:

- **Marketing:** To attract potential customers, you must inform them about your business and establish and maintain a customer base. Your target market is a defined group of people who may use your business.
- **Promotion:** To market a business, you must communicate your messages to the public. This is promotion. You tell or show people about your business by joining business associations and networking groups or participating in trade shows.
- **Advertising:** Advertising consists of an aired, rehearsed script on radio, television, or the Internet, and printed descriptive text and/or pictures that convey your message in publications, mail, or faxes.
- **Sales:** Marketing brings potential customers through the doors but does not close a sale. Selling is the process of convincing customers that you can best fulfill their needs. A complete transaction involves the exchange of money in return for a service or a product.

The components of a marketing plan

Marketing is not placing an advertisement in the paper and waiting for the telephone to ring—you will have a long wait. A successful marketing strategy is an intrinsic combination of carefully planned components. The more you know about your industry, the better you can market your business. A well-researched marketing plan details your strategies, timing, costs, and expected results.

QUICK Tip

Be Constantly Creative: Your various techniques should always be changing, dependent on their success rates, the time of year, and the economy. Be creative and make your marketing ideas stand out from the crowd. It takes time to learn what works for your business, and just as you think you have the answer, you may have to find new methods because the old ones stop working effectively. Never stop thinking of creative ways to market your business.

A marketing plan is a map of your ideas and timelines. As discussed in this chapter, your plan should detail your plans for:

- Clearly defining the product or service you are selling
- Knowing your target market and developing an "ideal customer" profile
- Knowing your competitive edge—your Unique Selling Proposition (USP)
- Setting pricing structures
- Knowing where your product is positioned in customers' minds
- Deciding how to distribute your product/service
- Branding your business and developing a corporate image
- Planning promotional strategies
- Preparing a marketing budget

What Are the Four Ps of Marketing?

Chapter 4 explains how to research the market to ensure that there is a place for your business and that it can withstand trends, time, and the competition. By performing the SWOT analysis and doing a consumer market survey, you should feel confident that there is a market for your business. Now to tell people about how great you are. Because there are many factors involved in marketing, let's break it down into "the Four Ps of Marketing."

1. Product
2. Price
3. Place
4. Promotion

1. Product: What are you selling?

Now is the time to refine your product definition so you have a clear picture of what you are selling to whom. There are many types of accountants or lawyers, but most specialize in one area, such as corporate taxes or immigration law. New entrepreneurs often make the mistake of trying to cater to everyone and do not specialize in one area.

To become known as the expert in your field—your ultimate goal—you must narrow down your product specifications. What is your product's position in relationship to the rest of the market? For a service business, you are the product, so you may need to further focus on your marketable expertise.

Who is your market and where are they? Who will use your product? This is your target market and includes the people or businesses you will market to. Most small businesses rely on their community for sales, so learn everything you can about the people who will use your business. You can then develop an ideal customer profile.

A woman selling midpriced makeup may initially think her market is every woman. Yet upon narrowing down her market, she discovers that some women don't use makeup. Others prefer a particular brand, while some use either cheap or expensive makeup. Some have skin allergies and have to use medicated or hypoallergenic products.

Don't waste money marketing to people who don't want or need your business. Define your potential consumers through research and by completing the questions in Figure 10.1. Depending on your type of business, you may have to modify the questions.

Target your ideal customers You can now build a profile of your ideal customer. The most successful businesses know exactly who their product or service appeals to. Once you know who you are targeting, you then research the best marketing methods to reach them.

If your ideal customer reads gardening magazines, then advertise there. If they live mainly in apartments, don't advertise in rural areas. Match your geographic marketing to your ideal customers' lifestyles, and promote through the media they are most likely to read, hear, or watch. As discussed, you will need to use a strategic mixture of media to reach your target market.

Figure 10.1: WHO IS YOUR TARGET MARKET? (RETAIL EXAMPLE)

Find out...	**Answer**
1. Are most of them male or female?	________
2. Are they an even mix of male and female?	________
3. What is their average income bracket?	________
4. Where do these consumers generally congregate?	________
5. Do they live in apartments, houses, or rural areas?	________
6. Which radio stations would they most likely listen to?	________
7. Which magazines are they most likely to read?	________
8. Where would they most likely shop?	________
9. What is their average age?	________
10. What type of work do they do?	________
11. What is the average family size?	________
12. What are their interests?	________
13. Do you know your business' geographic boundaries?	________
14. Are you targeting retail, residential, or commercial markets?	________

Watch the market in action Study consumers' purchasing habits. Visit busy malls, strip malls, out-of-the way locations, megastores, and businesses similar to yours. Note when they are busy or quiet. Watch which products people buy that are similar to yours and what they are willing to pay. Note which weekdays are busy and which seasonal times of the year affect your industry either positively or negatively. Attend industry trade shows, noting which booths attract the most people.

Develop your "Unique Selling Proposition" An important part of marketing is knowing your position in relationship to other similar businesses. Many businesses offer the same services or products, so you must know what your competition offers and then decide how you can better position your business to attract customers. Analyze what you are selling. Will what you offer appeal to this market? What sets you apart from your competitors? It may be superior after-sales service, online ordering and delivery, or in-home, after-hours consulting. This is called your Unique Selling Proposition (USP). Once your USP is clearly defined, you use it as the basis for your marketing strategies.

On asking a group of seasoned business owners what their USP was, few could clearly define theirs. Most said "service." Ask yourself: What is *so special* about my service that sets me apart? This is your USP.

CASE STUDY: Underselling Her USP

Marjory's Beauty Salon had operated for two years, offering hairstyling, manicures, makeovers, tanning, and waxing. Although it was busy, the salon needed a more stable customer base. One Saturday, a relatively new customer was reading Marjory's brochure and saw in small print that the salon offered an in-home service and 24/7 appointments.

"You should have this splashed across the window and in large print everywhere to attract us busy professionals," commented the customer. "No one else in town offers this service." Marjory had a Unique Selling Proposition and didn't even realize it. She took her customer's advice, focused her marketing strategy around promoting these services, and in a short few months, her business dramatically increased.

2. Price: How do you establish competitive pricing?

Establish a pricing policy in line with your industry that is competitive but not the cheapest in town—unless you are a discount store. There must be enough room to generate profits. If your research shows that you cannot compete or offer comparable quality, this business may not be a viable proposition. When your USP is well marketed, the perceived added value may allow you to marginally increase your prices over—or at least match—those of your competitors.

If prices are too low, consumers may think the quality is inferior. What are the deciding factors when you are price shopping? Do you choose the cheapest, midrange, or the most expensive? Knowing your ideal customer's profile and income level is important for product and price development. It's no use trying to sell expensive items to low-income earners or in an economically depressed region.

A bookkeeping service charging $15 an hour could be perceived by potential clients as "cheap—but what am I getting for that price?" Accounting clients expect to pay a certain amount for expertise. If the bookkeeping service is home-based, $20 to $25 an hour should be the minimum charge for quality work. However, if the service is located in an economically poor rural area, rates may have to be dropped accordingly, as competition is fierce when people are in survival mode. A bookkeeping service in a storefront setting has more overhead to absorb, so $35 an hour and up is acceptable as long as excellent service and expertise come with the package.

CASE STUDY: Not Snapping up the Snaps

A photographic studio chain tried pricing a glamor makeover—including makeup, hairstyling, and one 8x10-inch color print—for $25. The package was exceptionally hard to sell, even with extensive advertising. On expert advice, when the price was increased to $55, literally thousands of people booked appointments. At $25, the consumers' perception was that they wouldn't get good quality. At $55, the price was still cheap, but consumers were paying enough to put a perceived value on the quality of the package.

Compare prices Because the economy, competitors, and consumers are always changing, be sure to track price changes within your industry. It's not unusual to see price checkers strolling the supermarket aisles, because their sales are all about price—rarely service. Keep a close eye on your competitors and don't become complacent about your pricing. Closely monitor your customers. Do they buy only the advertised specials, or do they consistently purchase other products? A low-profit sale won't contribute much to the coffers. Your pricing should be reasonable and affordable to your target market.

3. Place: How will you distribute to your customers?

Setting distribution policies is key in marketing. You must understand where your business is placed or positioned in the market and how you can achieve a competitive edge. The way you provide your product or service to customers can give you that edge. Your ideal customer profile research should indicate how your product or service is purchased. Marjory's Beauty Salon provided a unique, in-home service to clients yet initially didn't promote this service in her marketing strategies.

If you are a service-oriented business, value-added customer service will set you apart from the competition. For example, will you offer:

- Normal trading hours only?
- After-hours appointments or servicing?
- In-home consulting?
- Same-day or emergency service?

Product-based businesses should know how they will get their goods to customers and ensure that this method is right for that clientele. Remembering that technology plays a large part in the way we now do business, your distribution methods need to be fast, efficient, cost-effective, and technologically terrific. Manufacturing and distribution businesses may need warehousing facilities. Can customers buy direct from the warehouse? Will you deliver or use the Internet for ordering? When you establish your positioning in the market, be clear about what you are offering and promote your features and benefits.

4. Promotion: How will you promote your business?

Telling the world about your business is complex. There are so many ways to promote, so this subject will be covered in more depth later in this chapter. First, we'll define the three elements that give your business its distinct identity—branding, customer service, and customer loyalty.

Out-Service the Competition: While my husband and I were shopping for a vehicle recently, one Ford dealership salesperson paid strict attention to our needs. Because my husband worked graveyard shifts, vehicle shopping was difficult. The salesperson offered to find only vehicles that perfectly suited our needs and deliver them to our door for a test drive. Can you beat that for service? What a wonderful USP. Yes, we'll tell the world about it. Be creative and cater to the busy consumer. Your efforts will generate repeat business and referrals.

What Is Branding?

1. Developing your corporate image, or "branding"

Every facet of your operation needs to be branded with your distinct identity to let people know who you are and what you do. A combination of your name, logo, slogan, mission statement, and corporate theme should be used extensively throughout your marketing. We all recognize large corporations' branding—such as Kodak or Sears—but even a small, one-person business can brand themselves and become well known. Consult with a graphic designer to help you project a professional image, as first impressions *are* important and open doors for you. Let's briefly look at the components of branding:

- **Name:** Make your name work for you and tell people what you do. ABC Enterprises says nothing about you, whereas Professional Personnel Services does. It also projects a professional image.

- **Logo:** A logo graphically expresses who you are. Although not necessary for a small business, it adds a professional touch and helps people identify your business. We all recognize those golden arches.

- **Slogan:** A short slogan becomes an extension of your name, further describing what you do. Think of the many slogans you instantly associate with larger companies. Living in a rural area, I never forget our local septic tank company's slogan, "Your Business Is Our Business."

- **Mission statement:** A short statement of your beliefs and goals describes your commitment to customers and commits you in writing to strive for those goals. Customers like to see mission statements because they silently imply "we care about you." Splash your commitment onto all promotional materials, business cards, and your website, then frame the words on the office wall.

- **Corporate color theme:** Choose a corporate color theme that remains consistent and is used on all correspondence, marketing materials, and signs. This cements your branding. Look around your community, in newspapers, and at advertisements to study various branding techniques.

It takes time to develop your branding. For example, it took me many years to hone my SmallBizPro branding. See Figure 10.2 on the next page for the final results, which have been quite successful.

2. Providing exceptional customer service

Customers can be demanding and impatient in our busy society. Some expect something for nothing and still complain, but mostly, people are easy to get along with if you take good care of them. For a small business, service is the one area where you *have* to excel to set yourself apart.

Clients expect both service and competitive prices. We all know how fast negative comments spread on the grapevine, so an unhappy client will spread negativity ten times faster than a positive referral. Your task is to perfect every aspect of your service, so review these important service components:

- **Guarantees:** Know what kind of guarantees you will offer and promote these in your marketing. Familiarize yourself with clients' needs and expectations, and if you can't meet them, tell customers before a sale rather than performing inadequately or selling them the wrong product.

Figure 10.2: THE COMPONENTS OF SUCCESSFUL BRANDING

Name:
SmallBizPro.com Services

Slogan:
"Helping people and businesses realize and achieve their maximum potential."

Logo:
Signifies learning through the written and spoken word, represented by pages and sound waves.

Web site:
www.smallbizpro.com

Mission statement:
"To promote the message of how to succeed in both business and personal life through my consulting, speaking, training, and writing. To help prevent business failure and to help people realize their dreams and maximum potential."

Corporate colors and theme:
Burgundy on parchment background, thin burgundy border on stationery, thicker border on promotional materials.

- **Personal service:** Remember, customers are always right, even when they are wrong, so don't argue with them. Treat them as you expect to be treated. Remember names, faces, and family details. This shows that you are attentive and care.

- **Telephone manners:** A sale can be lost or gained by that first call, so your communication skills must work overtime. Be polite, interested, friendly, and positive, and be available by phone. If your advertisements are on the radio at 7 p.m. every evening or the talk show you just appeared on is at 8 p.m., make sure your phone is answered at these times.

Thank Your Employees: Your employees are always marketing your business, and that is free advertising. Thank them at the end of the day and show them you appreciate their efforts. If you have to discipline an employee, do it privately without demeaning him or her in front of others. Everyone will respect you more and will usually work even harder to promote your business. Have an open door policy so that employees feel comfortable discussing their problems with you.

- **Employees:** Your receptionist or traffic controller—which may initially be you—is the direct link between you and your customers. Customers will either come to you or be diverted to the competition, dependent on how they are initially treated. Your employees must believe in you and your business and be willing to happily service customers. Train them well and treat them fairly—they are an important component of your business.

CASE STUDY: Cutting Down Business

A neighbor was having some trees cut down and removed. Another neighbor drove by and asked the worker if he would quote on trimming some overhanging branches. "You'll have to phone Bill, the boss," yelled the worker, without turning off the chipper. "The phone number's on the side of the truck." Had the employee stopped, turned off the machine, and handed the neighbor a business card, it would have generated a sale. As it was, the neighbor had no pen and drove off feeling slighted, later using another company.

Appearance is everything; it's the difference between whether people choose to use you or not. I called a trash removalist for a quote on cleaning up some unloved backyard items. What arrived at my gate was alarming; a large, unshaven man in greasy, ripped coveralls with long, unwashed hair and no smile. I wouldn't open the gate, informing him that I had already disposed of the goods. He was too scary for me.

- **Physical appearance:** Your employees, premises or office, vehicles, and *you* should always be clean and presentable.

- **Follow-up:** Contact customers after a sale to ask whether they are satisfied or if there were any problems. Honor time and price commitments, even if you have made a mistake. If promised delivery dates cannot be met, call your customer immediately, apologize, and reschedule.

3. Creating customer loyalty

Building a successful business means that you need repeat business. Unfortunately, for some, their loyalty lies with their bank accounts. You can't blame people for watching their shrinking dollars, so how are you going to keep customers? Use simple strategies, including excellent service. Offer incentives, such as additional discounts for regular business, a company coffee mug, or chocolates at Christmas. Thank them for coming in and have a coffee pot and cookies available.

Show That You Care: Be good to your customers and they will refer you. When this happens, send a thank-you card. If you meet on the street or at a dinner party, warmly acknowledge them. Even if you charge a little more than competitors, they'll become loyal to you. The fact that you took time out from your busy day to say thank-you or to chat is not forgotten. It's the small touches that make big impressions.

Think of simple ways to entice customers back. Our local bakery gives cookies to children. The deli gives a dozen buns free with orders over $9. The local independent supermarket always has free coffee available, along with drawing and suggestion boxes. Cashiers willingly pack and wheel your groceries to the car. Senior citizens get a 10 percent discount on Sundays and a free weekly grocery delivery service. These small stores have successfully sustained a strong customer base for twenty years.

Put Your Plan Together

To review progress in your marketing strategies, take a few minutes to answer the questions in Figure 10.3. Before you think about any form of marketing, you need to develop clear answers to the following six questions, as your marketing strategies will incorporate many of these answers. Use pencil because you may change some answers before your plan is finished.

Figure 10.3: COMPONENTS OF YOUR MARKETING PLAN

1. Clearly define the products or service that your business will focus on.

____

____

2. Describe your "ideal customer profile."

____

____

3. What is your Unique Selling Proposition?

____

____

4. How would you describe your pricing in relationship to your competitors?

____

____

5. How will you distribute your product/service to customers?

____

____

6. How would your customers perceive your business in relationship to others like yours?

____

____

7. What do you feel will be the most effective forms of promotion for your business?

____

____

8. Have you developed a slogan? If so, what is it?

____

____

9. What is your proposed mission statement or the message that it should carry?

____

____

10. What will you do to maintain and increase customer loyalty and repeat business?

____

____

How Do You Promote a Business?

Everything we have discussed under the four Ps is a form of marketing, but which strategies will work for you? There are many effective methods that don't involve a lot of money, but may require time.

Develop strong communication skills

Developing excellent written and verbal communication skills and applying these skills to your marketing will bring you long-term and repeat business. Successful businesses use a combination of techniques, and without a doubt, networking—combined with consistent community or market exposure—is the best type of promotion. To start, let's look at techniques that involve communication skills.

1. Networking—a powerful tool Networking is meeting people and telling them who you are and what you do. It is referring people with a need to reliable people or businesses. A true networker unselfishly helps others while actively promoting and meeting potential clients. They always look for ways to help others as well as themselves, because if you network purely for selfish reasons, it shows, and the results are far less effective.

Your networking success will be enhanced if you enjoy people and have enough confidence to express yourself. Start by developing a strong twenty-second infomercial about your business and yourself. When you meet a stranger, the first question is usually "What do you do?" Your mission is to have an informative answer ready. Start your introduction with "I am," not "My name is...," as in the following example:

> "Hi Peter, I am David Johnson, and my business is *Community Living Magazine,* which is now two years old and enjoyed and respected by the community. Our circulation has grown from an initial 10,000 to 35,000. We focus on community issues, biographies, places, and features of local interest. We have just started full-color advertising at extremely competitive rates."

David then presents his business card. In twenty seconds, he has introduced himself and his business, and explained his magazine, its community acceptance, and resulting growth in detail. The listener hasn't had time to get bored, yet in a short time knows much about David's business.

Part of networking is to first build a rapport and then a relationship. Give the other person a chance to tell you about themselves; show an interest in what they do. Ask for their business card "in case I know of someone needing your business." You are now a perfect audience and have made the first step toward building a relationship. If you're interested, call the next day, say how much you enjoyed meeting—how about coffee?

Network everywhere to build these important relationships—at meetings, trade shows, and in line at the bank. The opportunities are endless, although some tact and diplomacy should be practiced. You can't be all about business, but you can be looking to help others, at the same time letting people know who you are and what you do.

Join one or two specific networking organizations, such as women's networks (if you are a woman of course) or leads referral groups. Ask your chamber of commerce for details; they are aware of well-established groups in your area. As relationships build, network members turn to each other when they require help.

2. Join the chamber of commerce As a chamber of commerce member, you have the opportunity to use many benefits and discounts. Unfortunately, some people join and do nothing, so nothing happens. Attend dinners, seminars, and special events, such as business-after-business networking.

Offer your services to a committee, as chambers are mostly operated by volunteers. If you give time to your community, they in turn give back to you. You become known and referred, will expand your knowledge, meet businesspeople, and feel satisfied with your community contribution. Join Rotary or similar groups for the same rewards.

Before you commit your time, though, ensure you have the time to spare or can make the time, as chambers rely heavily on their committee members. Don't expect instant results or rewards; it takes time to become known in your community.

3. Display at trade shows Many people have the wrong expectations of exhibiting at trade shows, expecting people to flock to their table and place orders. Trade shows are excellent venues for meeting potential clients face-to-face and starting to build relationships. When your business is needed, you will probably be called. You also have the opportunity to glean creative ideas from other businesses and see what the competition is doing.

QUICK Tip

Exhibit, Inform, and Excite: When people visit your table, don't be aggressive. Be polite, excited about your business, and informative; ask them what they do. Have a drawing box on hand for business cards, and make sure they leave with a brochure, card, or handout. Don't forget the candy! The key to success is following up with a polite phone call, conveying how much you enjoyed meeting, and that you would be pleased to help, should the need arise. Touch base occasionally with industry news or specials that are of interest, but don't wear out your welcome.

4. Schedule personal appearances As your confidence grows, build your reputation as the expert by using your speaking skills. Apply to teach continuing education classes, design workshops, or speak at chamber of commerce events, networking groups, and anywhere you can get up in front of a group. Audiences consider you the expert and business will follow. Your name is networked not just within your own community, but further afield.

5. Attend conferences and seminars New entrepreneurs often say they don't have the time or money to spend on education. Mistake. By attending these industry-specific and business-related events, you learn more about your field and changing business management techniques, meet new people, and make new contacts, sometimes with the opportunity of setting up a display table. You would be surprised just how much business is transacted in conference hallways.

6. Contact the media You can't pay for the credibility that media interviews bring. Learn how to prepare a media kit and find creative ways to get interviews on either television or radio. Become known as the expert, the person the media calls for input. These interviews build both confidence and business, and seal your expert reputation. Media experience looks good on your résumé and corporate profile; it builds immediate credibility with potential clients.

QUICK Tip

Get More Big Ideas: Great verbal and written communication skills are a tremendous boost to marketing your business. Also read the companion to this book, *Taking Your Business to the Next Level* (Sourcebooks Inc.). Six chapters are devoted to marketing and sales, complete with many examples and with detailed information on how to build your communication skills.

7. Use evaluations and testimonials A book is often judged by the back-cover testimonials. They are powerful, no-cost marketing essentials. Ask satisfied clients if they would mind writing testimonials and thank them with a gift. Testimonials are invaluable business references. Collect them, and put them into a brag book. Use them on brochures and marketing materials (with written permission); frame them on the wall. I have seen whole walls of framed testimonials—most impressive. If you have a new product or service, find reputable clients who will test your product (you could offer it at cost price) in return for an evaluation or testimonial. Most people are happy to oblige.

8. Send out press releases Newspapers are always looking for interesting items. Create a unique approach to your business and learn how to send out press releases (see *Taking Your Business to the Next Level*). You may have a new environmentally friendly product or be holding a workshop of community interest. In one example, press releases promoting a one-day small business workshop were sent to newspapers, business networks, radio, and the chamber of commerce. Of those registered, 59 percent read about it, 9 percent heard through radio, and 32 percent through networking.

9. Write articles Submit well-written articles to business-related magazines, newspapers, or e-zines. Once you are published, your credibility as the expert increases. You can use these articles to build your portfolio and media kit, as informational handouts for customers, and to post on your website. If writing is not your strength, take a course on creative writing through your local community college. Have an experienced writer check your work before you submit it for publication.

Promote on a shoestring budget

It will take some trial and error to know which promotional methods work best for your business. You may be bombarded by advertisers vying for your business, so your task is to identify which methods are the least expensive and most effective to get your name quickly known. Consider the following methods as you plan your marketing budget. Some are "mass media" or "hit-and-miss marketing methods" because they rely on numbers and are not usually targeted at a particular market.

1. Newspaper advertising (nontargeted) If your community is your primary market, the local newspaper's classifieds is a good place to start. Because per-line rates vary according to the community size and the newspaper's reach, check with your local newspaper for the cost. The longer you run the advertisement, the cheaper the cost. Some newspapers run special display pages focusing on professional, home improvement, or home-based businesses. A cheaper rate is usually offered if you advertise for twelve weeks or longer.

Large display advertisements are expensive, one-shot, hit-and-miss options that are not often read by the public. Some local newspapers are so loaded with junk mail and flyers that it's difficult to find the newspaper. Consumers are on media-overload and can't possibly read all this advertising. You may receive only one or two calls from your expensive display ad. In one example, a women's network routinely placed a $400, quarter-page, monthly advertisement in the local paper. After eight months, research indicated that only a few members even noticed it.

Create a Sense of Urgency: Place a time limit on advertised specials and add a time-limited coupon to monitor results. This gives consumers a sense of urgency to *call now*. Note: if you use this technique in all your advertising, consumers eventually get smart.

2. Coupon books (nontargeted) Although coupon books give your advertisement a longer shelf (or drawer) life than newspaper advertising, you are again targeting a mass market. Costs vary, but count on spending at least $500 and more for a residential mail-out. The books are usually delivered with household mail or the local newspaper and can get lost in the junk mail. The response rate can be low (in one example, a run of thirty thousand netted the advertiser five calls, or 0.02 percent), but the per book cost of one to two cents is cheap.

As with all mass mail-outs, you have to reach the right consumer at the right time, with the right product, and when they can afford it and have time to shop. Ensure that you have enough product or the ability to service an influx of calls—you have to honor your advertisements. Coupon books are good for services such as dry cleaning, or for companies that have the staff to service the calls. Time limitations are important to monitor your response. Be prepared to advertise consistently to create consumer awareness, as people don't always respond to the first advertisement.

3. Flyers (nontargeted) Your flyer is usually circulated within other junk mail, so plan when and to whom you will send them. Flyers are great marketing tools to use at targeted trade shows or focused events. People do keep certain ones for reference, such as yard work or tree-topping, and will use your service when needed. Avoid summer for this type of advertising; in one example, a flyer circulation of thirteen hundred sent out during August had a response rate of three calls, a return of only 0.23 percent.

Try Consistency: A local store that consistently puts out a weekly flyer will draw repeat business. In one example, a new produce store circulates weekly flyers always advertising excellent prices, and they have developed a large, regular clientele. Try delivering one or two hundred regularly around the neighborhood and monitor the response.

Going door-to-door is best left to the professional salesperson who handles regular rejection well. For most, it's time-consuming and confidence-shattering. Local newspapers offer a flyer delivery service, with circulation broken down into specific areas, so call them for information.

The U.S. Postal Service offers a delivery service too, so call them for a quote or visit www.usps.com. Flyers are delivered with the mail, and you can choose delivery days. Smart entrepreneurs choose a day when the local paper (and flyers) aren't delivered—preferably near the end of the week—when people have more time to read and can call (or email) on the weekend or first thing Monday morning.

4. Brochures (targeted) A professional business brochure will encapsulate its services. They are invaluable for networking events, trade shows, mail-outs, correspondence, and promotions. Use a good graphic artist to design an appealing layout with lots of white space. Don't try to cram in too much information, as your brochure is a teaser. It should pique interest and generate a phone call. To be affordable, you need to order large quantities, which could become outdated. For smaller, customized runs, try a digital printer.

5. Handouts (targeted) This is the information age, so prepare informational handouts for networking events, trade shows, or seminars. Professional handouts help build that expert reputation. A garbage disposal business could prepare a handout on correct recycling, the benefits of composting, or reducing harmful household bacteria. A vacuum store could prepare one on household allergens and molds and how to eliminate them. Include all your contact information on the handout; you'll be surprised how they get passed around. Post handouts on your website.

CASE STUDY: Heating up Business

Sherri-Lee started a home-based ozone steam sauna business, offering first-time clients a free sauna. We met at a chamber of commerce dinner, and Sherri-Lee thanked me for previously suggesting that she write thank-you cards to new customers.

"It's a great idea," she said excitedly. "I write them while clients are in the sauna and mail them later. I include a coupon for a half-price visit and write on the card what the coupon is for. One client asked why I thanked her for a free visit. I explained that my clients are important to me. The client commented, 'It's amazing, nobody does that!'"

"I get 50 percent of first-time clients returning for the half-price session and 50 percent of those returning for at least two or more full-priced sessions, or they purchase a package deal," says Sherri-Lee. "It's the best marketing investment for repeat business I ever made. I haven't spent a lot on advertising, and probably every regular client refers at least one person."

6. Target marketing (definitely targeted) Service businesses such as those providing roofing, paving, or tree-pruning can prepare low-cost customized flyers on their computer, preferably fitting two to a page. Photocopy the master onto brightly colored paper and cut to size. Deliver fifty to one hundred flyers to homes in the vicinity of where you will be working, inviting, "Drive by 34534 Willow Drive on Tuesday and see us at work." This is an effective method of promoting residential services, as humans want what their neighbors have—or better. It's called "keeping up with the Joneses." One landscape curbing company eventually concreted eleven gardens in one cul-de-sac by doing this. It's a cheap method of promotion, and you can customize addresses as required.

7. Simply say thank-you (targeted) A week shouldn't go by without finding a reason to thank someone. It could be a new client, someone who referred a client, a newspaper that printed a press release, or an associate who helped you find a reliable service provider. Perhaps someone gave you some good advice or helped you when you needed it. Send a thank-you card, for they are the support system that keeps your business in business.

8. Birthday, holiday, and frequent user cards (targeted)

- **Birthday cards:** The personal touch goes a long way and people don't forget you when you remember them. Retail stores can ask new customers to register for the birthday club and have a sign and forms at the cash register. Then send a discount coupon for use during your customer's birthday month, along with a card. People love these cards, and will often return to use their coupon—and to purchase other products.

  One year (I guess no one loved me that year), the only birthday card I received in the mail was from the local saddle store. It included a discount coupon, which I promptly redeemed. Of course, I tell everyone how much I appreciated that gesture.
- **Holiday cards:** As an added touch that says, "We are thinking about you," send clients a handwritten seasonal greetings card. I look forward to cards each year from the local Cantonese restaurant and the family real estate agent. I tell everyone about the cards and refer the businesses to others.
- **Frequent user discounts:** Most people's wallets (including mine) are crammed with frequent user cards, whether it's for coffee, pizza, books, restaurants, dry cleaning, or photofinishing, to name a few. Consumers

use them because they love to get something free. The standard "buy ten, get one free" works. With all these discounted promotions, ensure that you have built the discounts into your costing and are not losing money.

9. Follow-up and service programs (targeted) The best way to get repeat business is to follow up and stay in touch with customers. Design a simple method of collecting new customer information—their address, phone number, birthday, and email address—and use a contact management system. Tell customers you like to stay in touch to notify them of specials or service dates. Follow up after a sale to ensure customer satisfaction.

Although the most simple way to build long-term customer loyalty and repeat business, many service-oriented businesses neglect ongoing, consistent follow up. Why? Most people I ask say that they are too busy and don't have the time. When business is waiting for you and you don't have to even look for it, why would you be too busy to pick up the phone?

Follow Up for Repeat Business: Touch base by telephone to see if you can help your customers. Many appliances and products need servicing, but without a reminder, often nothing happens. Car dealerships are diligent about sending our service reminders—sometimes two. They are assured of repeat business and your vehicle stays well maintained. Whether you are a hairdresser, vet, accountant, or computer servicing company, start a service/appointment reminder system. Not only are you assured of repeat business, you continue to build relationships. You would surprised at how few businesses use this simple, low-cost technique.

10. Ask for referrals (targeted) You no doubt do your best to please your customers, so why not politely ask them to spread the good word? Give each a few business cards or brochures. As you sow, so you shall reap, just as Sherri-Lee did in the earlier case study. People are always looking for "a good hairdresser" or "a good mechanic." Many businesses have built a solid client base using the referral method, which is cheap and effective. Thank clients who refer you with a card and small gift.

11. Crosspromote (targeted) Marketing is an expensive proposition, so why not share the cost? As you build relationships with other complementary businesses, discuss crosspromotion with them. You can then share advertising and promotion costs, hold joint events, and have each other's brochures and business cards on display. For example, a computer servicing business could crosspromote with a Web designer and an accountant. A hairdresser could crosspromote with a wedding shop, a photographer, and a beauty salon.

12. Send emails and newsletters (targeted) Email newsletters do solicit a positive response, and their cost is negligible. They shouldn't be fancy or wordy—they are there to inform and to keep in touch. Let customers know about special events, sales, and industry and product information. One small yet highly successful book retailer says that *short* emails to her customers about special in-store events and new book releases is one of her best marketing techniques.

13. The Yellow Pages (targeted) When people don't know who to turn to, they usually look in the Yellow Pages, so it pays to be listed. Before committing to an annual contract, study competitors' advertisements. If most are large displays, then obviously the Yellow Pages is working well for them. However, a smaller advertisement works just as well if you combine it with other marketing methods. People must be able to find you, but you don't need huge monthly advertising bills added to your phone account, so place an affordable advertisement and monitor the responses.

Which Advertising Media Should You Use?

Because you need to discover the advertising methods that work best for you, it is critical to monitor all responses in relationship to the dollars spent. Ask all customers, "Where did you hear about us?" and note their answers and the date—a simple way to monitor results.

When you start advertising, monitor every strategy. Sign up for ads in one magazine issue, one week of radio air time, and two newspaper insertions, and compare the results. Successful businesses not only take advantage of the most obvious form of advertising, they *create* consumer demand for their products through effective marketing strategies. Traditional advertising includes a variety of methods, including the following.

1. Point-of-purchase material

Point-of-purchase materials include posters, banners, table tents, brochures, displays, balloons, and in-store coupons displayed next to your product to increase its visibility. Take advantage of the people who walk by your display by making it stand out. How many times have you impulsively grabbed something at the checkout because it caught your attention?

QUICK Tip

Tell the Neighbors: If you perform a service that is visible to the public, get your customer's permission to place a sign telling the neighborhood which quality company this customer chose. Similar in concept to point-of-purchase material, this method is geared more to service-oriented businesses. Your sign can even contain a brochure holder so passers-by can take one home.

2. Radio and television

Radio and television advertising is usually recommended for promoting highly consumable items or special events and to establish consumer awareness. If you don't have a large inventory, several outlets, or fast-selling items such as hamburgers or computers, then use other forms of marketing. If you can afford radio or television air time, combine it with printed media. Used by itself, air time won't generate the expected business because it is short-lived. Getting the public to recognize your name takes repetition—and that is expensive. The cost is usually prohibitive for small businesses. Of course, a guest spot on a radio show as "the expert" costs nothing.

3. Transit advertising

For many larger businesses, transit advertising works well, but it is costly. The advertisements on the back or side of a bus are obviously visible. If you have sat behind a bus in traffic, you have probably read many. Smaller advertisements placed inside a train or bus are also effective—bored commuters often have nothing else to read. Large advertisements on the back of bus seats or inside shelters are effective, but be sure to advertise in the right geographic area.

4. The Internet

Marketing on the Internet is extensively discussed elsewhere, but suffice to say that competitive businesses keep up with technology and are accessible via email and their websites. A site gives you a 24/7 presence and can be utilized in many ways.

Consumers are now using the Internet for paying bills, ordering from reputable companies such as large office stationers, and for finding information. Even a business servicing a local market could benefit. For example, a local florist with an online catalog and secure ordering provides a convenience for our busy society.

Inform, Educate, and Sell: Surfers use the Internet to find specific information and to increase their knowledge. Sites offering free information get more visits, so include this component. For example, an accountant could prepare a series of articles such as "Ten Hot Tips for Saving on Your Taxes." By posting this information, a relationship of trust is already building with the user, who may also refer others to your site.

Those servicing a wider market—state, national, or international—should consider a website. Hotels, resorts, and bed and breakfasts gain regular international business this way. If you specialize in a product—for example, collector dolls—a website and secure ordering system is a great business booster.

People are still hesitant to buy over the Internet from unknown businesses, so be conservative about what you spend and monitor the results. Have a professional design the site and be prepared for a costly venture, depending on its size and bells and whistles. Consult first with other businesses and industry professionals. Splash your email and website address on everything—business cards, stationery, brochures, and all advertising, as consumers often visit a company's website first.

5. Specials

People love a deal and can't resist words like "sale," "special," "70 percent off," or "inventory clearance." Time-sensitive deals such as offering to pay the tax for the first twenty customers create an urgency to buy, particularly for higher-priced items. Specials will help clear out slow-moving inventory, stimulate cash flow, and increase market awareness, but should not be unprofitable.

6. Mix and match

You may have been told that the more you advertise, the more effective the results, or that your first advertisements may not work for you. The truth is, every advertisement should work for you if it is correctly planned and priced. The more you advertise, the better the results. Response rate should gradually increase, so don't expect the telephone to ring off the hook after the third advertisement.

Two or three techniques combined in the same time period generate a better response. A new business can't afford to wait for customers to magically appear. You need to become known—quickly. For example, an "informational" advertisement in a magazine and radio advertising may not prompt people to call, but adding coupon books or flyers will. Your market is now surrounded with your information. They are informed of your business's benefits with one type of advertising, and you are encouraging them to come in with another.

Don't deplete your marketing budget to do this. For better air-time rates, either buy the same day, all day, every week, using the same time slot, or use the same time slot every day on the same days every week. Magazine, flyer, and coupon advertising can be two-color instead of full color. Full color isn't necessary, unless you are selling high-end products.

How Do You Plan a Marketing Budget?

Planning a marketing budget involves asking five important questions.

1. How much can you supply?

Before you decide on how you are going to market, calculate how *much* you can sell. It's no use implementing a huge marketing campaign only to discover that you can't keep up with the work or that you don't have the working capital to finance a larger inventory. Once you know your capabilities—both physically and financially—you can then better identify what may work best for you. Some calculations are necessary for all businesses to complete their business plan projections.

2. Service businesses

A sole proprietor wears sixty hats, so you can't work religiously eight hours a day generating income. The accepted calculation is a maximum of four billable hours a day. If you deduct time for weekends, statutory holidays, vacations, administration, and education or conference days, you'll find you have about 185 working days available. If you bill $65 an hour for those 185 four-hour days, your maximum annual income—without extra help—is $48,000. Use this figure to calculate what percentage of income you are going to use for marketing. A new business should be prepared to spend between 10 and 20 percent of sales in the first year. What will you spend? At 15 percent, that is $7,200 a year, or $600 a month.

3. Product-based businesses

The calculation for sales projections for product-based businesses will be more complex. You must take into account the following factors to establish monthly sales projections and then calculate your marketing budget from there. Answer these questions:

- How much product can you physically house?
- How much product can you physically sell?
- How much product can you afford to purchase?
- Do you know your seasonal peaks and ebbs?
- Do you have the available manpower?

Try a simple marketing budget calculation using Figure 10.4 on the next page.

4. Plot your sales and marketing curve

For budgeting purposes, plot a month-by-month graph showing projected sales, join the dots, and create a sales curve. Ascertain when and how you

Figure 10.4: CALCULATING A MARKETING BUDGET

a) Annual working days: ______________________

b) x daily hours worked (service businesses): ____________

c) x hourly rate or daily sales: ____________________

Estimated annual income: $ ____________________

Marketing % (10 to 20%): ______________________

Total budget: $ __________________________

Monthly budget: $ ________________________

should be promoting your business to capitalize on seasonal times of the year, for example, Easter, Mother's Day, and back-to-school. If your product sells well on Valentine's Day, your marketing push should start a month before. Department stores start advertising Christmas as early as September, because advertising in December is too late. Magazines often have a two- to three-month copy deadline, while newspapers are weekly. Mall and trade show space must be booked and paid for months in advance. Timing and budgeting are crucial.

Although you need to capitalize on seasonal sales peaks, your first year's budget should make allowances for a stronger push when the business opens and during the first few months. It should also reflect periods when marketing for many businesses can be a waste of time, such as summer. Next, plot how much you can spend each month, based on the sales curve, and in which months you need to spend it.

Few businesses achieve their first year's projected sales because they were overly optimistic. Success is based on achieving close to these figures. Perhaps you will be one of the few who meet—or even surpass—your projections. Make sure you have the right product available at the right time and promote it the right way.

Plan Each Year: Reduce your second year's marketing budget to 7 to 10 percent of sales. By now, you will know more about your business, how it relates to the consumer, and which strategies work for you. Your third year's budget should be more accurate, based on the second year. By your fourth or fifth year, you should be able to reduce your marketing budget to as low as 4 or 5 percent of sales, but don't spend less than this.

5. Plan how you will spend

The last step is to look at each month's budget, combined with the seasonal projections, and decide how you will spend your marketing dollars. Some monthly expenses will be consistent, such as chamber of commerce dinners, monthly networking meetings, and a Yellow Pages advertisement. Your start-up marketing costs will be high, as they include expenses such as brochures, grand opening events, and advertising. Talk to others in similar businesses to see what works for them. Review and digest the low-cost, targeted options in this chapter before deciding how to spend your money. More detailed information can be found in *Taking Your Business to the Next Level.*

What Is the Next Step?

It's a subject that most people don't want to discuss and a chore they don't want to do—accounting. Yet you are in business to make money, and the only way you can ascertain whether you are or why you are not is to count the beans and be organized. The shoebox system doesn't work for most businesses, and flying by the seat of your pants only creates a giant hole. So get out the coffee pot again and perk up the brain to digest the basics about accounting.

Chapter 11

How Do You Organize Your Accounting, Time, and Paperwork?

She filed bills under "B" and letters under "L."
Where the rest of it went, who can really tell?

- **How do you organize your files?**
- **How do you organize your time and paperwork?**
- **How do you set up your accounting?**
- **What is a chart of accounts?**
- **What does your accountant require?**
- **How do you cost inventory?**
- **Which business expenses are tax deductible?**
- **What is a break-even point?**
- **How do you record vehicle expenses?**
- **Be nice to your accountant**

How Do You Organize Your Files?

No doubt about it, you have to be organized to keep on top of the paperwork. As soon as you start a business, you are inundated with a mountain of correspondence from various government agencies and an assortment of advertising. If you organize efficiently from the start, the paperwork won't bog you down. Too many people let papers pile up, leaving mail unopened for days and even weeks. They then hurriedly scan it without paying attention. This sloppy practice leads to mistakes.

Organization is an essential ingredient for a successful business, because as a business grows, so do the mountains of paperwork. Confusion causes lost documents and lost profits. You can't afford to forget follow-up, an appointment, or paying your accounts on time. Your reputation is at stake.

Start with a twenty-second filing cabinet

The more crowded your files, the less organized you are. Buy a four-drawer filing cabinet, suspension frames and different colored legal-sized hanging files and file folders for easy identification. Use tabs for visibility and follow Figure 11.1, which suggests the files you will need and which drawer to use. You will no doubt add to the list over time. This efficient filing system allows you to find any paper in twenty seconds or less. File paperwork as follows:

1. **Numerically:** File sales invoices both numerically and chronologically, with the latest number in front. Do this after they are posted (entered) to your books.
2. **Alphabetically:** For each accounts payable supplier, put the last paid invoice in front. The most recent purchases are now at your fingertips in chronological order.
3. **Chronologically:** All other files, including correspondence, are filed chronologically, the latest in front.
4. **Year-end:** After financial statements and taxes are completed, store the last twelve months' accounting in a storage box, and reuse the file folders. Keep your accounting records for seven years. Keep important information accessible, such as incorporation papers or asset purchases. Revisit all files and discard unnecessary papers during the year to keep necessary year-end cleanup to a minimum.

Figure 11.1: **YOUR TWENTY-SECOND FILING CABINET STRATEGY**

Top drawer:

- Payroll: one file for schedules, one for employee records
- State sales tax remittances and information
- Workers' compensation
- Accounts to be paid, organized alphabetically
- Check and deposit books, spare checks
- Posting file for accounting ready to be entered to books
- Quotations for work pending
- Quotations for purchases you make
- Monthly accounting papers and year-end documents
- Current credit card receipts and invoices

Second drawer:

- Incorporation papers and related correspondence
- Other licensing agencies
- Contracts and agreements with suppliers
- Telephone, cell, Yellow Pages contracts
- Bank account and credit card merchant documents
- Asset register and invoices for purchases over $200
- Business vehicle information and bills
- Expense reports, completed and spare sheets
- Completed job costings
- Client correspondence
- Business start-up information
- Insurance policies—a file per policy
- Contacts and leads information

continued

Third drawer:

- Paid accounts, a file for each main supplier, two for miscellaneous
- Reconciled bank statements and canceled checks
- Posted cash expenses for costs you personally paid
- Posted petty cash receipts
- Posted sales invoices or invoice books (use a three-ring binder for large quantities)
- Advertising information and rates

Fourth drawer:

- One previous year's accounting
- Spare credit card slips and information
- You'll find a use for the rest.

How Do You Organize Your Time and Paperwork?

Learn to work to routines

Keep on top of paperwork by dispensing with it as soon as possible. Keeping a daily and weekly routine helps achieve this goal.

Each day... When mail arrives, sort it into accounts to be paid, checks to be deposited, government correspondence, items requiring immediate attention, and the rest. Tackle one pile at a time. Check supplier accounts for correct pricing and note in your day planner or calendar the due date. Then file them alphabetically.

Match checks to be deposited with an invoice number, ensuring the full amount has been paid. Note any discounts taken, short payments, and the invoice number. Put the checks into your deposit book, ready to write up the deposit. Read all government correspondence, such as payroll or state tax remittances; note when payment is due and then file. Scan your advertising mail and either file or recycle it. Attend to the important things at once or you will probably forget.

QUICK Tip

Itemize Check Stubs: When you write checks, record the full amount on the stub; never leave the stub blank. Write a short description of the expense (e.g., office supplies). This saves you or your bookkeeper time, as the expense will be allocated to the right account, and it will save you accounting dollars.

Each week... Regularly review and pay your bills. When you pay an account, take it out of the accounts-to-be-paid file, write the check, then record the check number, date, and amount paid on the invoice. This is a cross-reference in case there is a dispute over payment. File the paid account. Review accounts receivable and make some collection calls. Service businesses should bill clients weekly. Put a copy of the mailed invoice into the posting file for entry to your books.

Empty your wallet weekly of those cash receipts for gas, lunches, stamps, and miscellaneous items. Put them into your posting file, clipped together. Separate petty cash items and balance the float. Staple the receipts together with a piece of paper detailing the amount, the check number, and date. If receipts are illegible, write on them what they are for. File in the posting file. Keep credit card receipts and invoices in a separate file so they can later be matched to the statement.

Each month... After month-end, sort through the posting file, putting the papers into the following order for entry to your books. If you use an accounting software system, either you or your bookkeeper should code each piece of paper using the correct chart of accounts number (shown later in Figure 11.3). Be diligent in coding the correct account numbers onto your documents or your accounting will be incorrect. Deal with each of the following categories:

1. **Sales invoices:** Batch sales invoices numerically, starting with the oldest. Locate missing invoice numbers. Attach a tape totaling the completed monthly invoices. They are now ready to enter to the books and you know how much you billed.
2. **Check stubs:** Remove the month's check stubs from your binder, carrying the balance forward to the next check. Clip the stubs together, filling in any missing information.
3. **Cash expenses:** Sort receipts into the various expense categories, staple together each expense type with a tape total, and indicate the type of expense.
4. **Bank deposits:** If possible, order a triplicate copy bank deposit book. Then remove a copy of each deposit, staple them together in date order,r and attach a tape of the monthly total. If you use the deposit book for posting, tape-list the deposits and staple the tape to the last deposit for the month.
5. **Miscellaneous:** Note or include anything else of relevance for the bookkeeper or your accountant.
6. **Credit card statements:** If you use credit cards for personal and business expenses, go through each statement when it arrives and highlight the business expenses. Take the credit card receipts and corresponding invoices and attach them to the statement in the order the charges appear

Alert!

Be Thorough with Credit Card Records: Detailed information is required of each credit card transaction, and for audit purposes, each charge must have an accompanying invoice. A common mistake is to include only the credit card slips with accounting records. No one can work from a credit card statement or the yellow slips, and accountants charge big bucks at year-end if all the necessary documents aren't presented.

Start a priority list

With so much to do, prioritizing is essential. Sometimes, work is overwhelming and you feel out of control. If organization is not your strength, use the weekly priority list system.

Using an eight-column pad, set up columns across the top titled Things to Do, Deadline, A+, A, B, and C priorities as shown in Figure 11.2. List all the things to do, decide on a deadline for each task (even if that task's deadline is weeks away), and then indicate the priority for each job. Work first on the A+ priorities, starting at the earliest deadline, crossing them off the list with a highlighter as completed.

Figure 11.2: **WEEKLY PRIORITY LIST**

THINGS TO DO: WEEK ENDING JUNE 15, XXXX

THINGS TO DO	DEADLINE	A+	A	B	C
Bill clients	June 9	✔			
Pay monthly accounts	June 9	✔			
Order business cards	June 12			✔	
Write thank-you cards	June 10		✔		
Clean filing cabinet	June 15				✔
Follow-up phone calls	June 11	✔			
Quotation for Mrs. Baxter	June 10		✔		

Review the list daily and add new priorities. You will be surprised at how many C priorities can eventually be crossed off without taking any action. Move outstanding chores to your new weekly list as necessary. There is a certain satisfaction at seeing work crossed off the list, which is also a constant reminder not to forget anything important. This simple system works efficiently—if you use it.

CASE STUDY: No Accounting for Taste

In my public practice, I am often presented with shoeboxes crammed with papers one week before the April tax deadline. These business owners don't have a clue where their businesses stand financially. Accounting has also arrived in fruit boxes, and zip-lock and grocery bags (both paper and plastic). The most repulsive scenario was a well-used, gravy-stained, family-sized cardboard fried chicken tub, complete with dried coleslaw on the bottom. Then there was the plastic bag, full of unopened mail, obviously swept off the kitchen table along with some sandwich crusts. Such filing systems say a lot about the business owners, who are also charged "dirt" time.

Unorganized people usually create cash flow problems for themselves. An unexpected tax bill for thousands of dollars, coupled with late government payments, soon puts such businesses in deep financial waters. Some people get so far over their head that bankruptcy is the only alternative. Not surprisingly, neither the chicken tub nor the sandwich crust business owners are in business now.

How Do You Set Up Your Accounting?

Each business has different accounting requirements, depending on its size and the volume of transactions, but the principles are the same for everyone. A small, one-person business may need only one journal to record all the monthly accounting. Once a business starts generating more paperwork, an accounting software program is a good idea. It's smart to start with a manual system so that the basic accounting concepts are understood before becoming technologically terrific.

Always get your accountant's help to set up and monitor your progress. Some people have a mental block about using their accountant for advice—and about paying their bills on time. Respect your accountant; he or she has your best interests at heart. Learn how to understand your accounting system and keep it up-to-date—the future of your business relies heavily on you being informed.

What accounting records do you need?

Many pieces make your accounting puzzle fit together. If you keep "source documents" (that is, every piece of paper) well organized, it's much easier to record your accounting information. Both a manual system and accounting software record the same transactions. Your accounting books should consist of the following:

1. **Sales journal:** records sales and taxes
2. **Cash receipts journal:** records all money coming into the business
3. **Cash disbursements journal:** records checks written, the expenses and bank charges, and automatic withdrawals
4. **Cash expenses journal:** records out-of-pocket and petty cash expenses
5. **Accounts payable journal:** records unpaid trade and supplier accounts
6. **General journal:** records adjustments made to your books, usually made by your accountant
7. **General ledger:** combines the above books, ready for the preparation of the financial statement
8. **Trial balance:** a listing of your financial accounts to show that the books balance
9. **Financial statements:** A compilation of all of the above, which reflects the financial situation of the business. If any entries in the above seven journals are incorrect, your statements will be wrong.

If you opt for a manual system, you use the first seven journals. For small businesses, the first five can be combined into one simple book. An accounting software program combines all the above functions with a one-time entry, eliminating the need for columns and cross-additions and posting the first six journals to the general ledger, which then has each page totaled and the whole book cross-balanced.

Data entry takes meticulous manual preparation. Information is posted in batches, which at month-end are balanced to an accounting control. Accounting means that every figure has to be entered to the books twice, thus the term double-entry bookkeeping. One entry acts as a control—either to the bank account, accounts receivable, or payable records—the other is descriptive and tells you what the amount is for.

QUICK Tip

Learn the Program First: Unless you have a thorough understanding of bookkeeping, don't even attempt to do your own accounting using a software program until you have formally learned how to use it with your accountant's guidance. If you enter a wrong account number or code an account incorrectly, your financial information will be wrong, and often, the mistakes are never picked up. Accountants make big bucks correcting records prepared by inexperienced bookkeepers, so don't practice false economy.

What Is a Chart of Accounts?

A chart of accounts is a directory of your accounting information, called accounts. Each one is usually allocated a three- or four-digit number, and the chart is listed in the order of a financial statement. Each business needs a slightly different chart of accounts. Figure 11.3 on the next page shows a simple chart of accounts for Jason's Garden Service. The following pages show examples of his accounting journals, with explanations to help you organize your system.

1. The sales journal (monthly sales invoices)

A sales journal records each invoice billed or daily cash sales, and is used to compile your accounts receivable records. Jason divided his sales into categories such as bark mulch, gravel, topsoil, sand, and delivery charges. Each month, his sales journal gives him the dollar value of goods sold (see Figure 11.4 on page 248). This information helps when he reorders supplies and indicates seasonal trends. State sales tax is also recorded.

Sales journal analysis Jason can now review his monthly sales to see which products sold well. He can also review his accounts receivable information by customer to study their buying patterns, both current and in the past. By utilizing an accounts receivable system, Jason can readily identify overdue accounts and keep on top of collections.

Figure 11.3: **CHART OF ACCOUNTS: JASON'S GARDEN SERVICE**

Current assets:

1000	Bank account
1020	Accounts receivable
1030	Inventory
1040	Prepaid expenses

Current liabilities:

2000	Accounts payable
2010	State tax payable
2020	Employee withholdings
2030	Employee taxes payable
2040	Bank loan payable
2050	Wages payable
2100	Loan payable–R. Davies

Fixed assets:

1200	Automotive equipment
1220	Office equipment
1230	Office furniture

Equity:

3000	Owner's capital
3010	Owner's draws
3030	Retained earnings (profit)

Income:

4000	Sales–supplies
4010	Sales–delivery
4020	Other income

Cost of sales:

4500	Material purchases
4510	Truck fuel
4520	Truck repairs
4530	Truck insurance
4540	Driver's wages
4550	Driver's benefits

Expenses:

5000	Accounting fees
5010	Advertising
5020	Bank charges
5030	Discounts
5040	Fees, licenses & taxes
5050	Insurance
5060	Loan interest
5080	Office supplies & printing
5090	Promotion–meals
5100	Rent & property taxes
5120	Telephones & Internet
5130	Travel & accommodation
5140	Utilities
5150	Workers' compensation

Figure 11.4: **SALES JOURNAL: JASON'S GARDEN SERVICE**

Sales Journal: September XXXX

DATE	NAME	INV. #	TOTAL Dr +	SAND Cr –	MULCH Cr –	SOIL Cr –	GRAVEL Cr –	DELIVERY Cr –	SST Cr –
09/01	J. Stein	2346	160.50	35.00	35.00	50.00		30.00	10.50
09/03	B. Jones	2347	909.50	150.00	200.00	200.00	200.00	100.00	59.50
09/15	I. Chow	2348	481.50				400.00	50.00	31.50
09/27	S. Bull	2349	207.00			165.00		35.00	7.00
TOTAL			**$1,758.50**	**$185.00**	**$235.00**	**$415.00**	**$600.00**	**$215.00**	**$108.50**
			=	+	+	+	+	+	+

The "*Dr* +" and "*Cr* –" signs under the headings denote debit and credit entries. When the columns are added across the page, the total debits should equal credits. If you calculate the totals on an adding machine tape, the balance should be zero. The plus (+) and minus (–) signs are there to help those challenged by bookkeeping. The accounting rule is: *add all debits and subtract all credits to balance your books.*

If you are recording sales from a retail operation where money is used from the till to pay various expenses, you can add these expense columns into the journal.

Jason can now convert sales figures into percentages to help with costing and budgets. For example, gravel is 36.4 percent of his total sales, before tax. Percentages are easily obtained by using the following formula, which is a quick and easy calculation:

$$\frac{\text{Gravel sales}}{\text{Total sales}} \quad \frac{\$\ 600.00}{\$1,650.00} \times 100.0\% = 36.4\%$$

2. The cash receipts journal (daily bank deposits)

This journal records everything deposited to your bank account and keeps a record of the money's origin, as not all funds are from sales. If you have more than one bank account, enter each one separately, either on another page or underneath the first completed one. If you enter two bank accounts together, your books will be a nightmare to correct!

Keeping an accurate cash receipts journal is simply a matter of clearly itemizing everything. To correctly record a bank deposit, follow these steps:

1. Match each payment to the paid invoice numbers, noting discounts or short payments. (You made these notes when sorting the mail.)
2. Put the checks into alphabetical order and enter them into the deposit book. Next to the payment or on the opposite page, note the invoice numbers being paid—the same applies to cash being deposited.
3. If other funds are deposited—such as capital, loans, or rebates on expenses—note in your deposit book whom the money came from and what it is for.
4. Now enter each daily deposit into the cash receipts journal using the correct columns (see Figure 11.5 on the next page):

    a) **Date:** The date of the bank deposit.
    b) **Invoice #:** The invoice number(s) being paid with each payment.
    c) **Total Bank:** The total of the daily deposit, which should equal the total of each payment listed in "bank in" column.
    d) **Bank In:** A line-by-line breakdown of each payment, which equals the "total bank" column.
    e) **Discount:** The amount of discount taken.
    f) **Accounts Receivable:** The total of the paid invoice including discounts. The total of the payment plus discount equals the total accounts receivable.
    g) **Account #:** The chart of accounts number, which identifies any deposits other than accounts receivable.
    h) **Amount:** The amount of the above deposit.
    i) **Description:** Note what this money is for.

Figure 11.5: **SALES JOURNAL: JASON'S GARDEN SERVICE**

Cash Receipts Journal: September XXXX

a)		b)	c)	d)	e)	f)	g)	h)	i)
DATE	NAME	INV. #	TOTAL BANK	BANK IN Dr +	DISC- Dr +	A/REC. Cr –	A/C #	AMOUNT Cr –	DESCR.
09/07	J. Stein	2346		167.58	3.42	171.00			
09/07	B. Jones	2347		949.62	19.38	969.00			
09/07	S. Swan	2333	1,667.20	550.00		550.00			
09/10	J. Darjeeling		1,000.00	1,000.00			(3000)	1,000.00	Capital
09/15	I. Chow	2348		513.00		513.00			
09/15	R. Davies		2,513.00	2,000.00			(2100)	2,000.00	Loan
09/27	S. Bull	2349		209.72	4.28	214.00			
09/27	J. Toms	2327	539.72	330.00		330.00			
	TOTALS:		**$5,719.92**	**$5,719.92**	**$27.08**	**$2,747.00**		**$3,000.00**	
			=	=	+	–		–	

The cash receipts journal should not be closed off at month-end until the bank statements are received. Then each deposit in the "total bank" column is checked against those on the bank statements because it is easy to make mistakes. The bank may issue a credit memo, or the account earn interest, which must be entered into the journal, ready for the bank reconciliation.

Some businesses operate on a revolving line of credit or use Internet banking for paying bills and moving funds between accounts. You need to record these transactions each month before you can reconcile the bank account. If you use Internet banking for transferring funds or paying bills, record each transaction in the appropriate journal.

3. The cash disbursements journal (checks written)

The cash disbursements journal records the details of every check you write and monthly automatic payments from the bank account, such as loans, car insurance, and bank charges. If you miss one item, your books won't agree with the bank statement.

Accounting software Your check stubs are, of course, well detailed. If you use accounting software, total all checks on a tape at month-end, highlight other deductions from the bank statement, and add these on to the tape. When the bank account is reconciled, then enter the checks. Ensure that each check stub is coded with the correct account number. When everything is entered, the bank account month-end total in your records must agree with the manual reconciliation.

Code as You Go: To avoid errors made while hurriedly coding a pile of checks at month-end, keep a copy of your chart of accounts in the plastic wallet of your check binder. When you write a check, code it immediately while you have the relevant information—such as the paid invoice—in front of you.

Manual systems Checks and automatic bank deductions are manually entered into the cash disbursements journal, and the bank reconciliation completed after month-end. A twenty-column journal is ample. Set out the columns according to the expenses you incur the most. Those you incur infrequently are entered into the miscellaneous column, along with a short description. Jason's main expenses are materials, truck costs, and wages. Figure 11.6 shows Jason's journal.

If you draw any money from the business for personal use, enter these amounts under the "draw" column. Cash money taken to pay business expenses is considered a draw until the actual expense is entered from a receipt into the cash expense journal.

Figure 11.6: CASH DISBURSEMENTS JOURNAL: JASON'S GARDEN SERVICE

Cash Disbursements Journal: September XXXX

DATE	NAME	CH. NO.	BANK OUT Cr −	MATERIAL Dr +	WAGES Dr +	TRUCK Dr +	DRAW Dr +	MISC. Dr +
09/01	Leasit Co.	024 ✔	700.00					700.00 Rent
09/01	FuelUp	025 ✔	930.00			930.00		
09/03	Office Co.	026 ✔	65.00					65.00 Office
09/03	Gravelpit	027 ✔	800.00	800.00				
09/08	Sandpile	028 ✔	400.00	400.00				
09/15	S. Jones	029 ✔	525.00		525.00			
09/15	D. Spence	030 ✔	650.00		650.00			
09/15	CCRA	031 ✔	730.00		730.00			
09/15	Min. Finance	032 ✔	350.00					350.00 Sales Tax
09/27	Supply Co.	033o/s	1,051.40	1,051.40				
09/30	J. Davies	034 ✔	500.00				500.00	
09/30	S. Jones	035o/s	525.00		525.00			
09/30	D. Spence	036o/s	600.00		600.00			
09/30	Loan	---✔	450.00					450.00 Bank loan
09/30	Charges	---✔	35.00					35.00 S/charges
09/30	Insurance	---✔	120.00					120.00 Insurance
TOTALS:				**$8,431.40**	**$2,251.40**	**$3,030.00**	**$930.00**	**$500.00**
$1,720.00								
			=	+	+	+	+	+

4. Bank reconciliation (balancing the monthly bank account)

Reconciling your bank account monthly is a priority because it's the main bookkeeping control. It's easy to miss entries, transpose figures, or forget an automatic bank deduction. A reconciliation assures you that what you have written in both your cash receipts and disbursement journals balances to your bank statement. It doesn't mean you have allocated the expenses to the right account, but at least every cent is accounted for. Here's how to do it in five simple steps:

Check your accounting When the bank statements arrive for the previous month, close off by performing the following checks:

- All checks should be written in numerical order
- Voided checks should have the number recorded and marked "void"
- Ensure each expense is correctly coded or entered to the journal
- Don't close off either journal until the bank is reconciled
- Ensure all deposits are entered

Compare bank deposits Check each deposit in the cash receipts journal against the bank statement; check it off either with a highlighter or checkmark. Correct wrong or missed deposits and credit memos. Your deposits total should now agree with the bank statement.

Compare checks Sort the canceled checks from your bank statement into numerical order. Using the cash disbursements journal, check off each check under your bank statement's "debit" column against your records. Highlight entries on the bank statement not in your journal—such as service charges or NSF checks—and enter them. The checks in your journal not yet shown on the statement are marked with "o/s"(outstanding). Now total the "bank out" column. When the bank account is reconciled, you can total, cross-add, and balance both journals.

Prepare your manual reconciliation See how it's done for Jason's reconciliation in Figure 11.7 on the next page.

Figure 11.7: **BANK RECONCILIATION: JASON'S GARDEN SERVICE**

Bank Reconciliation: September 30, XXXX

Balance end of August:		$ 4,296.53
September deposits from cash receipts journal:		5,719.92
		10,016.45
September checks from disbursements journal:		(8,587.65)
Balance September 30 (Jason's books):		**$ 1,428.80**
Bank statement balance September 30:		3,678.80
Less outstanding checks:	033	($1,125.00)
	035	(525.00)
	036	(600.00)
Balance as per bank statement:		**$ 1,428.80**

Complete the reconciliation Correct your check book balance if it differs from the reconciliation. If one of the outstanding checks is not listed on the bank statement the following month, carry it forward on your next reconciliation as outstanding and phone the recipient. If the check has not been received, put a stop payment on it and issue another one. Reverse the old check out of your books by entering it in parentheses ($600.00) across the page, then deduct this amount from that month's totals.

5. Petty cash and out-of-pocket expenses

One journal—set up similar to cash disbursements—can record both petty cash and your out-of-pocket expenses. Figure 11.8 shows you how. Set up the expense columns to suit your business. Jason kept a petty cash float and spent some of his own money on business expenses. Initially, he often forgot to ask for a receipt or lost it somewhere in his vehicle. When his accountant explained that he would pay tax on unclaimed expenses, he quickly learned to keep them in order.

QUICK Tip

Maintain a Complete Paper Trail: It is important to keep all receipts for business expenses. It seems you are always digging in your pocket for something. However, with petty cash, ensure there is a valid receipt, not just an IOU, as employees sometimes put their fingers in the cashbox.

Figure 11.8: **PETTY CASH JOURNAL: JASON'S GARDEN SERVICE**

Petty Cash Journal: September 30, XXXX

DATE	PAID TO	PETTY CASH Cr –	CAPITAL IN Cr –	OFFICE Dr +	MATERIAL Dr +	GAS Dr +	OTHER Dr +
09/02	Gas-up	50.00				50.00	
09/04	Office World		45.00	45.00			
09/07	Harry's Place		25.00				25.00 Bus. Lunch
09/09	Haul-it	30.00					30.00 Delivery
09/11	Rockpit	60.00			60.00		
09/15	Drugmart	43.00		43.00			
09/18	Gas-up		20.00			20.00	
09/22	Spark 'N' Shine	15.00					15.00 Windows
09/27	Telemart	35.00					35.00 Phone
TOTALS		**$233.00**	**$90.00**	**$88.00**	**$60.00**	**$70.00**	**$105.00**
		=	=	+	+	+	+

6. Other journals

If you maintain these four journals above and reconcile your bank account monthly, most of your accounting information will be in excellent shape. By keeping your accounting updated, problems can be quickly resolved. If you leave it for a few months, you tend to forget important details and are operating in the dark.

Use the simple systems in this chapter to keep you organized and fiscally fit. Then, if you need a quick financial statement, your accountant can easily prepare one. Many small businesses manage quite efficiently using just one journal, the combined journal, which is explained on page 257.

Other accounting journal requirements are:

Accounts payable journal Most small businesses do not need an accounts payable journal; this system is used more by larger companies, although most accounting programs come with one built in. Whenever you need a financial statement, outstanding accounts payable should be recorded in this journal.

General journal Because this journal records transactions not usually recorded in other journals, these entries are normally prepared by your accountant at year-end or when a financial statement is required. These transactions include depreciation, adjusting prepaid expenses, the business portion of home office and vehicle expenses, corporate taxes due, and inventory changes. Leave these to your accountant—that's why you pay for this service. However, keep a file detailing unusual transactions, such as trades, and explain them to your accountant.

General ledger Monthly totals from all the above journals are entered to the general ledger, which is maintained in order of your chart of accounts and is used to prepare your financial statement. Accounting software enables accountants to take manually prepared journals, enter the monthly totals and other details into their own program, and prepare your general ledger. This is more efficient than spending hours—or even days—manually preparing the information. Because financial statements are prepared from this ledger, accounting information should be accurate. Remember: garbage in, garbage out.

Combined journal This method suits many small businesses with minimum paperwork. Your accountant can easily set one up and show you how it works. The combined journal is so called because sales, cash receipts, cash disbursements, and cash expenses are combined into one book. If you need a more detailed breakdown of sales or expenses, one journal may not work.

Some businesses record more detailed sales information in the back of the combined journal, as journals with more than twenty columns are awkward to use. You then have the cash receipts and disbursements in the front and sales information in the back. When the two meet in the middle, start a new journal; it's a simple system that works well for a small business.

What Does Your Accountant Require?

Your books are closed off to prepare a financial statement at year-end or if you need one during the year. Because a financial statement is a snapshot of your business taken at a particular date, there can be no loose ends. Figure 11.9 on the next page is a checklist of things to do for your accountant.

Your accountant will outline all the required information before a statement is prepared and can often pinpoint areas that appear incorrect. However, your statements could still be inaccurate in areas that your accountant has no control over. They are your responsibility. Here's why:

- Inventory could be incorrectly costed.
- Sales invoices may not have been entered.
- Supplier accounts in the mail are not recorded.
- Expenses are entered to the wrong account.

Mistakes every bookkeeper makes

Countless errors happen with bookkeeping, and I've made them all—repeatedly. After all, we're only human. No one is perfect, we get tired, the phone rings, it's boring, and we lose concentration. These are my excuses—you will undoubtedly create your own as you stumble through this exciting learning experience. Attending evening bookkeeping classes will turn on some light bulbs and convert this foreign language into something less formidable. Once you get the hang of it, it makes a lot of sense.

Figure 11.9: YEAR-END THINGS TO DO ACCOUNTING CHECKLIST

Task	Complete
1. Record all sales invoices and taxes collected.	☐
2. Record all bank deposits and correctly allocate.	☐
3. List outstanding accounts receivable, balanced to your books.	☐
4. Record all checks and correctly allocate.	☐
5. Reconcile bank accounts for the year.	☐
6. List accounts payable, amounts, and what they are for.	☐
7. Complete petty cash and proprietor's cash expense journal.	☐
8. Obtain annual loans statements from lenders and banks.	☐
9. Reconcile outstanding payroll and other tax accounts.	☐
10. List any prepaid expenses (your accountant will check this).	☐
11. Take an accurate physical inventory figure and cost.	☐
12. Prepare information for general journal entries.	☐
13. Total and cross-balance all manual journals.	☐
14. Prepare accountant's copy of computer-generated reports.	☐
15. List all home-office expenses and vehicle mileage.	☐
16. Calculate vehicle business usage.	☐

When your books don't balance, use a slow, methodical process of elimination to find the errors. Here are some common mistakes and their remedies:

- Simple addition and subtraction errors occur as a sales invoice, check, or bank deposit is broken down. Check extensions across the page, line-by-line, to ensure each line crossbalances.

- Figures are transposed. *Here's a hot tip:* If the amount you are out is divisible by 9, check your figures until you find the transposed one. For instance, if $325 is written as $352, the difference is 27, which is divisible by 9. Try this with any figure; it always works.

- You may have incorrectly added a column. Add it up once again.
- You added a credit balance or subtracted a debit balance. (This reverse psychology confuses those new to accounting because bank statements reflect the opposite principle. Ask your accountant or bookkeeper to explain it to you.)
- You incorrectly carried forward totals to the next page. Re-add the totals across the top of the page to ensure they balance.

How Do You Cost Inventory?

Counting and costing inventory are not enjoyable tasks, yet if you make errors, your financial figures will be way out. Inventory is just like having cash in the bank, only it is represented by material items. Although your business software may maintain a theoretical inventory, once a year, this dastardly chore still has to be done because theoretical figures are often wrong.

CASE STUDY: Not Counting the Losses

One retail company I knew carried a large inventory of small items with a valuation of approximately $150,000. They used an industry-specific software program that also recorded a theoretical inventory value. Because counting inventory meant closing the store for a few days, it had not been physically counted for many years. Yet something was wrong with the financial information. When inventory was finally counted, the theoretical figure was $30,000 higher than the physical count. The business immediately lost $30,000 in profit.

Here is the correct way to prepare your inventory:

1. Prepare inventory sheets ready to list each item, quantity, price ,and the extension total.
2. Have two people count each item together.

3. Record each item purchased for resale or used for manufacturing. Don't include fixed assets or stationery.
4. If you have partially completed manufactured or assembled goods, estimate their current value, including labor. These goods are called "work in progress."
5. List damaged, obsolete, or slow-moving items that should be devalued. Try selling them on clearance or dispose of them. Give your accountant a value and list of these goods.
6. Price items at your cost, not retail price.
7. Extend all calculations and have a second person check them. Ensure that handwritten calculations are legible.

What is a "landed cost"?

A landed cost is the total cost of purchasing, assembling, or manufacturing a product. You need this information to determine selling prices and to monitor gross profits and production. For example, if you import shafts and hardware to build garden umbrellas and have a stock of completed shafts, your costings would be calculated as in Figure 11.10.

Figure 11.10: COSTING PRODUCT—GARDEN UMBRELLA SHAFTS

Umbrella shafts, 2 feet long	.90 each
Umbrella shafts, 3 feet long	1.30 each
Metal tapers	.50 each
Hinges	.40 each
	3.10 each
Duty on shafts	.35 each
Duty on hinges & tapers	.25 each
Freight on components	.45 each
Landed cost:	**4.15 each**
Assembly	1.30 each
Completed cost of shaft:	**$5.45 each**

Which Business Expenses Are Tax Deductible?

Most expenses incurred to start and operate a business are deductible, although there are limits to some, and others are *not* allowable. The IRS prefers that you operate with the intention of making a profit and keep expenses within reason. A business making sales of $20,000 a year, incurring $4,000 in promotional meals and claiming a loss of $10,000 will eventually attract their attention. Here are the most common tax-deductible business costs:

1. **Research:** Literature, vehicle expenses, training, start-up kits, travel, and other expenses related to out-of-town conferences and seminars, consultations with professionals, educational courses.
2. **Start-up:** Building repairs, fees and licenses, legal, accounting, business plan, loan application, appraisal and financing fees, leases, telephone lines, printing and stationery, marketing, advertising, samples, promotions.

Leave the Cash under the Table: Don't fall for the trap of hiring people who ask to be paid "cash under the table." Every time you pay cash without getting a receipt, you are not only losing out on your tax deduction, you are understating business expenses and encouraging cheaters to abuse the system. Leave the tax liability to the subcontractor—it's their choice to be honest or not.

3. **Operational:** Costs related to manufacturing or purchasing products for resale. These include raw materials, freight, customs, duty, brokerage fees, inventory, equipment repairs and maintenance, wages, wastage, and damaged inventory.
4. **Direct:** Costs related directly to selling, including sales wages, commissions, referral fees, displays, samples, delivery, discounts, rebates, and coupons.
5. **Overhead:** Expenses incurred to sustain the day-to-day operation of the business. See Figure 11.11 on page 263 for a detailed list. Exceptions include:

- Research and start-up costs are considered capital expenses, deducted over the first five years. Your accountant can suggest ways to claim some of these expenses in the first year.

- Business meals are 50 percent deductible if you are entertaining a client for business purposes. As there are limits to claims for certain types of entertainment, talk to your accountant.
- Clothing and dry cleaning are not usually deductible, but uniforms or "promotional corporate clothing" bearing your business logo are.
- Subcontract and casual labor are deductible if you have a receipt.
- If you incur theft of cash or products, you can claim the portion not compensated by your insurance company.
- Passenger vehicle lease, loan interest, and depreciation—ask your accountant for the annual limits.

What Is a Break-Even Point?

Your break-even point is the amount of sales net of taxes that you must generate to cover all operating costs, excluding profits. Calculate a break-even point for your business plan projections, and once you are operating, recalculate it again based on actual costs. Revisit it regularly; calculating a simple break-even point every few months can ensure that your costs are not getting out of hand.

How do you calculate a break-even point?

If your business is product-based, you must know your approximate gross profit margin. For example, if you operate on a 35 percent gross profit margin—as does the retail furniture store example in Figure 11.11—you need to generate enough profit after purchases to cover all overhead costs. This 35 percent gross profit margin contributes $35 gross profit for each $100 in sales, which in turn pays for the overhead expenses. First list your estimated monthly overhead expenses.

For a service business, simply list the monthly operating costs plus a desired wage and you have your break-even point right there. Calculate your break-even point using Figure 11.11 as your guide.

Figure 11.11 **CALCULATING A SIMPLE MONTHLY BREAK-EVEN POINT**

Direct overhead costs:	
Wages to salesperson	$1,750.00
Delivery	300.00
Damaged goods	150.00
Freight in	75.00
Discounts	220.00
Total direct costs:	**$2,495.00**
Overhead costs:	
Accounting fees	100.00
Advertising	650.00
Bad debts	50.00
Bank charges	60.00
Employee benefits	260.00
Fees, licenses & taxes	30.00
Insurance	75.00
Loan interest	250.00
Promotion	75.00
Promotion–meals	75.00
Office supplies	150.00
Office salaries	1,500.00
Rent	850.00
Repairs–store	50.00
Repairs–equipment	30.00
Sign rental & security	65.00
Telephone, fax & cellular	260.00
Utilities	350.00
Vehicle–gas	110.00
Vehicle–repairs, insurance	200.00
Workers' compensation	35.00
Total overhead costs:	**5,225.00**
Combined overhead costs:	**$7,720.00**

continued

The combined monthly overhead costs are $7,720. This calculation does not include the cost of purchasing furniture, which is taken into the 35 percent gross profit calculation. Now make the following calculation:

$7,720.00 overhead divided by 35 and multiplied by 100 =

$22,057.14 (monthly gross sales)

Gross sales needed for month:	$22,057.00
Furniture cost (65 % of retail price):	14,337.00
Gross profit (35 %):	7,720.00
Overhead costs:	7,720.00
Break-even point:	**$22,057.00**

The store has to generate $22,057 in sales to cover all costs. If the profit margins decrease or expenses increase, a loss will occur. These calculations don't take into account the owner's wages. You must decide how much you need from the business monthly to cover your personal needs. If you need $2,500, calculate as follows:

Total overhead costs:	$7,720.00
Owner's wages:	2,500.00
Total new overhead:	10,220.00
$10,220 divided by 35 and multiplied by 100 =	**$29,200.00**

To pay a $2,500 owner's salary, the store has to generate an additional $7,143.00 in sales.

7,143.00 x 35% gross profit =	$2,500.00

Service business break-even point:

Monthly operating overhead costs:	$1,420.00
Monthly personal wage requirement:	3,000.00
Break-even point:	
	$4,420.00

Knowledge Builds Points: Once you know your break-even point, divide this figure by 4.33 to arrive at a weekly sales figure, or you can even break it down to a daily sales figure. Knowing your daily sales figure target should be motivational—because if you don't know where you are, there is no motivation to reach a goal. If sales are slow, it should motivate you to do something (panic excluded). It helps you to plan your cash flow, motivates you to collect outstanding accounts receivable, and encourages you to strive for better profits.

How Do You Record Vehicle Expenses?

Vehicle expenses are an accountant's nightmare because most people are alarmingly sloppy in this area. Because most proprietors use their personal vehicle for both business and personal use, the business portion of the expense must be calculated. The way this is done depends on the status of the vehicle and the business, including whether:

1. Your business is a proprietorship (or partnership) and you own the vehicle.
2. Your business is incorporated and the business owns the vehicle.
3. Your business is incorporated but you own the vehicle.

1. A proprietorship, you own the vehicle

You operate your vehicle for both business and personal use. How do you track expenses? Purchase an auto mileage log to keep in your vehicle. Note the starting reading on your odometer (for example, 120,000 miles). Each time you use the vehicle for a business-related trip, note the date, your destination and the mileage. At year-end, note the final miles traveled, and total the business miles. You can claim your vehicle expenses two ways (see below), so calculate which one is the better tax advantage for you. As there are many restrictions and exceptions, talk to your accountant or download Publication 463, "Travel, Entertainment, Gift, and Car Expenses" from www.irs.gov/publications.

a. Standard mileage rate In 2004, you can claim 37.5 cents per business-related mile. Commuting to the office does not count, unless you stop to do business; then the mileage begins. If you choose this method in the beginning, you can change the methods back and forth, but not if you start by claiming actual expenses. Makes no sense but that's the rules.

b. Actual expenses, prorated for business use Keep records of all vehicle costs, including gas, licenses, repairs, oil, registration, tires, lease payments, insurance, and loan interest. Your claim will be prorated based on the percentage that you use it for business. Business-related tolls, garage rent, and parking fees are 100 percent tax deductible.

At year-end, your accountant will prepare the following cost calculations. Here is a simple example.

Gas	$1,350	
Repairs and maintenance	850	
Insurance	1,220	
Loan interest	730	
Depreciation ($18,000 value, yr 2)	4,800	
Total costs:	**$8,950**	
Ending miles:	140,225	
Starting miles:	120,000	
Total miles for year:	20,225	
Business usage from log:	14,375	= 71.07%
Allowable claim, actual expenses:	**$ 8,950 x**	**71.07% = $6,360.77**
Allowable claim, standard mileage:	**14,375 x 37.5 cents**	**= $5,390.63**

You can see by this calculation that it is more beneficial to claim the actual expenses than by using the standard mileage calculation. However, if you use the vehicle less than 50 percent for business, you cannot claim a Section 179 deduction.

If you lose a receipt, you will pay more tax. A $20 lost gas receipt could increase your taxes by $5 to $8. The same applies for business miles not logged. The IRS demands that a log be kept for audit purposes or your vehicle claim could be denied. Keep it religiously up-to-date and log every business-related trip, including start-up travel, banking, or the garage for repairs. It mounts up surprisingly quickly.

2. Your incorporated company owns the vehicle

If your incorporated company owns the vehicle, expenses are paid by the corporation. Limitations and certain rulings apply, so talk to your accountant, who will also tell you about the tax implications of the personal usage portion. The IRS does not like people driving Mercedes and writing off all the costs against their businesses, so make the most of the depreciation allowance but be sensible in your vehicle selection.

3. An incorporated company, you own the vehicle

If you use your own vehicle for business in an incorporated company, you are usually considered an employee of the company, and there are options to the way vehicle expenses can be reimbursed. Reimbursements under an accountable plan do not have to be reported as pay, whereas reimbursements under a nonaccountable plan are reported as pay. It is best to consult your accountant for advice on how to best record these expenses.

Be Nice to Your Accountant

If you are still reading, congratulations on sticking with it. You have probably decided by now that the only way to avoid this tedious, time-consuming, brain-draining, paper-shuffling chicken-scratching is to hire a bookkeeper. That's not a bad idea—make it a short-term goal to build your business to be able to do just that. Then you can focus on growing your business. Until then, learn to do it yourself. A good manager understands the financial workings of the business and never completely relinquishes financial control to someone else.

Here is a lighter story from the other side—an accountant's perspective. Think about these poor people as you industriously prepare your year-end accounting, and do the very best job possible.

Accountants are mostly very nice people. It's not their fault they sometimes appear a little stoic or dry. Think about it—if you spent seven years or more studying this profession, you'd probably be a little staid yourself. It's a lot for the brain to digest, and accountants have a huge responsibility to their clients. Their life consists of number-crunching and shoebox sorting, one hand attached permanently to the adding machine, the other on the keyboard or telephone. Accountants have to be serious. Would you appreciate your accountant cracking a joke as he informs you that you are bankrupt?

Taxing Time for All: As January approaches, accountants prepare themselves for the four-month onslaught of paperwork that must be assembled, perfectly processed, and submitted by April 15. Do you, the tax-payer, ever stop to think about the trauma these poor people go through? As the deadline approaches, latecomers line up in droves, clutching piles of triplicate forms and miscellaneous mountains of official paraphernalia.

When all is said and done, accountants are only human, although they are expected to create godlike miracles with your tax returns, wondrously creating refunds from thin air. If taxes are due, of course it is the accountant's fault—don't you agree? There is also a serious misconception that accountants survive on no sleep for four months, work eight days a week, thirty hours a day, and do not make mistakes—all for a modest fee.

You may notice that as the tax deadline approaches, you are greeted by smiles forced through gritted teeth, accompanied by monosyllabic conversations and outsized sighs of despair. If you have acute hearing, you will catch under-the-breath mutterings as you leave the office. Other signs of ATTSS (Accountant's Tax-Time Stress Syndrome) are receivers slamming in clients' ears after their 10 p.m. late-filing phone calls. Don't confuse this with office doors slamming after tardy clients leave, or greetings on the accountant's voice mail informing clients who call at 11 p.m. Sunday evening that they are in Tahiti.

Trembling hands, baggy eyes, nicotine-stained fingers, coffee dribbles on clothes, and nervous twitches are all identifying signs of accountants who suffer this annual affliction. Most symptoms are a direct result of clients leaving their year-end until the last minute, then presenting the whole shooting match in a grocery bag—unsorted, of course—and demanding a refund.

Accountants survive on a different diet than do ordinary people. A real accountant needs five to six pots of coffee daily; half a bottle of stress tabs and assorted vitamins; two cartons of cigarettes; a two-for-one pizza order; and at least half a bottle of premium Scotch, followed by Prozac chasers. If these important daily dietary requirements are not met, your accountant will not survive this crucial time of year. There is no time allocated in the agenda for sleep—this process is time-consuming and the stand-down pay is lousy.

You can easily identify accountants on April 16. Visit the airport and study the departure areas for flights to Alaska, Iceland, Tahiti, Barbados, the Caribbean, Tibet, or Australia. Observe a long line of hunched, ragged robotic types, stumbling to check in. Fifty-five percent of all passengers will be accountants. Then check the bookings for the most desolate and isolated inaccessible fishing or health resorts. Fifteen percent of accountants will be heading for a bush hideaway. Twenty percent fly to Las Vegas with fiendish gleams in their eyes to gamble away your accounting fees. Sadly, if you check the admissions to private and mental health institutions, 5 percent of accountants will be newly registered. Last but not least, the obituary column will reveal the whereabouts of the final 5 percent of this loyal, devoted breed.

But you—yes, you—can help change these sad statistics! Visit your friendly accountant in early January with all your paperwork in neat, organized, and legible order. Stop our dollars from being heavily invested into other countries on accountants' recuperative vacations. Reduce mental health costs, and stop the unnecessary trauma of accountants' funerals and family grief. Make your New Year's resolution now—always be nice to your accountant, get your taxes in early, and don't gripe about your bill.

What Is the Next Step?

Well, this chapter probably put you off wanting a large business. In fact, not everyone wants a big business and the big headaches that can accompany it. Many opt for starting and staying at home—an idyllic place to have a small office and generate a nice little income in the comfort of one's pajamas. Or is it idyllic? Read on and see for yourself.

Chapter 12

Your Home Office—Heaven or Hell?

Home is where the heart (i.e., computer, fax, photocopier, answering machine, telephone, and dirty laundry) is.

- **Is a home office for you?**
- **What's heaven about a home office?**
- **When is a home office hell?**
- **What home office tax deductions are available?**
- **Can you handle the home office challenges?**

Is a Home Office for You?

As technology embraces the world and makes doing business from a bedroom an achievable goal, countless entrepreneurs of all ages opt for starting a home-based business. Approximately 50 percent of start-ups are operated from the home, as entrepreneurs seek low-cost, workable solutions to tackle the work/life balance and family demands.

Having worked in a storefront office for many years before moving my business home in 1986, I couldn't entertain the thought of working anywhere else. There is no substitute for living on a small acreage on a quiet and friendly street, surrounded by birds, horses, wildlife, trees, and peace and quiet. This serene atmosphere allows one the luxury of uninterrupted work without uninvited guests.

Did I say quiet and uninterrupted? Who am I fooling? This long-term SOHO (sole operator home office) stint has allowed me to experience just about every conceivable situation, both good and bad. Evaluate for yourself whether a home-based office will suit your needs, because working from home is not everyone's cup of mocha. Most people think it will be wonderful, until reality sets in and they experience the isolation and other inherent home-office problems. Read on to decide whether you are cut out for this lifestyle.

The dreamers

Starry-eyed entrepreneurs-to-be imagine an idyllic scenario—shuffling into the office in pajamas and slippers, sipping coffee and ready to start work at 9:30 a.m., or putting on the voice mail to slide off for a round of golf. Although there is nothing stopping you from doing this, to survive a home-office environment, you need military-style discipline and planning. You may start your day with good intentions, but "things" always happen that are beyond your control. Four stray cows on the front lawn will destroy your well-planned day. Mothers in particular find working from a home office a complex, frustrating, hectic, job-juggling experience requiring phenomenal patience and split-second time management.

What's heaven about a home office?

As times and people's lives change, a home office can be the solution to a multitude of problems and have the following advantages.

1. Low overhead

A home office eliminates many overhead expenses that even a small leased office incurs. Leases, phone lines, fancy office furniture, utilities, signs, and reception costs are expensive. First impressions are important when clients enter a business, and cheap furnishings don't make a good first impression. You have to generate high sales just to cover overhead costs. What a waste of profits. Wouldn't you prefer they go in your pocket rather than to the landlord?

The office should be staffed from nine to five. Nothing irritates a customer more than a sign reading "Closed for lunch—back in half an hour." A walk-in customer may not come back. Haven't you experienced this same frustration? A home-based office means you don't have to staff the office at lunchtime or eat a brown-bag lunch.

2. Home-office tax deductions

Just like any business, your home incurs operating costs. With a home-based office, a portion of these costs are claimed on your tax return (discussed later). The IRS only allows you to claim home-based office expenses if it is the business' head office, and there are exceptions and limitations.

3. Flexibility in planning

Family: The flexibility of operating a home office is attractive to parents, particularly mothers. You can take children to school and after-school activities, and if the school phones to say your daughter is ill, you can pick her up and take care of her at home. My daughter was ill for two weeks, and although her demanding presence was trying, working from home was a blessing.

Hours: If you are ill, you can use voice mail or take the cordless phone to bed. If you lose time during the day, can't meet a deadline, or the computer crashes, you can burn the midnight oil in pajamas and slippers. Client appointments can be organized around your schedule. If you are a late riser or a night owl, you can often book appointments at a time convenient to you. Portable phones make life easier: you can be in the garden (or the washroom) without using voice mail. The trap, of course, is the temptation to become a workaholic and let the business run you, instead of the other way around.

Break the Ice: If you think new clients may feel uncomfortable visiting a home-based office, make them feel at ease. When making the first appointment, ask whether they prefer tea or coffee and let them know a muffin is waiting. This strategy usually breaks the ice.

If you don't have a consulting room, keep one room comfortable and spotless and meet there. My clients like to sit in the bright and cheery family room, where they can watch (and sometimes visit) the horses and see an attractive garden. A comfortable setting usually relaxes first-time clients.

Lunch: You can use up leftovers for lunch instead of buying a calorie-laden lunch and read newspapers or open mail. You can walk around the garden or the block to get some energizing exercise and stress relief. My horse always neighs for his lunch at noon, so there is no option but to stop work, break out the hay, and then go for a brisk walk to refresh the brain.

Dress: When you are not expecting clients, you can dress casually instead of donning business attire, saving on your clothing costs. Dress neatly however—someone will catch you if you work in your robe until eleven in the morning. You won't work productively in your robe and without a shower.

4. Security and disaster control

Working at home brings a strong sense of security, as you know there won't be a burglary, which often happens when people are away at work. If something goes wrong, you can immediately deal with it. I have dealt with disasters ranging from freezing and flooding to snowbound famine; malfunctioning appliances, toilets, and garage doors; burst pipes, overflowing gutters, sick animals, and children; lost puppies, stray cows, and injured family members. As inconvenient as it is, it's good to be there when disaster strikes, although when your spouse arrives home asking, "Did you have a nice day dear?" the answer is not always yes.

5. Safety in inclement weather

Driving during freezing rain, black ice, whiteouts, blizzards, flooding, wind, ice storms, and heavy snowfalls is potentially life-threatening. With a home office, you can continue working in these conditions without taking one step outside into the danger zone. Feel deep sympathy for those brave entrepreneurs who must open their doors on these treacherous mornings.

6. Parents can be parented

An increasing number of baby boomers have the added responsibility of caring for their aging parents in their home. A home-based office caters to this need. Although aging parents can be demanding and time-consuming, it is peace of mind to know that they are close should an emergency arise. My dear mother—aged ninety-five, bless her heart—is now an important part of our family.

When Is a Home Office Hell?

So far it's all sounding heavenly, so what is hellish about a home office? A majority of home-based businesses don't fly because of lack of structure, discipline, and self-motivation. It's not easy being stuck alone in a small bedroom office—particularly if you have come from a corporate environment. You might notice that this list of potential problems is longer than the "heavenly" one.

1. Business is not taken seriously

Only you can set your goals and decide whether you are going to get serious about your business. Many people putter along at home without goals, business plans, or structure. Because you work alone, you must design a structured working environment. If you don't take your business seriously, how can you expect your family, clients, and friends to?Learn to practice the three Rs:

- Routine: set a daily routine and follow it
- Rules: instigate work rules for your family
- Reinforce: both of the above regularly

Hold a family meeting to stress to your spouse and children that your work at home is important to you. Ask them to respect the ground rules—and be patient. It may take everyone time to adjust to the new situation. Once you set the rules, don't bend them or you will lose the family's respect.

Part-time operators should allocate two or three set days for work and others for family. Inform family that on your "at-home" days, you are completely available for them and their interests. On workdays, always make quality time for your children afterward. You will accomplish more by structuring your time and won't feel guilty for ignoring the children.

Use a Full Day: If you have children, plan to work beyond school hours by organizing a babysitter or after-school care. Otherwise, you will lose valuable work time through days being constantly interrupted. During those workdays, make every hour productive or you will never feel any sense of accomplishment.

2. Families may not be "trained"

Before you start a home-based office, sit down with your spouse and discuss the business, as you will need his or her complete support. Then talk about it with your children. Working from home can affect family routines and lifestyles, and their support is necessary. It can be difficult to ignore their demands. You have to train them to respect the fact that you are working, and this is no easy task.

Younger children often find your working at home a difficult concept to grasp. Mothers will need more help with household chores to prevent burnout, so allocate chores to both spouse and children, even if you have to increase allowances to get this help. Instill the entrepreneurial spirit into your children at a young age.

Circumstances will arise when children do answer the telephone, so for these occasions, teach them to answer politely with the business name. With so many choices in modern communication and technology, there are inexpensive options to help solve the home office telephone problems.

Get Phone Smart: Teach children telephone etiquette and use a "smart ring"phone system, where one ring denotes a business call and the other a personal call. Don't give friends your business number. You then have the choice of whether to answer the home line while you are working. Instruct your children not to pick up the telephone when it rings during business hours, as it sounds unprofessional to the caller and you could lose a potential customer.

3. Neighbors can be a nuisance

If your neighbors are a friendly bunch, you will have to train them too. The hardest ones to train are those who don't work, as they can't relate to a structured home-office environment. They have a habit of dropping by for a quick cup of coffee and staying forever.

When the doorbell rings and it's a neighbor, answer wearing glasses, holding a pen, a pile of papers, and the portable phone. Answer the door with, "Oh, hi Julie, can't talk, I have a strict deadline to meet. My how I envy you not having to work!"

When neighbors phone to chat, tell them, "I'm up to my ears in paperwork, can I call you after supper?" or "I have a deadline to meet, I work Fridays, you know." After much practice you will get these lines down pat and the message will eventually get through. Learn to be tough.

4. Home chores tempt the weak

It's difficult to ignore all the chores beckoning you. You may be tempted to load the laundry while you are working—but don't do it! You don't need any distractions. Abandon all thoughts of housework. If you can't complete chores before nine in the morning, leave them until after five. Just ensure the house or office is presentable if clients are expected. The rest can—and must—wait.

If you don't keep to a regular schedule, working at home will become a stressful nightmare. Many women try to be Supermom by running their business and trying to do all the chores. It doesn't work. Budget a few dollars every two weeks and bring in a housecleaner.

5. You are easily isolated

Isolation is a common and difficult problem to overcome, and it takes a real effort to become visible to both clients and your business community. Marketing is difficult enough for any business, but it's even harder from a home-based office. To stay in touch with the business world and to find and network with potential clients, you have to get out of your home office.

QUICK Tip

Get Out of the 10 x 12: The phone won't ring unless you create action. A reminder: join associations, networks, the chamber of commerce or Rotary, and become visible. Find one organization that really interests you, so you can also enjoy a social life. Initially, it's easier to network among friends and acquaintances than in a room full of strangers. Make a point of attending a business-related function or having a lunch or coffee meeting at least once a week.

6. Lack of motivation

You are now the boss, the only person who decides the future of your business. Motivation is synonymous with goal setting, passion, organization, confidence, and communication. No one else cares whether your business is working or not—this is your job. An organized, structured routine, a sound and workable business plan, and a love for your work are all motivational factors that should inspire you to move forward.

Here are some words to delete from your vocabulary: "later," "lethargy," "apathy," "I can't," "tomorrow," "I'm scared," "no time," and "it can wait." Keeping a positive attitude is so necessary. Instead, add these words to your daily vocabulary: "drive," "positive," "organized," "incentive," "inspirational," "initiative," "ambitious," "priorities," "I can," and "now." Even more important, remember your dreams and goals and affirm them daily.

7. Good weather means playtime

As silly as it sounds, fine weather makes working at home difficult. If your office or work space becomes stuffy, concentration levels drop and thoughts of going outside become urgent. If the temptation is too great, plan to work to a certain time and take a couple of hours off to enjoy the sun. You will achieve more by motivating yourself to finish in time, you'll not feel cheated of some playtime, and you will probably work twice as hard.

The alternative is to start work earlier, take a sun break, or work in the evenings. During the summer I sometimes ride my horse in the cool of the morning. I achieve more by not depriving myself of this ultimate pleasure. If you can successfully combine work and play, do it. You will feel motivated, exercised, relaxed, and ready to toil again.

8. Difficult to keep to routines

A home office requires strict self-discipline. Businesses remain mediocre without a disciplined mind; working at home compounds the problem. Start at the same time each morning, take regular mini-breaks and a lunch break, and don't finish until 5 p.m. Something will always interrupt your work, so deal with unscheduled dilemmas as they occur. Ensure you put in at least six productive hours a day.

CASE STUDY: The Corporate Commute

A corporate executive of many decades was downsized and decided to consult from home. No matter how hard he tried, he couldn't adjust to walking from the bedroom to the corporate home office. He couldn't focus, concentrate, or get motivated. In desperation, he dressed for the old office each morning, made his coffee, and got into his car, drove a few miles, in traffic and "arrived" at his corporate home office, ready to start work. The "commute" enabled him to get his mind into gear as he had done for so many years sitting in traffic. Do whatever works for you.

9. You eat, sleep, and breathe work

You may close your office door, but switching off the brain is not as easy. It's so important to establish a daily routine whereby you mentally switch off at the same time each day. If you work in the evenings, stop in time to mentally wind down before sleep. Do some stretches to relax and read a novel in bed before going to sleep.

Clients forget that you have another life besides work and will call at all hours unless you train them. Most new entrepreneurs make the mistake of allowing after-hours calls rather than offending new clients—we have all been guilty of that.

QUICK Tip

Get Physical: Plan some daily physical activity—do a little gardening, take a short walk, or go swimming. Pursue some home interests that are strictly yours, such as painting, reading, carpentry, or working out in your home gym. Find at least one personal interest that gets you out of the house to refresh and relax your racing brain cells.

Don't accept business calls after hours, excluding emergencies. Inform new clients of your working hours and tell them that quality family time is a priority. Most people respect this. If clients call on evenings or weekends, tell them you are busy and will return their call in the morning. If you have to work at night, stop by 9 p.m. and relax for an hour or two before bedtime. Otherwise, your brain will work all night and you'll awaken feeling exhausted, listless, and unmotivated. Remember: We work to live, not live to work.

10. Business outgrows the home

Growth can become a big headache if your business suddenly needs more space and there is nowhere in the home to expand. You also may not be large enough to move out of your incubator and into larger, leased premises. Your work becomes hampered by a disorganized work space. Your mind becomes as cluttered as your desk

When reaching this stage, some people impulsively rent commercial space without being financially or mentally ready for this huge step. This is why planning your future goals and cash flow projections is crucial. In the planning stages, estimate the maximum space needed to reach your projected sales working from home.

Crunch the Numbers: Determine by the projected sales figures when you will need larger premises or employees—or both, and research and know this information before start-up. You will then know if those sales can support the extra overhead. If they can't, think how you could reorganize your home space or research other alternatives.

What Home Office Tax Deductions Are Available?

Because your home office replaces leased or purchased space, most costs related to that space are tax deductible. There are limitations to what is considered business use and also a deduction limit for part-year use. Discuss this with your accountant and read the IRS's downloadable Publication 587, "Business Use of Your Home." Deductions are calculated proportionately, based on the number of square feet your home business occupies. This includes storage sheds or outbuildings used for business purposes. First measure the home's total square footage including outbuildings to be used. Then, calculate the square footage of the business portion. Figure 12.1 on the next page demonstrates how this calculation is done.

Major repairs, such as replacing a roof, will be amortized by your accountant over a number of years as the full cost cannot be written off in a one-year period. The same rule applies to major renovations specifically for housing the business, such as an extension to your office.

Maintain good records

Keep all home-related expenses in a file for year-end so your accountant can include them in both your accounting records and your business tax

Figure 12.1: CALCULATING HOME OFFICE USE

Your office is 12' x 14', and you use a 15' x 12' garage as work space, so the business portion of your home is 348 square feet. The house is 1,750 square feet in total, so the business portion is calculated as a percentage of the whole home, in this case 19.89 percent. Deductible expenses are:

1. Mortgage interest (or rent)	$ 5,700
2. Real estate taxes	2,120
3. Utilities	2,310
4. Security system	470
5. Repairs and maintenance	1,630
6. House insurance	770
7. Depreciation	170
Total annual costs:	**$ 13,170**

Business portion: $\frac{\$13{,}170 \times 348 \text{ sq. ft.}}{1{,}750 \text{ sq. ft.}} = \$2{,}618.95$ **or 19.89%**

return. As home-maintenance costs mount up quickly, keep good records of all costs. Small items such as vacuum bags, garden maintenance costs, cleaners, and coffee for clients constitute part of your home-office expenses.

If you don't have a business telephone line, you can't claim the first residential line rental. When the telephone bill arrives, separate out the business portion, pay that portion of the bill with a business check, and pay the personal portion with a personal check. At year-end, prepare these costs for your accountant as per Figure 12.1 above, including the square footage. This saves your accountant time and you money.

Home usage exceptions

There are some exceptions to home-based business usage and its space calculations. One example is a daycare business, which is calculated on a different formula:

$$\frac{1{,}350 \text{ sq. ft.}}{1{,}800 \text{ sq. ft.}} \times \frac{12 \text{ hours}}{24 \text{ hours}} \times \frac{5 \text{ days}}{7 \text{ days}} \times \frac{50 \text{ weeks}}{52 \text{ weeks}} \times \underline{\$7{,}000} = \$1{,}802.88$$

This formula takes into account the number of rooms used for daycare, over the total square footage, multiplied by the number of hours in a day the home is used for business, multiplied by the number of days a week the business is open, multiplied by the number of weeks in a year it is operated, multiplied by the total home expenses! Your accountant will figure it out.

Snacking Short Cut: Keeping tabs on the cost of food for your daycare business can be an accounting nightmare. Use the IRS's standard meal and snack rates and a daily log. See page 29 of Publication 587 for an excellent downloadable weekly log.

Filing your tax return

A proprietorship must file a Schedule C (Form 1040), "Profit or Loss from Business," to report income and expenses, along with a Form 8829, "Expenses for Business Use of the Home," plus a Form 4562, "Depreciation and Amortization." The deductions can be used to bring your profit to zero but cannot be used to create a loss situation. If your business makes a loss before these deductions or the deductions exceed your profit, the remaining home-office deductions are carried forward to a year when they can be utilized. Some businesses often have thousands of dollars in unusable home-office deductions because their profit never exceeds their operating expenses.

Can You Handle the Home Office Challenges?

Working from home suits many people, but for others, it's a disaster. Running a successful SOHO takes practice. Think carefully and complete the checklist in Figure 12.2 on the following page before making a decision. Revisit it after operating for a few months and compare answers. Will your home office be heaven—or hell?

Figure 12.2: **CAN I HANDLE THE HOME OFFICE CHALLENGES?**

Can you answer yes to at least fifteen questions?	**Yes**	**No**
1. I have discussed having a home-based business with my family.	☐	☐
2. My spouse/partner fully supports my business.	☐	☐
3. I have focused goals and timelines.	☐	☐
4. I have, and will use, my business plan.	☐	☐
5. I intend to take this business seriously.	☐	☐
6. I have given my children chores and responsibilities.	☐	☐
7. I have organized a professional phone answering system.	☐	☐
8. My family understands the telephone rules.	☐	☐
9. I have informed neighbors and friends of my working hours.	☐	☐
10. I have structured set working hours and days.	☐	☐
11. I have organized after-school care on those days.	☐	☐
12. I will not do home chores during working hours.	☐	☐
13. I have joined business/networking associations.	☐	☐
14. I have joined a club/organization of personal interest.	☐	☐
15. I will ensure that I get enough physical activity.	☐	☐
16. I will plan quality family time daily.	☐	☐
17. I will maintain a positive attitude.	☐	☐
18. I will close the office door at least two hours before bed.	☐	☐
19. I will inform new clients of my working hours.	☐	☐
20. I have organized support services for my aging parents.	☐	☐
21. I have enough space to operate the business for two years.	☐	☐
22. I have calculated when the business will outgrow this space.	☐	☐

23. I have additional residential space I can use as I grow.	☐	☐
24. I checked regulations to see if I can hire employees at home.	☐	☐
25. I know the sales point and cost of moving to larger premises.	☐	☐

What Is the Next Step?

Well, you are nearly there—on the way to becoming a successful entrepreneur. This book is your companion and guide to help ensure that each step you take is a step in the right direction. Consider setbacks as challenges you can conquer, turn adversity into an advantage, keep positive, and keep learning. We don't stop learning until we start pushing up daisies. The next chapter highlights some successful entrepreneurs who each have experienced all the pitfalls and pleasures of self-employment. Be inspired by their stories. The next step is up to you.

Chapter 13

What Will Your Story Be?

Now make your dream a reality, because you know where you are going and what you are doing.

- **Traveling the entrepreneurial road**
- **Las Vegas SBDC clients are all winners**
- **Some food for thought**
- **Lost job, found passion**
- **Kilts to the hilt**
- **Cashing in on chores**
- **In closing**

Traveling the Entrepreneurial Road

There's a lot of information in this book that takes time to digest. You'll probably want to read it a few times to absorb the messages. If you follow the advice and your business choice is sound, you are on your way to a new, exciting way of life. Don't expect your path to be easy; a new business takes hard work and commitment. You will grow as you learn and be enriched with new knowledge and skills.

To further inspire you, here are some entrepreneurs' stories that run the gamut, from a man's kilt manufacturer in Seattle, Washington, to a concierge and errand consulting business in Apex, North Carolina. Read of their battles, victories, and success secrets as they travel their entrepreneurial roads.

These stories focus on business owners who for the most part have used the services of the U.S. Small Business Administration (SBA) and Small Business Development Centers (SBDCs) across America to successfully start and grow their businesses. There are three from Nevada. I was so impressed with them all that I couldn't choose which one to include, so they all became a part of this book. The final story is a tale of sheer persistence and lessons learned from the school of hard knocks. It highlights some familiar battles that many entrepreneurs experience and will no doubt relate to. However, this story is different. Where many would have quit, this couple turned what could have been a story of failure into a remarkably diversified business with a niche.

My intent in this chapter is to encourage you to follow your dreams and consult with professionals; the rewards are bountiful. These businesses are not large, yet each person and their partners had a vision, had the desire to succeed, and had identified unique niches that needed filling. Enjoy and be inspired.

Las Vegas SBDC Clients Are All Winners

In a city renowned for gambling, where losers far outweigh winners, the Nevada Small Business Development Center beats those odds hands down. Here are the stories of three winning entrepreneurs who readily credit their success to the support and help of the staff at the SBDC. Passionate about what they do, each business owner derives inner rewards by solving people's problems.

It's Simple.biz

A stay-at-home mom living in rural Montana with an eighteen-month-old child, Susan Jamerson was devastated when her husband suddenly died of a heart attack. With fifteen years documentary filmmaking under her belt and now widowed, Susan tried procuring government filmmaking contracts, but the process was difficult.

She had lived four blocks from a SBDC office but had never noticed it. By working with the center, she discovered a grant was available to help people in rural communities through the U.S. Department of Agriculture's Innovative Research Program. Susan's idea started to take shape.

After traveling to Nevada to meet with various agencies, she moved to Reno, started Jamerson & Associates LLC, and secured two USDA grants—a first-time accomplishment for a Nevada business.

After performing in-depth market research and holding focus groups for a year, Susan produced a video, *Starting a Business in Nevada*, funded by the Nevada Commission on Economic Development. The second grant funded the building of her website, www.itssimple.biz. The site, which took two years to build, officially launched nationally in October 2003.

The site is packed with resources and every tool a new entrepreneur could ever need. It is most comprehensive. Susan's aim was to produce a portal to help people in rural areas who didn't have access to mentoring or formal training facilities. Still new to cyberspace, the site boasts 125,000 visitors a month.

As her business developed, Susan has worked hand-in-hand with SBDC and SBA offices across America, working particularly closely with the Reno and Nevada offices. "Michael Graham, the deputy state director of the Las Vegas office, has been my mentor," says Susan. "In fact, he changed my life with his advice. The SCORE counselors and SBA staff are all my partners."

Susan and her new husband purchased and renovated a building and have two employees. There are future exciting plans to partner with SBDCs to launch online distance training in three states, with the goal of going national.

A real winner who earned her jackpot, Susan was honored in 2003, receiving the U.S. Small Business Administration's Nevada Small Business Research Award. Don't miss her website at www.itssimple.biz.

Housing Helpers®

After moving from Denver, Colorado in 1999, Don Twining started Housing Helpers after his research showed Las Vegas to be the second-fastest-growing city in the United States—a winning decision. Don has had ongoing help, guidance, support, and financing from the SBDC and SBA, and his annual sales have amazingly increased, going from $10,000 to $130,000 a month. His original staff of three, including his partner and wife Susan, has increased to thirteen employees.

Initially a roommate matching service, Housing Helpers now offers a wide range of services catering to people on the move. Free long-term housing relocation and rental finding assistance—including apartments, condos, and houses—furnished corporate and vacation rentals, and a full-service real estate company round out a smorgasbord of relocation services encompassing Denver, Boulder, Las Vegas, and surrounding communities.

A year after Don started, he found a wealth of help and hands-on support through the Nevada SBDC. "By following Michael Graham's advice on signage and attending the sign expos he sent me to, choosing and retaining the right employees, and other business strategies, my business dramatically increased," says Don. "My recently installed exterior sign is forty feet high and cost $40,000. I'm positive that it will more than pay for itself in the first year."

When Don needed a CPA to understand his needs and better structure the accounting, the SBDC provided an advisor to find the right accountant. When he needed to purchase an office building, the SBDC helped him to acquire a 7(a) loan through the SBA. That property has more than doubled in value.

Don credits his successful growth to extensive research, having a good business plan with the money to support it, and by setting daily, weekly, monthly, and yearly goals, which he writes down and revisits daily. "Goal-setting really works," says Don. "I also work with the SBDC all the time. My next big challenge is knowing how to take the next big step to help us grow the business even more."

With Don's business acumen and willingness to work with and listen to professionals, it's in the cards that his next step will be a winning hand. Learn more at www.housinghelpers.com.

Moms in Business Network

Gina Robison-Billups's business filled a necessary niche quite by accident. While working in her family's entertainment business—and trying to juggle the demands of a baby and young family—Gina discovered the isolation and frustration of being a working mom. She also discovered that there wasn't a support system in place in Nevada to help. Deciding to start a working moms' network, Gina placed one small announcement in a local newspaper. Thirty phone calls later, the first professional organization for working mothers was born, the Moms in Business Network (MIBN).

When Gina was discouraged after a few meetings with low attendance, her mother suggested she try just one more month. At that meeting, Gina was offered a free booth at a women's expo, where she gathered names from two hundred interested women. This confirmed her research: help with the work/business/life/family balance was not readily available through other organizations.

In just a couple of short years, the interest in and growth of MIBN has been phenomenal. From fifteen people at the first meeting, MIBN now boasts over eight thousand members and subscribers from across the country, with the potential of another forty thousand members through one company currently being negotiated. MIBN members include entrepreneurial and employed mothers, foster and stepmothers, single dads, and stay-at-home-moms, as well as companies that support working mothers by providing membership benefits to their employees.

Membership includes a host of benefits, seminars, workshops, conferences, and discounts. Gina is now working with the SBDC Disadvantaged Outreach Program to develop a program to help women become certified business owners and apply for government contracts. She recently formed an alliance with the National Federation of Independent Businesses (NIFB).

The need for Gina's network is already nationally proven and her work recognized. She was named the 2003 U.S. Small Business Administration's Home-Based Business Advocate of the Year for the state of Nevada. "The SBDC is a huge source of support," says Gina, "They are my cheerleaders. Michael Graham and Hank Pinto think that what I am doing is so important, they won't let me quit. The people are amazing; they show a lot of pride and caring." Learn more about Gina and the MIBN at www.mibn.org.

As millions of gamblers lose their shirts to Nevada casinos each year, the SBDCs work hard to ensure that their entrepreneurial clients are well educated against the risks and pitfalls of owning a business. Although the stakes are high, their failure rate is low and their clients are the winners.

Some Food for Thought: Family Food Distributors Inc.

When Patricia Mendez met her husband John Rivas in 1999, they shared a common passion—food. Patricia had thirteen years' management experience in the food distribution industry, and John had owned a supermarket and his family a restaurant.

An immigrant from Ecuador in 1989, Patricia recognized a niche that needed filling: supplying nostalgic food products to Ecuadorian immigrants who missed their favorite homeland foods. John and Patricia's daughter Andrea were eager to start a family business.

With little money, they purchased their first vehicle, an old van for $700. Initially a partnership, Family Food Distributors Inc. of Kearny, New Jersey, was now open for business. They began operations in February 2002 from their home. Within two months, the house became crammed with pallets of products. Patricia found a warehousing company that rented them affordable space for two to three pallets, which quickly grew to two to three truckloads.

Research indicated that competition was less fierce in outlying areas such as Connecticut, so they marketed to areas outside of the larger cities, selling into supermarkets, specialty stores, and travel agencies. "Smaller stores move as much product as large ones," says Patricia. "They are as important to us, and we give great customer service. We aren't and don't want to be the cheapest, but we do supply a complete line of products."

After two years, the warehousing company was moving, so the business had to move. In summer 2003, needing help and financing, Patricia met with assistant director Dennis Rasugu of the New Jersey Small Business Development Center in Newark. Dennis asked if she had a business plan. "No," answered Patricia. "What's that?"

Under Dennis's guidance, Patricia enrolled in an eight-week course at the Entrepreneurial Training Institute, learning valuable business skills and how to prepare a business plan. Upon graduation, she was assigned a mentor for eighteen months. Good things started to happen. *The Star Ledger,* New Jersey's largest newspaper, wrote an article about the business. James E. McGreevey, the governor of New Jersey, was announcing at a conference employment statistics that the state had helped to create. Inviting the family, they were cited as great examples of a business creating jobs.

Currently, Dennis is helping the business obtain commercial financing through the New Jersey Economic Development Agency. "The SBDC has been so resourceful and helpful," says Patricia, "and their help is free. You have to be persistent and willing to work hard—we work twelve to sixteen hours a day. My daughter Andrea is twenty-three, and she works full-time with us and studies business management full-time at Rutgers University."

Family Food Distributors Inc. now has an office and warehouse of five thousand square feet, a subleased truck and new van, and six full-time and two part-time employees. Its continued growth and success of should give new entrepreneurs some real food for a thought. Contact Patricia at familyfooddist@aol.com.

Lost Job, Found Passion: PR Enterprises LLC

"We're going to dinner to celebrate!" said Pam to Elizabeth, her ten-year-old daughter, when she picked her up from school one day in January of 2000.

"Why are we celebrating?" asked Elizabeth.

"Because I just lost my job," replied Pam.

"You've lost your mind!" quipped her daughter.

"No dear, we're starting my new business, PR Enterprises, today."

Starting a business wasn't a sudden decision for Pam; she had long been thinking about it. Her ten years' relationship sales and marketing experience for nonprofit organizations, plus seven years in trust sales and small business banking, made her well equipped to start a marketing business.

In September 1999, at the time a single mother, Pam had attended a Women Mean Business conference sponsored by the Small Business Development Center in Lexington, Kentucky. She met a business coach who asked her in-depth questions about her business idea. It seemed like a viable proposition. After losing her job twice in three years due to corporate downsizing, Pam was finally ready to go it alone six months later, starting on Saint Patrick's Day, 2000.

Through volunteer work, she met an attorney whose firm needed marketing help, so she had her first client. They are still clients today. Pam had also been referring small business clients from the bank to the SBDC, who in turn became one of her first clients when they hired her to help coordinate the Women Mean Business conference.

With help and advice from the SBDC, Pam put together her business plan to offer event planning, sales and marketing consulting, etiquette training, and coaching to businesses. The SBDC guided her through many challenges, including assessing the competition, setting her prices, and looking at the big picture. She continues to seek their advice with ongoing growth strategies. The relationship paid dividends. In 2002, Pam was recognized as the New Business Owner of the Year by the Lexington chapter of the National Association of Women Business Owners.

Today Pam has grown her home-based business enough to utilize the services of six independent contractors plus a part-time administrative assistant. "My business plan certainly looks different than it did four years ago," says Pam Berryman Larson. She is now happily remarried, with a supportive husband, and her daughter helps Pam with her Mystery By Design events. "Nearly half of my business comes from coaching, and we have refined our services to etiquette programs for businesses and the murder mystery events, which are popular with corporations conventions, and even motor coach tours," Pam adds with pride, "I didn't borrow any money for three-and-a-half years, but now I utilize a business line of credit."

Her's is a real success story for someone who was a single, out-of-work mom just a few short years ago. By leveraging her passion and expertise and by consulting with the professionals at the SBDC, Pam is carefully building an enjoyable, profitable family business and is now publishing the Lexington Women's Magazine. Learn more about what she does at www.p-r-e.com.

Kilts to the Hilt—Building on Change: The Utilikilts Company

From Glasgow, Scotland, to Sydney, Australia, the unique concept of men in skirts attracts enormous global coverage. The Utilikilts Company was a struggling two-person business in 2000; it has since grown to fifteen employees, with sales projected at $2 million for 2004.

Such growth was not Steven Villegas's plan when he sold his first kilt in 2000. Nor were men's skirts a part of his dream in 1996 when he wanted to launch a traveling theater housed in a convoy of double-decker buses with a goal of heightening social awareness. Instead, over thirty thousand kilts later, the Utilikilts Co. is realizing a dream of making positive social change through selling skirts to men and instigating socially aware corporate policies and practices.

Utilikilts is succeeding because Steven, and Utilikilts cofounder Megan Haas, share a business philosophy in which standards, ideals, and positive change are paramount. Their mission statement clearly defines their goals. "Utilikilts seeks to set a global example, defining 'business with a conscience' and channeling company gains and resources back into the community."

The concept of men in kilts is not new, but the concept of contemporary men wearing skirts and kilts to work and play does attract ongoing worldwide attention. Yet when the Utilikilts Company needed money to grow its Seattle business, the banks were not interested. The product was different, as were the founders' business and life philosophies.

Steven attended a U.S. Small Business Administration workshop on obtaining financing, but he says, "It wasn't for me, it sounded too complicated." In the fall of 2000, his sister Danielle Villegas, now the company's chief operating officer, joined the team, and with the help of another new employee, Bill Geurts, a former bank controller, the company put together a business plan to present to the Seattle SBA. The plan and paperwork took a few frustrating months to complete—months of being short of operating capital before their first microloan was approved.

"The SBA took us on when no one else would," says Steven, "and they advanced another 7(a) loan for over $100,000 a couple of years ago." Now, Utilikilts is the Levi's of kilts, the largest kilt/skirt manufacturer in the world. The company was recently awarded the Mayor of Seattle's 2004 Small Business Award and the Better Business Bureau's 2004 Innovative Business Practices Award.

Utilikilt customers love the product, the company, and what it stands for. "Our customers are so supportive," says Megan. "In return, we created the Northwest Kilt Exchange, a program where customers can volunteer to nonprofits and receive a kilt in exchange. We're represented in the media solely by our customers, and our message, when it comes to our product and our views on social responsibility, is that everyone has a choice."

Using a business plan to raise funding for start-up and growth and having key, experienced people on board have provided the company with a solid foundation. This story presents only a glimpse of a unique and inspiring success story. Few business owners achieve the winning combination of experiencing business success and fulfilling their social values and goals. Discover more about Utilikilts' global success at www.utilikilts.com.

Cashing in on Chores: Triangle Concierge Inc.

How did two entrepreneurs who admit to doing many things wrong successfully turn their business around? It took the combination of having a powerful partnership, refocusing, having strong ethics, and "niching" into a relatively new industry.

It's fine to be on the cutting edge of a trend, but when you are part of creating that trend, the battle is slow and frustrating. Katharine Giovanni is the cofounder of a unique global organization, the International Concierge and Errand Association. She and her husband Ron Giovanni operate four home-based businesses, the principal one being Triangle Concierge Inc.

What is a concierge? According to the association's brochure, a concierge does everything, "a jack-of-all-trades, time broker, the great equalizer, convenience services, a magician, and meaningful relief." In such busy times, all are necessary services for both small businesses and large corporations.

Katharine and Ron became involved quite by accident. Katharine had ten years' meeting planning experience and Ron twelve years of sales experience. In 1993, they decided to start Meeting Planners Plus in New Jersey. Factor in two children, no formal business experience or professional help, plus a move to North Carolina, growing their business was not an easy road to travel.

In 1996, they realized that a large component of their meeting planners business involved concierge work. Research exposed few similar businesses and even fewer people willing to impart information, so start-up was difficult. Katharine designed and launched their website. A few months later, they began to get calls from people wanting start-up advice.

"Why are you giving so much free advice?" Ron asked Katharine one day as she hung up from another call. "You should be charging for it."

That was the business's turning point: finding a niche within a niche. They have since diversified into three more businesses: New-Road Publishing, Triangle International, and the latest addition (of which Katharine is president) XPACS (Xtreme Professional Athletic Concierge Services). She also authored four books.

"We did everything wrong," reflects Katharine. "We have a master's degree from the school of hard knocks. At times, bankruptcy would have been an easy alternative, but the thought of quitting never occurred to us. We're proud to say we never used a bank loan and made it through the dark days."

With a comprehensive website offering articles, resources, consulting, workshops, books, and concierge start-up packages the couple has developed, the business now has over two thousand clients in thirty countries. "We don't advertise," says Katharine. "Our biggest success is in answering phone calls and emails promptly. We run our business on honesty, caring, love, and respect—all the pillars of ethics. We have a reputation for that."

Theirs is a rags to riches story with a happy ending. While Ron was born into a poor family and Katharine wasn't, they both nearly ended up in rags. By persevering, learning from previous lessons, diversifying, and having strong principles, they have cashed in on chores and brilliantly filled a niche within a niche. Visit their website at www.triangleconcierge.com.

In Closing

These entrepreneurs excite and inspire me. I hope that having read these stories, you too will be inspired and understand that the entrepreneurial road is not an easy one, but it is paved with many inner rewards.

Follow the step-by-step start-up information in this book, take your time in choosing the right business, do your research and homework thoroughly, prepare and use a business plan, work on developing excellent communication skills, and keep focused. Set those goals, give them a defined time, and don't let even the sky be your limit—you can achieve anything you believe in.

Follow those dreams; *make* them happen. May your path be smooth yet exciting, paved with learning, not filled with potholes. May each corner you turn bring you steps closer to inner happiness and success.

I wonder what *your* story will be?

Appendix

Small Business Telephone and Internet Directory

Where do I go, who do I call?
I hope this directory will have it all.

Secretary of State Offices

Following are listed the main website addresses and telephone numbers for each secretary of state office or the equivalent agency. Of course, telephone numbers and Web addresses do change, but one or the other should give you the information you need. Most websites are loaded with useful resources, information, links, online publications, and in many states, the ability to register online with the necessary local, state, and federal agencies.

State	Website address	Telephone
Alabama	www.sos.state.al.us	(334) 242-5324
Alaska	www.dced.state.ak.us/bsc/corps.htm	(907) 465-2530
Arizona	www.azsos.gov	1-800-458-5842
Arkansas	www.sosweb.state.ar.us	(501) 682-1010
California	www.ss.ca.gov	(916) 657-5448

State	Website address	Telephone
Colorado	www.sos.state.co.us	(303) 894-2200
Connecticut	www.sots.state.ct.us	(860) 509-6003
Delaware	www.state.de.us/sos	(302) 739-3073
Dist. of Columbia	www.dc.gov	(202) 727-1000
Florida	www.dos.state.fl.us	1-800-755-5111
Georgia	www.sos.state.ga.us	(404) 656-2817
Hawaii	www.state.hi.us	(808) 586-2744
Idaho	www.idsos.state.id.us	(208) 334-2300
Illinois	www.sos.state.il.us	1-800-252-8980
Indiana	www.state.in.us/sos	(317) 232-6576
Iowa	www.sos.state.ia.us	(515) 281-5204
Kansas	www.kssos.org/business	(785) 296-4564
Kentucky	www.sos.state.ky.us	(502) 564-3490
Louisiana	www.sec.state.la.us	(225) 342-4479
Maine	www.maine.gov/sos/cec/corp	(207) 624-7752
Maryland	www.dat.state.md.us	(410) 767-1184
Massachusetts	www.sec.state.ma.us	(617) 727-9640
Michigan	www.michigan.gov/doingbusiness	(517) 241-6470
Minnesota	www.sos.state.mn.us	1-877-551-6767
Mississippi	www.sos.state.ms.us	(601) 359-1350
Missouri	www.state.mo.us	(573) 751-4153
Montana	http://sos.state.mt.us	(406) 444-3665
Nebraska	www.sos.state.ne.us	(402) 471-4079
Nevada	http://sos.state.nv.us	(775) 684-5708
New Hampshire	www.sos.nh.gov	(603) 271-3244
New Jersey	www.state.nj.us/state	(609) 292-9292
New Mexico	www.sos.state.nm.us	1-800-477-3632
New York	www.dos.state.ny.us	(518) 473-2492
North Carolina	www.secstate.state.nc.us	1-800-228-8443
North Dakota	www.state.nd.us/sec	(701) 328-4284
Ohio	www.sos.state.oh.us/sos	1-877-767-3453
Oklahoma	www.sos.state.ok.us	(405) 521-3912
Oregon	www.sos.state.or.us	(503) 986-2200
Pennsylvania	www.dos.state.pa.us	(717) 787-1057

State	Website address	Telephone
Rhode Island	www.state.ri.us	(401) 222-3040
South Carolina	www.scsos.com	(803) 734-2158
South Dakota	www.sdsos.gov	(605) 773-4845
Tennessee	www.state.tn.us/sos	(615) 741-2286
Texas	www.sos.state.tx.us	(512) 475-2755
Utah	www.commerce.state.ut.us	1-877-526-3994
Vermont	www.sec.state.vt.us	(802) 828-2386
Virginia	www.soc.state.va.us	1-866-722-2551
Washington	www.secstate.wa.gov	(360) 902-4151
West Virginia	www.wvsos.com	(304) 558-8000
Wisconsin	www.state.wi.us/agencies/sos	(608) 261-7577
Wyoming	http://soswy.state.wy.us	(307) 777-7311

Websites and Contact Information

Here is a list by topic of the websites and resource contact information referenced in this book.

Topic	Contact information
Accounting and tax: CPA	Donald Starr, CPA: www.dstarr.com
Business law: lawyer	Christopher Fletcher: Phone 360-332-5558
Business plans	www.bplans.com www.businessplans.org www.entrepreneur.com www.planware.org/busplan.htm www.sbdcnet.utsa.edu.SBIC/bplans.htm
Credit and background checks	www.backgroundcheckgateway.com
Export guide	www.sba.gov/managing/marketing/exportguide.html
Incorporation	www.companiesinc.com
Insurance: business	http://info.insure.com/business/homebizoffice.html
Insurance: life	www.lifeinsurancequote.com

Topic	Contact information
Internal Revenue Service	www.irs.gov/businesses
Small business	www.irs.gov/businesses/small
Printable guides	www.irs.gov/publications
Legal information	http://w3.abanet.org/home.cfm
Loan calculator	www.bankrate.com
Loan financing	www.businesstown.com/finance/money.asp
Loans: venture capital	www.vfinance.com
Name search: example	www.sos.state.ia.us/dbsearch/index.html
Statistics and demographics	www.fedstats.com
Success stories:	
Family Food Distributors	email: familyfooddist@aol.com
Housing Helpers®	www.housinghelpers.com
It's Simple.biz	www.itssimple.biz
Moms in Business Network	www.mibn.org
PR Enterprises LLC	www.p-r-e.com
Triangle Concierge Inc.	www.triangleconcierge.com
The Utilikilts Company	www.utilikilts.com
Trademarks and patents	www.uspto.gov
U.S. Small Business	www.sba.gov
Administration and locations	www.sba.gov/sbdc/sbdcnear.html

Useful Small Business Websites

There are hundreds of excellent, informative sites for small businesses to surf. Here are a few to get you started.

Association of Small Business Development Centers: *www.asbdc-us.org*

The umbrella organization for the large network of SBDCs across the country, its small business information center contains links to dozens of important, resource-packed sites about everything from women in business and minorities to tax and legal information.

Biz Office: *www.bizoffice.com*

Apart from a huge resource library, forms, templates and letters, Web marketing opportunities, and government grant information, this site also offers numerous links to other small business sites and resources.

Business Plans.com: *www.bplans.com*

Information on all areas of small business plus many online tools and resources, including a business plan and financing wizard, as well as many sample business, marketing, and advertising plans.

Entrepreneur Magazine: *www.entrepreneurmag.com*

New articles each month on everything a small business owner needs to know, from marketing, money, and management to e-business and business opportunities, plus an archive of past issues.

Inc.Com: *www.inc.com*

This online magazine will keep you up-to-date with what is happening in the world of small business. It features tons of resources and articles for start-up and growth plus many other tools and services.

It's Simple.biz: *www.itssimple.biz*

As quoted in Chapter 13, Susan Jamerson's site is a cornucopia of resources, articles, online quizzes, and small business information. It includes a national map highlighting each city, which then links you to a list of local small business resource centers and secretary of state offices. Don't miss this site.

Moms in Business Network: *www.mibn.org*

Another success story from Chapter 13, Gina Robison-Billups's site links isolated working mothers across the country, offering them the opportunity to join a network that offers loads of seminars, resources, and benefits not usually accessible to working moms, one-person start-ups, and small businesses.

The Small Business Advisor: *www.isquare.com*

This excellent site contains book reviews, links, a glossary, U.S. government business links, tax advice, and resource books. It offers weekly marketing, accounting, tax, and other helpful tips, plus a host of information and articles.

SmallBizPro.com Services: *www.smallbizpro.com*

My small business site isn't as big as some of the others mentioned here, but it contains many helpful articles, tips, free book chapters, links, two very popular online entrepreneurial quizzes, free online consulting, fun and fitness tips, recipes on the run, and even a video so you can see me in action.

U.S. Business Advisor: www.business.gov

Here is where you will find the right answers to those questions about laws and regulations, financing, taxes, workplace issues, international trade, and more.

U.S. Chamber of Commerce: *www.uschamber.com*

Find the nearest chamber of commerce on this site, review the various business resources, and see how joining a chamber of commerce can help your business grow.

U.S. Small Business Administration: www.sbaonline.sba.gov

The SBA has offices across the United States, and its site offers detailed information on a multitude of small business programs and many necessary resources, such as laws and regulations, plus online classrooms and counseling. A definite must-surf for new entrepreneurs.

Working From Home: www.homeworks.com

Popular small business authors Paul and Sarah Edwards have designed a site full of help for the home-based business. It includes a self-assessment test, loads of tips, free book excerpts, and information on how to successfully operate a home-based business.

Index

D

E

Q

R

T

About the Author

Frances McGuckin is an award-winning and bestselling author, small business expert, professional speaker, and columnist. Traveling across North America, she delivers passionate, powerful, and information-packed messages to associations whose membership comprises largely of small businesses, to small business development center conferences, and to corporate conferences where the corporation's bottom line relies on the success of their small business dealers or distributors.

Business for Beginners, Frances's first book, has sold over 130,000 copies in its three Canadian editions. It is used to teach entrepreneurship and as a resource in many business programs, high schools, colleges, and small business development centers. Rights have been sold to Indonesia, Thailand, and Saudi Arabia, a Russian edition was published in January 2004, and the book has been electronically published by Intuit Canada in four business and tax programs. It was also distributed for six years in business planning software products across North America. The sequel and companion book, *Taking Your Business to the Next Level* (Sourcebooks Inc.) will be published in five languages in 2005.

Recognized as a small business expert in both the United States and Canada, Frances is often interviewed by many small business publications, including the *New York Times, Home Business Journal, Black Enterprise Magazine, Hispanic Trends, Self-Employment America, The Chicago Tribune*, and *Entrepreneur*. She writes columns for various business publications and websites, including the International Association of Floor Care and Sewing Professionals, based in Iowa, and *Business in Vancouver*. In mid-2004, Visa Canada selected Frances to represent them nationally as their small business expert.

Frances has been recognized for her contributions to women in business and small businesses. Her recent accolades include the 2003 Volunteer of the Year Award from her chapter of the Canadian Association of

Professional Speakers and the Surrey International Writers' Conference 2003 Special Achievement Award. She was honored as one of Vancouver's 2002 five most influential women in business, and as a 2004 YWCA Women of Distinction nominee. As an active participant in the Prime Minister's Task Force on Women Entrepreneurs in 2003, Frances had some of her recommendations adopted federally in the final report.

Her home-based businesses, SmallBizPro.com Services and Eastleigh Publications, are in their twenty-second year. She has been actively teaching entrepreneurship for nineteen years, including teaching an accredited Equine Entrepreneurship course at Kwantlen University College. She founded a Toastmasters group and was a founding member and coordinator of the Langley, B.C., chapter of the Valley Women's Network, which has since sponsored eight chapters.

A strong believer in giving back to her community and small business, Frances was a chamber of commerce director in Langley for five years, founding and chairing the Small Business Advancement Committee. Working with the chamber and local municipality government, she realized her dream of changing local, antiquated home-based zoning and operating bylaws in 2000, earning her community one of three national Most Friendly Home-Based Business Community awards.

As an active Rotary International member and treasurer for three years for the Vancouver chapter of CAPS, Frances believes wholeheartedly that we are here on this earth to give to each other—and to have fun doing it!

Frances cares for her ninety-five-year-old mother, has a teenage daughter, a thirty-five-year-old son, and is a grandmother of two. In her spare time, she practices daily fitness and makes quality time for her rather large family of people, horses, and other pets. Bubble baths are not often in her schedule. For more information, visit her website at www.smallbizpro.com.